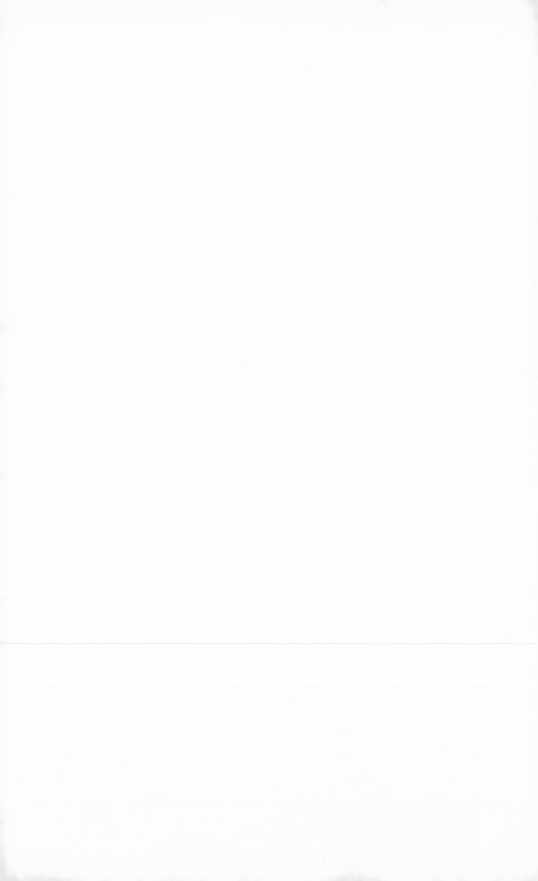

STRATEGIC
ORGANIZATION
PLANNING

Recent Titles from Quorum Books

STRATEGIC ORGANIZATION PLANNING
Downsizing for Survival

DAVID C. DOUGHERTY

Foreword by JOHN B. JOYNT

Q

Quorum Books

NEW YORK • WESTPORT, CONNECTICUT • LONDON

Library of Congress Cataloging-in-Publication Data

Dougherty, David C. (David Carson), 1912-
    Strategic organization planning : downsizing for survival / David
C. Dougherty ; foreword by John B. Joynt.
        p.   cm.
    Bibliography: p.
    Includes index.
    ISBN 0-89930-339-0 (lib. bdg. : alk. paper)
    1. Strategic planning.   I. Title.
HD30.28.D68   1989
658.4'012—dc19   88-11355

British Library Cataloguing in Publication Data is available.

Library of Congress Catalog Card Number: 88-11355
ISBN: 0-89930-339-0

First published in 1989 by Quorum Books

Greenwood Press, Inc.
88 Post Road West, Westport, Connecticut 06881

Printed in the United States of America

The paper used in this book complies with the
Permanent Paper Standard issued by the National
Information Standards Organization (Z39.48-1984).

10 9 8 7 6 5 4 3 2 1

DEDICATED WITH MUCH LOVE TO
MY WIFE, BONNIE, AND TO
OUR SON AND DAUGHTER, DAVID AND LEE

Contents

Exhibits

Foreword

This book is a guide to managers who, in all organizations, wish to improve organization structure and increase organizational effectiveness. Its purpose is to show how the managements of corporations and other organizations can cope with growth and change, whether planned or unpredicted.

Because of external influences and the rate of change, which cannot be projected with accuracy, there is a continuing need to review organization and plans and to integrate the goals and objectives of the enterprise with the results to be achieved by each supporting organizational unit. Also integrating organizational goals with the personal goals of key individuals becomes increasingly important to organization development.

Organization is further complicated by interdepartmental relationships, need for coordination, and team building in order to maximize results. In the light of these developments, top executives periodically reexamine their existing organization, giving more attention to results delegation versus activity delegation so as to build a well-balanced results-oriented organization, structure, and people. Conceptually, each organizational unit should become a "results center."

Mr. Dougherty's book goes beyond the traditional approach to organization by bringing together the elements of organization analysis and development needed to ensure that the organization is adequate to meet current and future needs. His book should be reviewed at the executive level and by all managers, as it sets forth the key factors in building a strong organization.

John B. Joynt, President
The Joynt Group, Incorporated, Management Consultants

Preface

Because of ill-defined and poorly designed organization structures, many mixups of great importance take place daily—even in our largest and best-managed corporations. The causes of these mixups, although not obvious, are failure to define who does what, who has what authority, and who reports to whom. The results are duplication, waste effort, delay, frustration, or relaxing and letting the other fellow do it. Many such mixups in a company bring about ineffective performance, needlessly high costs, loss of competitive position, low morale, lost opportunities to develop executives, and bankruptcy. Such results throughout our economy add up to a staggering waste of our national human resources. The purpose of this book is to help reduce this waste.

Organization planning has its philosophers and its practitioners just as automotive engineering has its research scientists and its mechanics. Many books on organization have been written by management philosophers and college professors. This is one of the first, to my knowledge, to be written by a mechanic. I have a philosophy, of course, but my objective has always been to make something work. For over thirty years I have tinkered with the structures of organizations that were having, or were about to have, serious survival problems. During this experience I have tried out most of the accepted tools of organization analysis and applied most of the principles. I have even fashioned a few tools of my own. I have found out the hard way which ones work and which ones do not—and why. This book is a result of my desire to share this experience.

It contains actual cases from this experience. The names of the companies and individuals have been disguised for obvious reasons. These cases are complex because modern business organizations, regardless of size, are complex. They are far more complex than the old corner drug store; just as the modern racing car is more complex than the old Model T Ford. But a mechanic who is willing to put in the time and effort can learn to repair a racing car.

This is a how-to-do-it manual on modern organization repair for the practicing manager. If he will diligently pursue this book to the end, he will learn how to analyze, design, and control today's organization structure to satisfy its need for:

1. *Economy of effort* to maintain control and minimize friction
2. *Direction of vision* toward the product rather than toward the process—toward the results rather than toward the effort
3. *Understanding* by each individual of his own task as well as that of the organization as a whole
4. *Effective decision-making* that focuses on the right issues, is action-oriented, and is carried out at the lowest feasible level of management
5. *Stability*, as opposed to rigidity, to survive the turmoil and adaptability to learn from it
6. *Perpetuation and self-renewal* to help it grow, develop, and keep up-to-date as changes in objectives and strategy require

Organization structure means different things to different people. To some, it means the interpersonal behavior between specific individuals in small face-to-face groups; to others it means a chart, a mere piece of paper. As used in this book, it means much more than that.

Achieving business objectives in balance requires both personal work and also constructive work relationships. For every position this involves a clear reporting relationship with one manager and interactions with individuals in other positions. An organization structure is the definition and description of both the work and the teamwork for all the management positions needed to achieve business objectives. It is the basic framework through which the managers direct, coordinate, and control the business. If it is poorly defined or if it is a makeshift arrangement that has grown up over the years without plan to accommodate individuals, then management is rendered difficult and ineffective. If, on the other hand, the structure is logical, clear-cut, stabilized, and streamlined to meet present-day objectives, then the first prerequisite of sound management has been achieved. Effective planning and control of the structure can help both managers and individual contributors to achieve better business results by:

1. Grouping the work in easy-to-understand arrangements so that it is easier to perform work within the structure

2. Holding to minimum voids in work and making sure that needed work is assigned to some position

3. Identifying and eliminating unnecessary work, overlap and duplication, management layers, positions, and the like, to avoid unneeded cost for achieving the same or a lesser result

4. Helping to carry out a consistent, equitable, and competitive compensation plan by permitting the logical determination of values added by various types of work

5. Stabilizing the structure sufficiently to permit an individual to evaluate personally the results he has achieved in a position and to plan a career over a reasonable period of time

6. Attracting, motivating, developing, and holding competent employees

In addition, the business can stay up-to-date more easily, carry out its strategy and objectives, apply advanced technology, and plan for changes in work assignments. In such a structure, it is much easier for each person to know what results are expected of him, when and why they should be achieved, and what it should cost.

The impetus for this book came about when the author became deeply impressed with the difficult barriers limiting the successful performance of this vital managing process. In no area of management is there so great a gap between the discussion or writing about principles and their practical application; between the intent to organize and organizing. Even the word to "reorganize" has a distasteful connotation for many businessmen, and it is considered to be an act of last resort when all else fails. Yet the successful application of this skill no doubt will be of primary importance to the managers and planners of the future, who must design and control the structures of large organizations of increasing importance, size, and complexity.

Peter F. Drucker, in the *Age of Discontinuity* (page 211), sees the coming pluralist society as a society of large knowledge organizations. He says we are not likely to see a society that repudiates organizations; rather the concern will be with making an organization fully effective as a major instrument and tool of man and as a central organ of human society. We quote Drucker:

To satisfy its members is not and never will be the first task or test of an organization. It must satisfy people outside; it must serve a purpose outside; and it must achieve results outside the organization itself. At best it can integrate and harmonize the ends, values, and wants of its members with the demands of its mission. But the mission comes first. It is given. It is objective. It is impersonal. It is, at the same time, specific, limited and aimed at only one of the many needs and wants of the society, the community, and the individual. Clearly there is only one foundation for the authority our organizations and their managers must have—performance.

Helping managers achieve such performance is the purpose of this book. In closing, I wish to acknowledge a special debt I owe to some old friends in management: Luther Gulick, former President of the Institute of Public Administration; Lounsbury Fish, former Organization Counsel for the Standard Oil Company of California; Ewing W. Reilley, Marvin Bower, and Richard F. Neuschel of McKinsey & Company, management consultants; Carl Heyel of Carl Heyel & Associates; and John B. Joynt of the Joynt Group. This book rests on the thought and work of these men—and many others—in which they have allowed me to share. Above all, I wish to acknowledge the debt this book and I owe to Donald R. Booz of Donald R. Booz & Associates. It was at his suggestion that I undertook the monumental task of writing it. He gave to this book his counsel and help freely and far beyond the call of friendship.

The following members of the Chicago Affiliate of the Organization Development Council reviewed and commented on specific chapters of the manuscript: Robert Baldaste and Robert Dinerstein of the Organization Department of the Standard Oil Company of Indiana; Robert A. Meyers, Director of Organization Planning, United States Gypsum Company; and Robert P. Seass, Director of Planning, the Harris Trust and Savings Bank.

Finally, an outline of the book was sent for comment to the heads of organization planning staffs in over fifty national companies. Their ideas also helped mold the shape of this book. It is hoped that its publication will make their crucial and difficult tasks a little bit easier and more effective.

In writing this book I have attempted to refer to managers as being both male and female. If the reader finds any instance where I have not done so, it is because I find the repeated use of the word "he/she" awkward and not because of any disrespect for the outstanding women I have known over the years in the field of professional management.

Last, I must express my appreciation to Richard Griffin, Financial Editor of the *Chicago Sun-Times*, and to Robert H. Siepka and his wife, Elaine, for their generous help in the massive job of editing and typing the manuscript. And to Eric Valentine, my editor, and Jane Jordan Browne, my agent, for their belief and counsel. Without it this book would not have been published.

Part I

Principles and Techniques of Organization Planning

1

What Is Organization Planning?

In the General Electric studies[1] of professional management in 1954, "organizing" was recognized as one of the four activities of a professional manager along with planning, integrating, and measuring. However, "organization planning" as a differentiated staff function was in its infancy. It is a relative newcomer on the organization charts of large divisionalized companies.

An organization section first appeared as a staff function on the General Motors organization chart of 1920. The functions of the organization section included: To make a study of and at all times be throughly familiar with the corporation's various organizations; have complete records on hand pertaining thereto, including authority charts; to advise, when called upon by any operation, the best form of organization for getting certain desired results and do such other development work referring to form of organization as may be desired.

In 1941, a research study[2] of thirty-one large companies reported that only four had organization planning staffs. Their functions were as follows:

1. To develop an objective, rational plan of organization
2. To review changes in the current authorized plan of organization against the objective plan and recommend appropriate action
3. To make a periodic audit of the informal organization against the authorized plan and report lack of conformance or revise the formal plan
4. To make organization surveys to determine the objectives, the essential work, the work structure, and staffing requirements

5. To have an important voice in the design of the policy structure and decision-making controls required to make the work structure effective
6. To appraise job values; to determine wage and salary structures outside the company; and to recommend inside salary levels

Two of these staffs were assigned control over salaried manpower (salaries) and other related budgeted costs. None of the four had the entire range of functions.

In 1962 there was an in-depth study[3] of the strategies of seventy of the largest corporations in the United States and what impact strategy had on the organization structures of these corporations. We can see the influence of growth and product diversification that led to profit center divisionalization as we know it today. Four companies in particular were studied in great depth—Du Pont, General Motors, Standard Oil of New Jersey, and Sears, Roebuck. It was the conclusion of the author that a new strategy required a new—or at least refashioned—structure if the enlarged enterprise was to be operated efficiently. The subsequent growth, diversification, and enduring financial success of both Du Pont and General Motors was attributed to a large degree to the redesign of their organization structures. Growth and diversification were the critical factors causing the need for structural change. Since that time, there have been well-publicized cases where the survival of two large automobile companies (Ford and Chrysler) was a direct result of the divisionalization of their structures. National management associations (American Management Association [AMA] and The Conference Board) have conducted extensive research studies of organization structures and organization planning practices of their member companies and reported on the results.

In an AMA survey[4] of organization planning in 1971 involving 209 large companies, 115 executives replied to the questionnaire.

In spite of all the attention and study given to the subject of organization, however, there is considerable evidence that organization planning, as a staff activity, is still in the developmental stage. Few such staffs have achieved a full range of activities or an ultimate, stable and continuing role in the structure of their companies. Although a few companies have discontinued the function, many more have recently started it and even more plan to start one in the near future. In many companies it is currently closely associated with executive development and compensation. Growth, diversification, effectiveness, and even the survival of large companies in the future may well depend on the success of their efforts to achieve and maintain a logical, well-designed structure.

WHAT IS AN ORGANIZATION?

One of the most important problems facing the individual, the family, and the nation as well as business, social, and political institutions is to learn how to organize the work and teamwork of a human group so as to achieve effectively common purposes. This has been true ever since cavemen learned that they were more successful when they hunted in groups than when they hunted alone. We are all members of not one but many organizations. We perform our work in these organizations without realizing how complex the coordination of human work really is. On Saturday we watch the Chicago Bears play a football game on television and marvel at the apparent ease with which eleven men coordinate their activities to defeat the opposing team. How infinitely more difficult it is to orchestrate the efforts of more than 800,000 employees of General Motors in order to create and deliver the products that win preference in the market place over the products of their competitors: Ford, Chrysler, and the Japanese automakers. Only when a company gets into trouble—as Ford did in the forties, Chrysler in the fifties, and American Motors in the sixties—do the public and even the executives of these companies suspect that something is wrong with the organization structure. A close analysis of work processes in these companies would have disclosed the pulling, hauling, and cancellation of instructions that are common in poorly designed and poorly defined organizations. So broad in scope and complex are organization problems that they are not obvious even to those directly involved.

MISCONCEPTIONS ABOUT ORGANIZATION PLANNING

As a result of such complexity there are many misconceptions about the function of organization planning. Here are a few:

1. *Misconception:* Organization improvement results from a one-time project rather than from a continuing activity.

   Fact: Organization structure is dynamic and requires constant attention and control if a simple and logical pattern of work is to be achieved and maintained.

2. *Misconception:* A well-designed organization structure is an end in itself and is more important than the people who staff it. It guarantees good performance.

   Fact: Organization structure is only a tool for helping people to work together more effectively. It cannot guarantee successful performance beyond the capabilities of the people involved. An outmoded structure may, however, be a guarantee of poor performance.

3. *Misconception:* If a corporate organization planning staff has been established, it should perform all the organization planning in the company.

   Fact: Organizing is one of the primary activities of all managers. The chief executive officer, the top manager, plays a crucial role in the overall organization planning process. He must, with the help of his staff, coordinate the organizing activities of all his key managers so as to achieve a sound, rational structure.

4. *Misconception:* Organization documents (charts, position descriptions, man

specifications, and the like) are confidential and their use should be carefully restricted.

Fact: The current approved organization structure should be known to all if effective group performance is to be achieved. This means that all documents defining it, such as charts, position descriptions, organization and policy manuals, notices, instructions, and the like, should be available to all employees.

5. *Misconception:* An organization structure that is successful in one organization can be used without change in another.

Fact: Successful organization structures are unique. Organizations with the same mission, such as hospitals, may appear to have broad functions that are similar, but they must be arranged in a unique way to achieve unique goals.

6. *Misconception:* An organization planning staff usurps the organizing authority of the division managers.

Fact: Organization planning is a staff activity established to help the chief executive officer. It should train division heads to make their own organization surveys and review their resulting proposals for conformance to the overall organization policies, principles, and structure of the chief executive.

7. *Misconception:* Organization planning is theoretical fol-de-rol of no practical value.

Fact: Many practical benefits can be derived from organization planning as is illustrated by the case experiences related in Part II of this book. Massive and important companies like Ford and Chrysler would not have survived their crises without organization planning staffs. Some benefits of sound structure such as the elimination of unneeded positions are easy to quantify in financial terms. Reduction of losses owing to interdepartmental bickering, confusion, poor performance, high turnover, overly complex procedures, and the like, is difficult if not impossible to quantify, but no less substantial.

8. *Misconception:* An organization structure restricts the creative ability and initiative of a strong, aggressive entrepreneur.

Fact: An organization structure should no more restrict a manager than a script restricts an actor. Structure can always be changed to take advantage of a person's particular talents. Care must be exercised, however, to ensure that the change does not cause hidden complications and complexities that adversely affect the work of others and that outweigh over the long-term the apparent immediate advantages.

BARRIERS TO ORGANIZATION IMPROVEMENT AND CONTROL

Why do important companies like Ford get into serious trouble before their executives take a critical and analytical look at themselves and their organization structures? Among the problems that most organizations face in trying to improve their organization structures are the following:

1. *Poor organization like many other management practices is not obvious.* The symptoms—declining market share and earnings—may be

obvious but their basic causes are not. Outmoded organization structure is seldom as apparent as a broken machine or a pile of scrap. More often than not, the symptoms of poor organization are recognized only when mounting dissension becomes apparent at top levels or when a capable man is fired for incompetence. Profits decline, good men leave the company for lesser jobs for no apparent reason. The executive turnover rate reaches a high level. Often, the frustrated executive himself is unaware that he is trying to please two bosses; that he has not been given the authority to achieve the performance expected of him; or that he has been given unrealistic goals or time limitations.

2. *Chief executive officers are not as a rule organization-minded. Many do not consider themselves professional managers.* Few chief executive officers and division general managers are members of professional management societies. Many chief executives do not even realize that organizing is one of the major functions of managing. They tend to concentrate more on operational areas of their jobs on which they believe they will be judged by the board of directors and the shareholders. As long as the market share and profit results are satisfactory without obvious machine breakdowns, strikes, or customer complaints, they seldom think of analyzing the organization structure to seek better, simpler, less-expensive ways to achieve the same or better results.

3. *Chief executive officers seldom fully understand and appreciate the nature of organization planning and the practical value of good organization practices in achieving and maintaining a profitable, growing, healthy, and competitive business.* A chief executive, learning over a cocktail that a competitor has an organization manual, may decide on the spot that his company should have one, too. Who should get the assignment? The personnel director uses job descriptions for evaluating salaried jobs. He is just the man to do it. The president then summons his personnel director, who typically has had little experience in organization planning, and asks him to have someone write an organization manual. At the same time he cautions the personnel man not to disturb the busy executives too much in the process. Thus, organization planning is begun without understanding or plan. Even if the organization manual is completed, the chief executive often doesn't read it, much less use it as a guide in making duty assignments among his key executives. The manual soon becomes obsolete and useless as a management tool to improve the structure. Senior executives complain (correctly) that the exercise was a waste of their time. The whole function of organization planning is in this way discredited. It is obvious that, without the chief executive's understanding, support, and participation, the function should not have been established in the first place.

4. *Departmentalization makes basic organization improvement difficult to achieve.* Duplication of functions, voids, and fuzzy divisions of work usually involve more than one major division. Teamwork between

them is difficult to accomplish except by the chief executive who has jurisdiction over both. At this level, the knowledge of the facts and the means for analyzing them rarely exist without an organization planning staff. While the various staffs and operating divisions may usually be well run as individual units, there still may be voids, duplication, and jurisdictional conflicts among them. A strong executive may easily thwart advisable organization planning in his division merely by saying, "I want to run my own division without outside staff interference. If I do not do my job to suit you, then get someone else." This is enough to discourage the chief executive if he is not a sophisticated manager.

5. *Pressure of operating responsibilities and "emergencies" causes continuous postponement of more important, but less urgent, broad-scale organization studies.* Where a basic organization problem does exist, it is often sufficiently troublesome to make current operations more difficult and demanding of the chief executive's time and attention. Thus, the operating problems caused by poor organization structure are often the very factors that delay their correction. How often have we heard a manager who is drowning in the details that he should be delegating say that he does not have the time to do organization planning or review job descriptions? He does not have the time to plan his work because he is too busy doing it. This is frequently the sign of a poor manager.

6. *Chief executives and key senior executives lack organization planning know-how.* Management training courses and seminars are not designed to train executives in the techniques of organization planning and analysis on a broad scale. There are few practical books on organization planning written out of experience by practicing organization planners. Business schools rarely teach practical courses on the subject.

7. *There is no comprehensive organization plan or a systematic method for making changes in it.* In such companies, changes in the overall organization structure are made extemporaneously, without a study in sufficient depth of the interrelationship or grouping of activities or the long-range result of a change on the effectiveness and profits of the organization as a whole. These changes, once made, are irreversible. It is not practical to eliminate the public relations staff during a cost-cutting program and then set it up again when the profit picture improves. Capable technical men in this field are usually not easy to attract if they see an unstable prior organization history, and executive recruiters do not charge small fees for their services. The division manager making the organization change—if he takes the matter up with the chief executive at all—will present his side of the story so convincingly that he will have no trouble in obtaining approval for the change regardless of its effect on other departments. This is particularly true if he is a strong capable executive who is interested in taking over any function that needs to be performed, regardless of whether or not it is part of his logical "ticket" or

not. It is difficult to prevent such a power play without a systematic procedure for analysis and review of organization changes by a qualified organization planner and without the support of a strong thoughtful professional manager in the role of chief executive.

8. *Desire for protection causes duplication and overlap of functions and generates resistance against corrective action.* If a division head wants a job done but believes that the corporate staff that has been delegated the responsibility to do it will not perform in a way that will satisfy him, he will establish his own staff to do the job rather than complain about another executive's work. Then, once his own staff is established, he will not give it up without a fight.

THE IDEAL ORGANIZATION PLANNING ENVIRONMENT

In the ideal environment for overcoming these barriers, the chief executive officer will be a thoughtful manager who recognizes and plays his crucial role in the organization planning process. He will be a professional manager in the best sense of the word. He will belong to at least one professional management association. He will keep up with the latest techniques in the field of management. He will be an emotionally mature man of unquestioned integrity with a rational, analytical mind. On his desk will be an organization manual with up-to-date job descriptions and specifications in it. Combined with this will be a corporate policy manual. In a small company, he may make his own organization studies and write or review the position descriptions before they are issued in the manual. He issues the organization change notices and the executive directory. When he finds that this organizing function is requiring too much of his time, however, he will consider employing a trained organization planning staff to help him. If it is possible that this staff will grow, the staff head will not only be an experienced organization analyst, he will also have had some previous experience in directing an organization planning staff.

ORGANIZING AN ORGANIZATION PLANNING STAFF

Before a chief executive appoints anyone to help him with his organization planning, however, he should take the following steps:

1. Define the objectives, scope, and functions of the organization planning staff in a charter
2. Develop organization planning policies necessary for the staff to achieve its objectives
3. Fix the responsibility; that is, design the special staff job or jobs necessary to achieve the objectives
4. Work out a comprehensive approach and plan of action for the staff

5. Arrange for proven organization planning techniques to be applied to the work undertaken
6. Maintain project control over the work assignments through some positive means of measuring the results achieved
7. Recruit highly qualified individuals.

DEFINING OBJECTIVES, SCOPE, AND FUNCTIONS OF THE STAFF

The objectives of such a staff have already been discussed. They may be restated here as helping the chief executive officer develop and maintain a simple, effective organization structure for the purpose of:

1. Improving the effectiveness, functioning, and economy of the organization as a whole
2. Cutting salary costs
3. Improving customer service
4. Increasing the effectiveness of executive, sales, and technical personnel
5. Raising employee morale
6. Reducing executive turnover
7. Reducing the executive failure rate
8. Compensating for shortages in qualified management, technical, and clerical employees
9. Improving policy and procedure execution
10. Developing teamwork among departments and avoiding overlaps, jurisdictional conflicts, and duplication of functions and staffs
11. Maintaining competitive and equitable salary structures and relationships

The mere definition of objectives in a charter, however, is not enough. The duties of the staff should be included in the organization manual together with the organization change policies and procedures and the organization principles and criteria to be applied in the structuring of the organization or in reviewing change proposals. If necessary, an organization survey guide should also be issued defining the techniques to be used by the staff in planning and making their organization surveys.

THE PROACTIVE INSTEAD OF REACTIVE APPROACH

To be fully effective, the organization planning program should be based on the following top management concept. Organization planning and improvement work must be proactive and continuous, not reactive, intermittent, or expedient. In its reactive form, it is confined to: (1) development of a new organization structure whenever required to carry out a change in corporate stratgegy or to conform to newly enacted legislation; and (2) revision of the existing organization structure as operating experience reveals the need for change. This is a euphemistic way of saying "to put out fires."

In its proactive form, organization planning is concerned with the continuous observation and analysis of the organization structure and job values aimed at forestalling operating and compensation problems caused by poor organization, long before their magnitude compels attention, and at uncovering new opportunities for organization improvement that would otherwise remain hidden or obscure.

If the initiation of organizational improvements awaits the point of crisis or the compulsion of competition, as in the case of the Automobile Company (see Chapter 6), a major reorganization is required under difficult financial pressures. Substantial opportunities for controlling costs or for improving performance and profits frequently remain neglected until the symptoms of poor organization cause serious market share and profit decline. Sometimes at that advanced stage the problem is like a cancer. When it hurts enough for the patient to be willing to undergo an operation, it is often too late to save him.

It is worth emphasizing again that the first essential policy is that the staff's approach to the development and improvement of the organization structure should not be limited to a reactive approach that becomes active only when an organization change is requested by a senior executive or by the chief executive officer. It should provide for a proactive approach involving the continuous review of the corporate organization structure and proposed changes in it so as to detect evidence of inadequate policy and functional control, unnecessary levels, voids, unneeded functions, functions needing strengthening, functions improperly positioned in the structure, overly complex procedures, new policies required, or excessive costs of any one function in comparison to the effectiveness and value of the results.

A COMPLETE PROGRAM

The second concept, a derivative of the first, is the organization program should be complete. It cannot be limited to the preparation of job descriptions and specifications used solely for job evaluation, as is sometimes the case when the function is a subordinate part of the personnel activity. It should encompass the rational design of all work, regardless of the function.

RESPONSIBILITY FOR INTRADEPARTMENTAL ORGANIZATIONAL PLANNING

When a change in organization is clearly intradepartmental in nature and affects no other department or division, then the corporate organization planning department should be available to advise the department head only. If he wishes to help in conducting the fact-finding survey itself, then the organization planning staff should conduct the survey for a fee, just as an outside management consultant would. The staff must not become trapped into providing free organization consulting services for the division general managers and corporate staff department heads. It should train them in techniques of organization planning and review their organization change proposals for the chief executive before he approves them to see that the principles and techniques have been properly applied.

BENEFITS WHEN DIVISION AND STAFF HEADS DO THEIR OWN ORGANIZATION PLANNING

Following are the benefits of requiring division and staff heads to do their own planning:

1. Organization planning proposals are likely to be more practical from an operating viewpoint.
2. When a proposed organization plan is developed by the division head, who must live and work under the plan, a natural pride of authorship accrues to it. He is then far more likely to make his assignments in accordance with the plan than if it is developed by the top organization planning staff.
3. When the division head and his own staff work together on the organization change proposal, this staff will serve him better than will the organization planning staff of the chief executive officer. Not only can he work with them more easily, but they are available to him on a continuous basis to help with the installation of the approved changes and the subsequent follow-up.
4. The department head is more likely to recognize organization planning as one of his reserved management responsibilities and he will get valuable management training by participating in carrying out the function personally.

ASSIGNMENT OF THE ORGANIZATION PLANNING RESPONSIBILITY TO THE HEAD OF A TRADITIONAL STAFF DIVISION

Companies that have not adopted a proactive approach to organization planning have commonly assigned the function to one of the traditional divisions of the business. Although the assignment varies considerably from business to business, it is most commonly delegated to the personnel director or the controller. The selection of any of these positions is supported by a number of arguments, most of them quite obvious but irrelevant. The personnel director uses position descriptions and specifications for evaluating jobs and for hiring, training, evalutating the performance of, and compensating the executive personnel. The controller is concerned with the control of manpower and related costs and an organization planning staff quickly becomes adept in helping him in the control of manpower. The controller is sometimes—like the one at the Hard Rubber Company (see chapter 5)—a trained management analyst who can provide sound direction for such a staff. In evaluating these alternatives, however, it is helpful to consider the points already discussed:

1. The chief executive frequently makes organization changes that involve the very division to which the function is assigned; having the staff assigned to one of them raises questions of apparent, if not actual, lack of objectivity.

2. Interdepartmental organization studies are many times employed as a means for adjudicating jurisdictional conflicts and overlaps. One of the parties in the dispute should not be responsible for helping the chief executive perform the job of adjudication.

A CHARTER FOR THE ORGANIZATION PLANNING STAFF

So far, our discussion of organization planning has concerned the positioning of the organization planning staff in the company structure and concepts that should be considered in defining the role of the staff. The final step in setting up for organization planning is to spell out the staff's specific responsibilities in writing in a charter: policies, procedures, and related documents. One of the causes of ineffectiveness and frustration among organization planners is the great variation in the functions of organization planning staffs. To avoid this problem the chief executive should reach clear-cut decisions on what the staff is supposed to accomplish and how it is supposed to operate by determining (1) the basic mission; (2) its authority for initiating organization studies; and (3) the scope of its coverage of the organization structure.

In deciding what the basic functions of the staff should be, the chief executive should use the following as a guide:

1. Recording existing organization planning practices and structure by developing and maintaining an organization manual

2. Achieving more effective integration and teamwork among the various units of the organization

3. Developing, and taking steps to achieve, a more objective, rational plan of organization

4. Reviewing changes in the current authorized plan against the "objective plan," applying organization planning principles, and recommending appropriate action

5. Making organization surveys to determine the objectives, as well as the essential work, organization structure, job values, and staffing requirements of a new or changed component

6. Having an important voice in the design of the policy and other decision-making controls required to make the organization structure effective
7. Appraising jobs and determining job values; surveying wage and salary structures outside the company; recommending inside salary levels
8. Developing and maintaining the corporate policy manual
9. Advising on the control of salaried manpower and related costs

Specifically a decision should be made by the chief executive between these two approaches for the staff.

1. *The Reactive Internal Consultant Approach.* Under this method of operation, the organization planning staff would work like an outside consultant, primarily only on problems raised or projects requested by the chief executive.
2. *The Proactive Functional Control Approach.* Under this alternative, the staff would initiate most of its own studies and maintain the means for auditing and identifying the major organization improvement opportunities of the business. It also would provide functional control and review major organization planning and change proposals of an intradepartmental nature initiated by the staff of operating divisions.

THE SCOPE OF THE STAFF'S WORK

Finally, to complete writing the staff's charter, the area of the organization covered by the corporate staff needs to be spelled out in terms of specific levels. The scope, for example, may cover two reporting levels below the corporate staff heads and one reporting level below the division and plant heads. Also, the charter should specify how deep the staff's work should be in terms of the administrative tools and elements to be included in their studies.

Should it deal with all the factors affecting the complexity or cost of the administrative process including policies, procedures, forms, reports, and other management tools whenever they have a bearing on the effectiveness of the organization unit being studied? Many companies have systems staffs with these responsibilities.

Or should the department's work be limited to the study of major functions and jobs and their positioning in the organization structure?

NOTES

1. *Professional Management in General Electric* (New York: General Electric Company, 1954).

2. Paul E. Holden, Lounsbury S. Fish, and Hubert L. Smith, *Top Management Organization and Control* (Stanford, Calif.: Stanford University Press, 1941).

3. Alfred D. Chandler, Jr., *Strategy and Structure* (Cambridge, Mass.: The MIT Press, 1962).

4. William F. Glueck, *Organization Planning and Development* (New York: American Management Association, 1971).

Exhibit 1.1
The Principles of Organization

(For a discussion of the application of these principles see Chapter 4.)

I. *PRINCIPLE OF THE OBJECTIVE*

Every organization and every part of an organization must be an expression of the undertaking or it is useless.

Application of this principle results in carefully defining in writing what an organization wants to become and what it wants to accomplish, and when. Then every element of the organization must be periodically appraised in terms of what it is contributing to realize the objectives, policies, and goals of the enterprise. If it is not contributing, it should be eliminated. On the other hand, if to achieve these goals there are activities required that are not being performed, then they should be activated.

II. *PRINCIPLE OF SPECIALIZATION*

The work of every position in management should be confined to the performance of a single leading function.

Application of this principle means that, at the working level, functions whose objectives conflict with the defined basic objectives, management principles, and goals of the component and require dissimilar abilities, professional knowledge, and experience should be segregated and assigned to a more suitable reporting relationship and grouping of functions in the structure.

III. *PRINCIPLE OF COORDINATION*

Functions and positions that are related by common objective should be grouped together in order to secure coordination and unity of effort. Those that are unrelated or have conflicting objectives should be segregated.

In grouping functions for the purposes of management coordination, it is often necessary, in the interest of achieving a common business objective, to combine into units unlike functions, rather than to design units that consist of similar functions. In this way, managerial control and unity of action necessary to achieve objectives can be achieved. For example, selecting employees, inspecting products, and accounting for profits are dissimilar functions, but they are coordinated at plant, division, and corporate levels in the overall structure for the purpose of achieving a common business objective.

IV. *PRINCIPLE OF RESPONSIBILITY AND AUTHORITY*

In every organized group the supreme authority must rest somewhere. There must be a clear line of responsibility and authority from the supreme authority to every position in the group.

Staff associates must be careful not to issue direct orders to line associates. This confuses people at the lower levels in the organization structure so that they do not know where the directions are coming from.

V. *PRINCIPLE OF ACCOUNTABILITY*

Accountability of the superior for the acts of his subordinates is absolute. No person can effectively report to and be accountable to more than one direct superior. Organization structure should be planned in such a way that each manager has full and undivided authority over those subordinate to him, subject to the overall framework of approved policies, procedures, methods, and organization documents established by higher authority. In turn, the manager is absolutely accountable for the acts of his subordinates. It is not proper for a manager to complain to his superiors about the performance of his subordinates. As long as they are his subordinates, he should be loyal to them. It is surprising what a difference it makes when subordinates know they are getting that kind of support.

VI. PRINCIPLE OF DEFINITION

The responsibilities, authorities, and accountabilities of each key position and its relationships to other positions should be clearly defined in writing and distributed to all concerned.

Clear definition and accurate titling of key positions and units are particularly essential in the effective communication of organization information in a complex and rapidly changing, divisionalized, line-and-staff organization. Employees like to know what they or their line superiors are accountable for so they can make a maximum contribution. Definition is also a great safeguard against an incompetent superior and provides a sound basis for reaching common agreement on basic objectives, goals, and standards of performance. Authoritative organization documents, if effectively used, can channel the use of scarce management talent and effort toward achieving the most profitable and desirable results for the organization as a whole.

VII. PRINCIPLE OF CORRESPONDENCE

The responsibility, authority, and accountability in any position should correspond. A manager cannot be held accountable for results if he does not have enough responsibility and authority to take the actions necessary to achieve these results.

VIII. PRINCIPLE OF SPAN OF MANAGEMENT CONTROL

The span of management responsibility should not be too narrow. There is also a limit to the number of positions that can be accountable to a single superior.

The number of persons reporting to the same superior should be neither more nor less than the number that can reasonably well be directed, coordinated, measured, and supported by a qualified superior. At the lower levels in the line structure where the work may be reasonably standardized and repetitive, it is sometimes possible for a large number of employees to be directly managed by one superior. At the higher levels of the structure (that is, the plant, division, or corporate levels) where many complex interlocking relationships between dissimilar functions are involved, the span of management responsibility over line subordinates should be less. If the span of control is too broad, some activities may not receive the managerial support and attention they require. If the span is too narrow, the superior may perform work that he had delegated to subordinates, thus creating confusion and unsound floatback of decision-making responsibility and authority.

IX. *PRINCIPLE OF BALANCE*

It is essential that the various units of an organization be kept in balance. No one element of the organization structure should be too strong. There should be equal apportionment of strength and authority.

It is not proper for a superior to give or appear to give all the support attention, responsibility, authority, and accountability to one subordinate and little or none to another. This results in giving too much attention to certain areas and in unintentional or apparent favoritism, imbalance in workloads, poor communications, and other organizational malfunctions.

X. *PRINCIPLE OF CONTINUITY*

Organization and reorganization is a continuous process. Organizational means to assure that this is accomplished on a rational basis should be provided within the structure of every organization. If this is not done, the organization may function perfectly well for two or three years with a static structure, while the business environment and strategy have been inexorably changing. Little bits of reorganization that should have been done during this time will accumulate and finally require a major reorganization; or, the enterprise may collapse and go out of business. This is unnecessary. Every organization should be continuously reorganizing and adjusting the structure to meet changes in objectives, goals, policies, and circumstances, reallocating functions, and so on. A healthy business has some built-in organizational means for doing so.

This means the head of the organization, if it is sufficiently large, should seek the help of someone without day-to-day operating responsibilities, to ensure that organization planning and control get the attention they need. If the job is given to anyone with more urgent but less important operating duties, organization structure will surely be forgotten in the pressure of daily work.

XI. *PRINCIPLE OF MINIMUM LEVELS*

The chain of command should be as short as possible. The number of levels of managerial responsibility and authority should be kept to a minimum.

Each added level of management tends to slow further the downward flow of directions and communications and the upward flow of reports and recommendations for decision and action. This line of communication must be kept flowing freely. In the interest of expediting decisions, maintaining good communications, and maximizing overall economies, unnecessary management levels and positions should be eliminated.

XII. *PRINCIPLE OF FUNCTIONAL GROWTH*

As an organization grows, the various functions that must be performed increase in their scope and complexity as do the amount of work that is necessary and the technical requirements for the organization's performance.

Every effort must be made to keep the structure as simple as possible in keeping with its stage of growth and its basic organizational pattern (that is, customer type, physical location, product, production process, or physical equipment).

XIII. *PRINCIPLE OF CENTRALIZATION*

Responsibility, authority, and accountability should be centralized within the structure when necessary to provide authority, leadership, accountability, and consistency of action, and to provide the means to deal with emergencies or exceptional situations.

Centralization in a diversified, divisionalized structure normally exists at the plant, division, and corporate level.

XIV. *PRINCIPLE OF DELEGATION*

Responsibility and authority should be delegated within necessary central control to the position that is as close as practical to the point of required action where the decision can be reached with maximum competence. Also, the decision-making position should be provided with the work elements necessary to implement such responsibility. Such authority must not be delegated below the level where the information and work elements are provided to make the decision effectively.

This should be done in the interest of achieving quicker and better decisions. All other things being equal, the closer the decision is made to the location where it will be carried out (and where the facts on impact and results are known), the better the results will be. In the case of decisions with broad impact, the decision should be made at higher levels in the structure, where all the pertinent facts on the results of this impact can be quickly obtained and the specialized staff skills can economically be provided to help line management investigate all feasible alternatives, and select the one that will provide the most profitable results for the corporation as a whole.

XV. *PRINCIPLE OF SEPARATING LONG-RANGE WORK FROM SHORT-RANGE WORK*

Accountability for long-range work should be separated from that for short-range work at the highest level in the structure. Urgent, fire-fighting work will drive out long-range, more important—but less urgent—work if both are included in the responsibilities of the same position or component.

It should be clearly known and understood which positions and functions are primarily line (operating) and which are staff (planning and control). Line and staff functions should be separated at the highest level possible within the corporate, division, and plant structures. Line and staff functions should not be combined in one position or unit.

Exhibit 1.2
Corporate Policy. Planning of Organization Structure:
Large Divisionalized Corporation

I. *NEED FOR A POLICY*
  A. Reaching corporate goals involves individual work and productive team-work. In each job this requires a well-defined reporting relationship with one superior. Organization structure is the definition and description of both the work and teamwork for all required positions.
  B. A well-designed structure can help supervisors and individual contributors get improved results. For example, a company can:
    1. *Increase return on investment.* Successful corporations have demonstrated that a higher level of performance can be achieved using a well-designed organization structure.
    2. *Realize its growth goals.* A sound structure helps employees perform the work needed to carry out whatever strategic plan has been selected.
    3. *Keep abreast of technological advances.* A sound structure facilitates the application of new technology by permitting its introduction into existing work in a systematic way. This involves redesign of jobs and skill specifications.
    4. *Adapt to changes in job requirements.* Employees are more productive when jurisdictional problems are eliminated. They can take the initiative and solve their own problems more quickly when each one clearly understands what his goals are and what help he can expect from his associates.
  C. A sound structure makes a specific contribution to achieving result goals by:
    1. Creating a rational and understandable grouping of activities so that the plan of organization is clear to those working within it.
    2. Assuring that necessary activities are provided for and unnecessary activities are abolished.
    3. Eliminating voids in work so as to ensure that every required accountability has been assigned to some position.
    4. Facilitating the execution of an equitable and competitive salary administration program by establishing logical relations between values added by various types of work.
    5. Identifying and abolishing work overlap and duplications to avoid increasing the expense for achieving the same or a lesser result.
    6. Attracting, motivating, developing, and retaining high-talent personnel by providing increasingly more responsible positions as opportunities for promotion; by providing enough stability for an employee to appraise the results he has achieved in his job; and by making it possible for him to plan his career over an adequate time span.
  D. Well-defined and documented understanding of job duties. Charts and job descriptions should be kept simple and understandable, yet the

structure should be described in writing fully enough to permit the achievement of the results outlined above. Concise but adequate documents help to:

1. Confirm verbal decisions.
2. Transmit accurately and promptly changes in work to all employees involved.
3. Record organization decisions for use when further changes are required.

II. STATEMENT OF POLICY

It is, therefore, corporate policy:

A. To have each operating and staff division head prepare and maintain a soundly designed, well-defined, and appropriately documented organization structure. This structure should specify supervisory reporting relationships and work relationships and provide the structure within which the unit head and his associates can successfully carry out their result goals.

B. In order to assure that this structure has been thoroughly thought through and is based on logical assumptions, to have each division head ensure that the organization structure:
1. Is based on the goals of his division charter or his position description.
2. Tries to achieve maximum added product value at minimum cost.
3. Is practical, rational, well defined, and based on sound principles of organization.
4. Can be staffed with qualified personnel in a reasonable and practical length of time.
5. Takes into consideration the work of closely related units.
6. Is understood and generally supported by the supervisors and individual contributors that must work within it.
7. Is in accord with pertinent corporate and division policies.

III. APPLICATION OF POLICY

A. Minimum factual information concerning a new unit or a major change in organization structure will generally encompass the following:
1. Facts about present conditions and need for the change.
2. Current charter or position description of the division head or the latest draft noting status.
3. Present and proposed structure in chart form including exempt positions, position and unit titles, and names of present incumbents.
4. Present and proposed functional charts showing the work for each component.
5. Written supporting analysis covering:
   (a) present work and as proposed, describing work to be simplified, eliminated, or added. Major realignment of activities and work processes, where these can be planned.
   (b) reason for changes and why they should bring about the results desired.
   (c) comments of other units substantially affected.

6. Estimated changes in the positions and evaluations resulting from the proposal.
7. Estimated changes in total base salary costs, present and proposed, and an explanation for the difference.
8. Recommended plans to staff the new structure.
9. Comments of corporate functional staffs when their areas of expertise are involved.

IV. *TITLES*

A. Experience has demonstrated the importance of using similar titles for units and positions doing similar work.

B. Documenting of an organization change includes titling the resulting units and positions. Poor communication of organization information would result from too varied a selection of such titles. Titles should be selected that are consistent with titles generally existing elsewhere in the company and are meaningful outside the company. This will facilitate communications.

V. *DELEGATION OF RESPONSIBILITIES*

A. Division Head
1. Plan major changes in the organization structure of his division and recommend them to his superior.
2. Request written counsel and comments as outlined in this policy.

B. Division Head's Superior
1. Approve major changes in structure.

C. Functional Staffs
1. Supply specialized comments and counsel at the request of those preparing and recommending changes in organization. Comments are normally provided or confirmed in writing.

VI. *DEFINITION OF "MAJOR CHANGE"*

A. In implementing this policy normally what constitutes a major change in organization structure can best be made by the unit head recommending the change.

B. Certain changes are usually important enough to require thorough fact-finding and analysis, careful review, and application of specialized functional know-how from a variety of staffs, as described above. Examples include those concerning:
1. Greatly increased compensation requirements.
2. Substantially reduced staffing levels with attendant morale problems and out-placement.
3. Need for knowledge, experience, and skills at present scarce within the company.
4. Work processes and functional groupings that are substantially changed from those currently existing.
5. Substantial changes in authorized plans and budgets.
6. Major changes in the division charter or product lines.

C. Usually merely adding or dropping one position, or in some cases even several positions, would not be considered a major change as used in this policy. Such changes do, however, require the approval of the new or changed job descriptions as prescribed in the Exempt Salary Administration Policy.

ISSUED BY:
Chairman of the Board
DATE ISSUED:
12/21/87

**Exhibit 1.3
Excerpt from an Organization Design Manual:
Large Divisionalized Corporation**

ORGANIZATION PRINCIPLES FOR PLANNING THE MANUFACTURING
SECTION OF A PRODUCT DIVISION

I. *INTRODUCTION*

Two categories of organization principles will be included:

A. General principles covered in the preceding sections of this manual.

B. Principles peculiar to a manufacturing organization, but that should be given equal consideration in designing the structure.

1. *The Manufacturing Function*

Manufacturing is the activity that is accountable for procuring, processing, and delivery of the physical products sold or ordered by marketing in line with specifications prepared by engineering at the lowest real cost, with minimum capital investment and with minimum delivery time, consistent with good quality, working conditions, employee and public relations, and which contribute to the long-range strategic goals of the company and the division. Manufacturing is also accountable for:

(a) Continuous improvement of processes and facilities to achieve lower costs and delivery times.

(b) Planning and obtaining facilities as required to meet growth and changing requirements of the division.

(c) Proposing to division sales and engineering functions, changes in processes, product design, or delivery requirements to improve quality, reduce total costs, and increase profits, or meet customer needs.

2. *The Organizing Process*

(a) Account for all the basic work elements in the manufacturing function.

(b) Define this work and minimize—or eliminate—all semantic problems.

(c) Arrange these work elements into groups requiring similar experience, skills, and activities.

(d) Further group or segregate these activities to realize a balanced workload for each employee, optimum spans of responsibility for supervisors, and a proper "pyramiding" of objectives.

(e) Allocate these activity groupings to the most appropriate components and establish a proper working relationship between them.

II. *PRINCIPLES FOR ORGANIZING THE MANUFACTURING SECTION OF A PRODUCT DIVISION*

A. *Basic Principles*

1. The manufacturing section head should consider each of the following fields, which should account for all of the work in manufacturing:

(a) Manufacturing engineering
(b) Purchasing
(c) Quality control
(d) Plant facilities
(e) Shop operations
(f) Administration
(g) Personnel
   (If these activities are not delegated to a separate manager, they are to be retained by the manufacturing section head. This does not prevent the establishment of specialist positions in personnel or administration when managerial accountability is reserved.)
   Principle of balance. Effective performance of the total work of manufacturing requires balanced managing of these specialized and interlocking activities.

2. Decision-making accountability should be delegated to the position that is closest to the point of action. Also this position should be provided with activities required to carry out this delegation.
   Principle of delegation. Provision of the tools required to carry out authority at the lowest practical level generally results in more decisions being made at that level and more quickly. This frees up higher management levels for planning and decision-making of broader scope.

3. Accountability for short-range work should be separated from long-range work at the highest practical level in the structure. *Principle of separating long-range work from short-range work.* It is generally accepted that less important short-range "urgent" work will drive out more important less urgent long-range work if they are both included in the same position or component.
   NOTE: Some principles are in conflict with each other. This is true of numbers 1, 2, and 3 above. For example, number 1 (Basic Functional Fields) indicates that these activities, since they are homogeneous within themselves, are not homogeneous with each other and should not be mixed, i.e., all purchasing activities should be assigned to the manager-purchasing.
   Principle 2 (Delegation) on the contrary indicates that, if the manager of shop operations is to have maximum decision-making authority, he should have some elements of purchasing, manufacturing engineering, and quality control.
   Principle 3 (Separating Long-Range from Short-Range) tends to support Principle 2 in that it places all short-range work in one component, i.e., shop operations, leaving other components to handle long-range work. Such conflicts create the need for qualifying principles.

B. *Qualifying Principles*
   Separation of the following principles from those noted as "basic" does not indicate secondary importance, but notes that these principles are helpful in reaching the right compromise in specific cases in the applica-

tion of conflicting principles and even between conflicts in the qualifying principles themselves.

1. *Principle of specialization.* Work that requires similar skills (education, training, and experience) and types of activity should be grouped together for assignment to positions and units.

   Principle of specialization. Competence of individuals is increased by specialization and by close work contacts with other specialists in the same field; maximum flexibility in work assignments is possible and thus fewer employees may be required.

2. *Separation of managerial work from other kinds of work.* Positions and structures should be designed so that managerial work is clearly separated from non-managerial work and should not be combined in the same position.

   Principle of managerial work as a specialized field. Managerial work is a specialized field itself and requires its own special skills and training. These skills are most effectively used in positions requiring these skills only. Also the value of the work of each specialist is increased by his concentration on that field only and by the direction of his efforts by someone skilled in managing.

3. *Balanced accountability between fields of work.* Activities should be grouped so that no one component has an unduly heavy share of the total work of manufacturing.

   Principle of balance. Each field represents an important part of the total work of manufacturing. Balanced emphasis by the section head, manufacturing, on each of these functions is achieved by balancing the scope of the positions reporting to him. To do otherwise invites imbalance, distortion, and overloads.

   For example, in situations where shop operations require one manager, assignment to this position of all short-range manufacturing engineering, purchasing, and quality control work may create an overload position and one similar in scope to the one of his superior, the section head, manufacturing. This also reduces the scope of the work of the other positions.

4. *Spans of management control.* Each management position should directly supervise the number of positions that requires the skill of a competent individual to manage on a full-time basis. This varies from five to six at higher levels of the structure involving complex work and many interlocking work relationships up to perhaps forty or fifty at lower levels, where the work is simple and repetitive.

   Principle of span of management control. Broad spans make it possible and needed for the incumbent to spend full-time planning, organizing, leading, and controlling. Excessively broad spans, however, result in some work not being properly planned and directed. Too narrow spans provide insufficient managerial workload. The incumbent then tends to do some of the work that should be assigned to those under his supervision, thus encroaching on their responsibilities.

5. *Minimum levels of management.* Structure should be designed so as to minimize the number of levels of management. The objective within the company is to hold the structure to a maximum of eight levels. This normally sets a limit of two to four in manufacturing as follows:

Level No.	Component Title	Position Title
4	manufacturing	section head
3	shop operations subsection	superintendent
2	shop operations unit	general foreman
1	shop operations subunit	foreman
—	workers	—

Principle of minimum levels. Levels of management restrict the free flow of authority and information downward through the structure and the flow of reports coming back up. Minimizing the number of levels to simplify the structure is essential in a large divisionalized company to match the market responsiveness of smaller competitors. Reducing levels tends to broaden spans of control and reduce the ratio of managers to individual contributors.

In other fields such as manufacturing engineering and purchasing, there is such a variety of work requirements that generalizing on the maximum number of levels is inappropriate. The important point is to achieve the minimum number of levels regardless of the number of levels required in parallel functions.

6. *Flexibility.* The structure should be designed to provide sufficient flexibility to meet the short- and long-range fluctuations in each field.

Principle of manufacturing flexibility. Workloads are seldom static and thus reassignment of employees is required to meet such fluctuations. Fluctuations are of three types:

(a) *Very short-range*—due to variations in orders, manufacturing difficulties, and the like.

(b) *Medium-range*—due to seasonal variations in demand for products.

(c) *Long-range*—due to changes resulting from the business cycle and the long-term growth—or decline—in the business of the division.

NOTE: The structure should be designed so "a" and "b" above have no impact on the structure, and "c" has a minimum impact.

7. *Objectives and economy.* The structure should be designed to achieve the total objectives of the division most economically.

Principle of the objective. Real economy involves the measurement of results as well as the apparent cost. For this reason, the objectives of a component must be established before the costs can be appraised against the results expected. The following tests of structural economy can be applied:

(a) Does the structure require a minimum number of supervisory and specialist positions?

(b) Does it provide a maximum number of positions that requires employees to use their full skills instead of doing work of a lower skill because a lower level position is not provided?

8. *Single lines of responsibility and authority.* Each position should derive its responsibility and authority from—and be accountable for its performance to—only one other position. Relationships with other associated positions should be clear and understandable.

Principle of responsibility and authority. Understanding is better and conflict is minimized when each position is responsible and accountable to only one other position, and by clearly defining relationships with other positions.

9. *Product volume.* The organization structure should be appropriate to the division's type of manufacturing process as measured by product volume. ("Volume" as used here is the number of identical—or highly similar—units produced.)

Principle of product volume manufactured. If the product line consists of a number of types or sizes—but all are produced at high volumes—it is essentially a mass production process. In such cases the major workload falls on manufacturing engineering, purchasing, and quality control, rather than on shop operations. Where volume of products is low, the heavy amount of workload—not necessarily skill—falls on shop operations.

Many divisions are combinations of these two processes using mass production for some lines and job shop for others. As a matter of principle, facilities and organization structures for these two types should be segregated where practical, to permit performance of each to be measured against standards most applicable to the particular process.

10. *Shop arrangement.* The structure should be designed in accord with the basic concept of shop layout or arrangement.

Principle of shop layout. In theory, shop layout is temporary in nature. In practice, however, once established, the cost of major rearrangements cannot be justified unless there is a radical change or relocation that incurs the cost anyway, thus providing the opportunity to change the basic layout.

There are three fundamental arrangements:

(a) *By subproduct lines.*
This arrangement reduces the integration required between the units.

(b) *By function or production process.*
Physical operations and skills are grouped together as follows:
(1) Sheet metal fabrication
(2) Machining
(3) Winding
(4) Finishing
(5) Assembly
This arrangement requires maximum coordination of units

because of interlocking work relationships. Therefore, it requires more of the overall effort in manufacturing engineering, purchasing, and quality control.

(c) *Combination of subproduct lines and function.* For example, common fabrication and machining units feeding into a series of subproduct assembly units.

NOTE: Sheer size of the manufacturing function and diversity or complexity of product lines have been considered by some as organization design principles. The only aspect of "size" that really affects organization structure is the number of employees required to carry out the functions. Larger numbers of people offer the maximum opportunity to use alternative organization structures without sacrificing the principles of the objective, grouping, minimum levels, and the like. These factors affect the size of the functions, but they are not themselves organization design principles.

2

The Chief Executive's Personal Role in Organization Planning

The preceding chapter deals with the history of the function; misconceptions about it and the organization planning staff; ingredients of a successful program; barriers to such a program; how to organize the staff; and how to write the staff charter. Although proper organization of the staff is important, it cannot guarantee a successful program. It can only provide the static framework within which dynamic action must take place. If the organization improvement effort is to produce the most fruitful results, this framework must be supported by a broad-gauged approach to the conduct of the work.

In this chapter we discuss in detail what the staff should do to overcome barriers to its success, specifically: (1) The viewpoint, the set of values, or the way of thinking that the individual organization planners must apply to their work; and (2) the way the staff tackles individual organization studies.

THE CHIEF EXECUTIVE'S VIEWPOINT

The most important point to remember always is the crucial personal role of the chief executive in organization planning. He truly is the head organization planner. Every time he assigns a task to one of his subordinate executives, he either does or does not conform to the authorized organization plan. If he deviates, and does so often, he has in effect changed the authorized plan of organization. This organization change has been made, consciously or unconsciously, planned or unplanned. Thus, the staff must become thoroughly familiar with the way the chief executive thinks about his organization structure. The identifying characteristic of this viewpoint is that it continuously focuses on the business as a whole and how the business system functions in the mind of the chief executive. True, the staff may frequently be concerned with a problem that is—or at first sight appears to be—limited to one part of the business. It will be concerned with such questions as these:

— What is the basic cause of this business problem?
— What effect will a change in this function have on other functions of the business?
— Is this function essential in achieving some major objective or goal of the business, or is it obsolete?
— What is the relationship of policy, procedure, forms, reports, and other administrative tools to this problem?
— Is establishing or strengthening this activity or function and the potential result worth what it is likely to cost to achieve it?

Among organization planners there are too many technicians and not enough generalists in management. A technician tends to strengthen one part of the organization at the expense of the performance of the business system as a whole. It is difficult for him to be thoroughly familiar with the best ways of organizing every major function of the business, including the new ones. But such knowledge is essential in a qualified organization planner. It is his work background and experience as a generalist in management that makes it possible for him to see a business organization as one integrated work system.

THE FACT-ORIENTED APPROACH

The fact-oriented approach should include:

1. Gathering historical information on the development of the organization structure and functions
2. Planning the survey
3. Getting the facts
4. Analyzing facts and preparing the proposal
5. Installing the approved proposal
6. Following up and auditing results

This involves getting minimum facts needed to answer the following questions:

1. How did the organization develop into its present form?

2. What are the major improvement opportunities?

3. What are the objectives of the organization?

4. What functions are essential to achieve these objectives effectively at minimum cost?

5. What implications does this have for establishing new functions and strengthening, reducing, or eliminating present ones? How should the remaining essential functions be grouped most effectively to pyramid objectives? How would the resulting structure conform to the generally accepted principles of organization and how would this affect the present cost, workflow process, or decision-making? Finally, the organization planner must determine the various ways of organizing the work to achieve the objectives and evaluate the alternatives against the established criteria as a guide to the chief executive in selecting the best approach.

In the following chapter we will discuss some of the analytical tools the organization planner uses to arrive at answers to such complex questions.

THE FUNCTIONAL APPROACH

An organization of any kind, no matter how large or complex, is composed of not more than a few basic workflow processes and supporting activities. These should be carefully defined in writing. It is essential first for the organization planner to study the overall objectives, the interrelationship of the functions, and how they should hang on the organizational "Christmas tree." He then should study each function regardless of the number of persons carrying it out or their place in the overall structure of the organization.

Another popular approach is to study individual departments or divisions. This, however, is a piecemeal attack that can produce only piecemeal results. The total organization approach or functional approach, although offering just as great an opportunity to improve organization and control manpower, also throws the spotlight on the effect of the change on the entire organizational activity system.

An example of this is found in the survey of the Art Association (see Chapter 11). Since the primary objective of this study was to reduce costs, it was essential for the task force to analyze in some detail the work and workload of essentially every job to see what could be eliminated without reducing the productivity of the organization and its effectiveness. More important, the serious financial difficulties of the association, due to limited revenue, were found to lie outside the scope of the survey as originally planned. Only a chief executive's approach to this study would have uncovered this.

ACHIEVEMENT OF THE OBJECTIVE

A primary purpose of organization planning is to improve the performance and economy of an organization as a whole. Until satisfactory results are achieved, it is premature and unwise to concentrate on chopping heads. However attractive these apparent short-term savings may be, they are often secondary to the long-term benefits of stronger overall performance, more profits and better products, that accrue from the total organization effort. Unless these manpower savings are evaluated in terms of their long-term effect on the total output of the organization, the savings and economy may be more apparent than real. A low-cost means of attaining an unsatisfactory end result is still an extravagance. It is better to abolish the activity.

RELATIONS BETWEEN THE ORGANIZATION PLANNING STAFF AND CHIEF EXECUTIVE

Once an organization planning staff has been brought into being, its success will depend on the establishment and maintenance of a sound and close working relationship with the chief executive officer. This relationship is a reciprocal one. It cannot flourish unless each renders to the other. It requires that the chief executive give active support to the organization planning staff that serves him. In turn, it requires the staff to earn the confidence of the chief executive by the professional caliber of its work. This is not a new thought, but rarely does anyone using the term "support" explain what it consists of for either party in this reciprocal arrangement.

WHAT CHIEF EXECUTIVE SUPPORT MEANS

Chief executive support of an organization planning staff really is the belief in and cultivation of an idea. This is the idea that continuous stabilization, adaptation, simplification, and development of a rational organization structure is essential to operating effectiveness, the achievement of business objectives, and the execution of strategic plans. The efforts of all managers and key senior executives must be carefully planned, integrated, and coordinated to this end. Diffusion of this idea throughout an organization cannot be accomplished passively. It requires sustained action of a kind that only the chief executive has the power and prestige to take and without which organization planning work must be carried on under almost insuperable difficulties. Let us list what the chief executive officer should do to fulfill his crucial role in supporting his staff.

1. *Stimulate among senior management personnel an understanding of the problem and the opportunities it holds for sound organization planning and a*

will for united action to realize these benefits. It is not enough for the chief executive to accept an idea; he must show that he really believes in it by his actions. It is the way he communicates and interprets this idea to his key executives who must carry it out that gives it real meaning. Organizational efficiency, coordination, and control begin with the chief executive's determination to have it. He not only must enforce the organization planning policy, he must comply with it himself. It helps for the chief executive to show his interest in the organization planning staff and the organization improvement program when it is instituted, but the real problem is to ensure the durability and intelligent application of the concept by gradually building it into the thinking habits of his key management executives. This is a management training job of a high order. It cannot be achieved by any means other than by consistent, demanding leadership on the part of the chief executive. He must have the will to organize and manage;[1] without it the organization planning staff has little possibility of real success. Following are some of the specific attitudes and characteristics the chief executive should seek to foster through this process of management training:

A. Appreciation throughout the entire organization of the vital role that sound organization planning plays in the success and profits of the business.

B. Recognition of the need for continuously questioning and improving organization structures and adapting them to changed strategies, objectives, and conditions. To help achieve this end the chief executive must encourage the development of a bold, challenging proactive point of view instead of the traditionally reactive one toward the design and control of organization structure.

C. Understanding of the responsibilities of both line and staff for the success of organization planning. It is not enough to use the services of an organization planning staff, but each executive must realize that organization planning is a reserved function of every manager, and that he must not completely delegate this function to any staff specialist. At the same time, if the organization planning process in a large organization is to be orderly, integrated, continuous, and company-wide in scope, it must be planned, guided, controlled, reviewed, and spearheaded by one or more staff organization planners.

D. Knowledge of how widespread the scope and objectives of the organization planning program are. This is essentially the job of dispelling the concept that results from the program must be limited to the office area, job evaluation, or the reduction of manpower costs. The opportunities shown in the case studies in Part II should be helpful in raising the organization's sights in this matter.

E. Determination that the organization planning program is not a reactive posture of waiting for someone to request an organization improvement study from a free internal organization consulting service, while having the staff sit on their collective hands between times. Instead, the staff should be the top proactive functional control unit and dynamic contributing force in the management of the business. Since all the results of the business are achieved through the organization structure, the planning, stabilization, and communication of this structure is at least on a par with—and in some ways perhaps even more important than—the management of the company's sales and production operations. In addition, everyone should clearly understand that, if the organization planning program is to have any real substance, the greatest payout comes, not from changing the organization structure, but from consistently cashing in on these changes in terms of tangible results; for example, changes in organization structure mean nothing until the company ultimately realizes improved business performance and profit results. In achieving such results, the soundest organization plan means little unless it is capably staffed.

F. Insistence that the entire organization acquire the habit of thinking critically and objectively about the true profit-making value of the work each component does against its cost.

G. Recognition that the most significant manpower savings cannot be achieved without cost. Ordinarily, a price must be paid in terms of giving things up, taking some risks, and making some courageous decisions affecting status symbols.

H. Realization that the chief executive has a continuing interest in the function of organization planning. Organization planning is not a one-time project but a continuing process. One of the most practical means of demonstrating this interest is exemplified when the chief executive personally praises the key department head who does an outstanding job both in studying his organization structure and in presenting the organization change proposal for approval before he staffs the structure. This is the only step that will ensure the continuing vitality of the organization planning function. Regardless of the enthusiasm with which an organization planning staff is started, operating personnel will know whether the chief executive means what he says by the way he acts toward the organization planning staff when he makes significant organization changes.

2. *Ensure that the organization planning staff has sufficient time to prove itself.* The cases in Part II show how long it takes to make overall organization changes and achieve anticipated profit and market results. If the organization planning activity is being conducted in a company where executives have little experience in applying the skills of organization analysis, the staff will have a long and difficult management training job to do. The staff must win the confidence of long-service employees. For this reason the chief executive must realize that, if the organization planning staff is to build soundly, it must build slowly. Unless the chief executive is serious about adopting and holding to this long-range view, it would be better to forget about establishing any organization improvement activity at all. To start the program and after a time audit it, abolish it, or change directions for want of spectacular results would do more harm than good (see Chapter 6).

3. *Facilitate decision-making on the staff's proposals.* This is a matter of agreeing with the staff and division heads on a simple procedure for approving organization changes and keying up the appropriate executives to make adequate organization studies and reviews within a reasonable length of time before any change and staffing commitments are made. Some staffs have to spend more time winning approval of their proposals than conducting their organization studies and guiding the implementation of approved changes.

THE STAFF'S RESPONSIBILITY FOR RELATIONSHIPS
WITH THE CHIEF EXECUTIVE

If the staff is to merit the chief executive's support, what must it do to earn his confidence? His confidence will be influenced by the technical proficiency of the staff and the soundness of the relationships it has developed with the operating personnel and key senior executives with whom it works. These are some of the things the staff head must do:

1. Learn the chief executive's veiwpoint. Read his written pronouncements on company objectives. Learn his goals, his ways of thinking, values, strategy, and interests. Guide the work of the staff so that its organization planning skills are used most effectively in helping the chief executive with his reserved organization planning work. This in no case means giving him recommendations he would like to hear, unless they are soundly based.

2. Achieve a frank understanding with him on the barriers to organization improvement as they exist in his company. Reach agreement on the roles he and the staff will play in overcoming or minimizing these barriers.

3. Make it easy for the chief executive to indoctrinate his key executives in the objectives, techniques, and importance of the organization planning program. Prepare materials he can use for this purpose, including speeches, presentations, articles, instructions, policies, and the like.

4. Give the chief executive current articles, books, and speeches by professional chief executives on the subject of organization planning.

5. Encourage him to associate with and visit these men and observe how they discharge their organization planning responsibilities on a day-to-day basis.

6. Encourage him to visit his organization planning staff frequently and participate with it in conducting overall organization studies, designing the organization structure, and debating the merits of various organization plans.

7. Plan the staff's program so that a large part of its effort is devoted to organization problems of real interest and importance to the chief executive.

8. Develop for him, at regular intervals, summary information on the program, progress, and results. Make factual and conservative claims when the results are not clearly the work of the staff alone.

9. Be sure the demands of the staff on the chief executive's time are necessary and purposeful. Don't pester him, but do keep him adequately informed of the progress on matters in which he is particularly interested. Discover early what these matters are. Generally, they will include the organization planning staff's master program and goals (see Exhibit 6.1); summary reports of progress; highlights of projects brought to completion; proposals on projects brought to completion; proposals on projects he has requested and progress on installations in connection with the proposals he has approved; as well as disagreements and jurisdictional conflicts that the staff has been unable to resolve.

10. Adhere strictly to the concept of completed staff work in bringing any organization change proposal to him for approval. Never bring him a problem

without assembling essential facts and presenting alternative solutions, thoroughly compared and evaluated, along with the recommendation of the staff as to the best solution.

TECHNICAL COMPETENCE OF THE ORGANIZATION PLANNING STAFF

Skill in the successful diagnosis and solution of organization problems is the product of three factors commonly regarded as prerequisites for successful business planning of any kind: (1) proper mental equipment; (2) specialized knowledge; and (3) perfected and proven techniques.

Mental Qualifications

Observation of the work habits and caliber of thinking of competent organization planners discloses the following basic mental faculties:

1. *A logical, analytical, and perceptive mind.* These qualities are apparent in the organization planner's ability to approach extremely complex business and organization problems, see beyond the symptoms to the root causes, approach the gathering and analysis of minimum data by orderly processes of thought and detect obscure but significant relationships among the data obtained.
2. *Ingenuity and creative imagination.* These are required not only in conceiving original solutions to the problems defined, but in conceptualizing and visualizing the probable consequences of the various alternative solutions proposed.
3. *Good judgment.* This is essential in evaluating the relative importance of factors bearing on the problem and in recognizing the practical business results of alternative courses of action.

These natural aptitudes and qualities of mind and mental processes can be strengthened through experience and training. They cannot, however, be created in this way. For this reason, they—together with a certain emotional maturity discussed later—must be considered as essential selection criteria to be included in an organization planner's position specification and not as a staff development or training objective.

Specialized Knowledge

The organization planner should be thoroughly experienced and trained in the fundamental principles of business organization and control, policy and procedures formulation, reports and forms design, and in the various types of office equipment and methods of work simplification. In addition, and far more important, he must be thoroughly and currently informed on the best ways of organizing all the major functions and subfunctions found in various types of businesses. He must know patterns of structure to be found in the outstandingly successful organizations of various types as well as the critical skills, motivations, and experience required to perform various types of work. This, of course, does not mean that it is necessary—or even desirable—for him to be skilled in actually performing all these kinds of work. In performing his surveys, however, he should have observed critically and analytically the work of those who are highly skilled in organizing various functional work areas.

Perfected Organization Planning Techniques

These techniques are demonstrated in the way the staff conducts its organization surveys. It is partly a matter of general approach to organization problems and partly a matter of technique. The following chapter will be devoted to the specific specialized techniques of organizational analysis. Although the sound general approach to organizational analysis is the more fundamental requirement, the development of systematic and perfected techniques of analysis and presentation is by no means unimportant. The gathering and analysis of organizational and functional data in a predetermined, orderly, and precise way, instead of haphazardly, have the three following benefits:

1. They speed up the performance of the assignment.
2. They improve the quality of the problem diagnosis and recommendations by promoting greater thoroughness and ensuring that all types of feasible solutions are explored and evaluated.
3. They do much to make division heads conscious of organization improvement opportunities and to educate them in making their own organization surveys using these same analytical techniques.

STAFF SELECTION AND TRAINING

Specialized organization planning knowledge and techniques should be viewed primarily as training needs both for the professional staff and line managers. It is essential, of course, to recruit the organization planning staff from those with considerable experience and demonstrated achievement in solving organization and compensation problems. However, this is secondary to the intellectual and personal qualifications the incumbent should bring to the job as the minimum criteria for selection, since the other skills can be acquired through training and experience on the job. Even when these basic qualifications are required of the staff, the organization planning staff head must not make the mistake of assuming that on-the-job coaching of the new members is in itself enough to overcome their deficiencies. If the technical competence of the staff is to be achieved and maintained, there must also be an organized and continuous work-time training program by and for the experienced senior staff members. This book seeks to help the chief executive, division heads, and senior staff men with their continuing training and self-development in organization planning techniques; at the end of this book, there is a bibliography on which they can draw to supplement their own experience in both the human relations and technical phases of their work. Many professional associations hold seminars to discuss the best ways of organizing to perform their particular functions more effectively. Finally, the staff should build a reference file on the charts, job descriptions, policies, procedures, principles, documents, manuals, and organization and management practices of successful competitors. They also should build a modern management reference library if there is not one elsewhere in the company.

RELATIONS WITH OPERATING PERSONNEL

In spite of the importance of technical competence, it is unfortunately true that the more competent the staff becomes in this respect, the more difficulty it is likely to have in winning the confidence of the operating personnel and division heads. Although a mediocre staff is not likely to initiate any significant and measurable organization changes, neither is it likely to disturb any established work habits and power or status relationships among the top executives. The more penetrating the organization planner's analysis and observations of functional voids and overlaps in the structure, the greater is the probability that his work will result in major organizational changes that will incite fear, avoidance reactions, suspicion, and resistance on the part of the top executives. This is particularly true if organizational changes in the past have resulted in layoffs of experienced and talented managerial personnel without any effort on the part of the company to help them obtain employment elsewhere. The danger that the program will result in some work elimination and personnel reductions cannot be easily avoided, for it is inherent in the nature of the organization planning and work simplification process. A division head often believes that the review of his organization structure by the staff amounts to a criticism of his own organizing ability. He is quick to point out the organization planner's lack of experience in performing the work he is analyzing and slow to appreciate the compensating value of having the time and ability to objectively and critically observe and analyze the work in considerable depth without also having the time-consuming job of doing it. If the staff sees its responsibility as consisting not only of developing organization improvement ideas, but also of winning their approval and guiding their installation, it will not ignore these occupational hazards nor regard them with undue pessimism. Rather, the staff will give just as careful thought to obtaining the emotional and intellectual approval for the execution of its proposals as it gives to the technical phases of its work. The cases in Part II emphasize the importance of this consideration. Without genuine acceptance of change in the work by the persons concerned, the organization changes proposed by the staff are unlikely to be carried out by those who must direct and work under the new plan of organization. Without changes in the work, the benefits of the change will not be realized and there will be no real payoff for the many hours of analysis spent by the staff. At best, the staff will suffer passive cooperation or indifference; at worst, it may encounter open antagonism, sabotage of its work, or the spreading of harmful rumors about its objectives or competence. This might result in its abolition or relegation to some dusty corner of the personnel department before the benefits of its work become apparent. Even when results are apparent, there are many others eager to take the credit. The willingness of the operating personnel to carry out the change proposals of the staff is directly related to the following factors: (1) their undertstanding of the staff's work; (2) their participation in that work; (3) the recognition they receive for their participation; (4) their confidence in the staff; and (5) demonstrated results achieved by the staff.

UNDERSTANDING

Only an exceptional organization change proposal makes its underlying objectives self-evident to those who have not participated in the study. Acceptance depends not so much on what change in work is required, but upon why it is required. The responsibility of the chief executive for bringing about this kind of understanding among his key executives has been discussed previously. The staff's educational and promotional effort must be focused on the objectives of the specific organization change as well as on the organizational improvement program as a whole, the need for it, and the logic of having the activity headed by a specialized staff group. But the real test of acceptance for the program will be found in the attitudes of senior executives toward organization change proposals that may adversely affect them personally, either by really or apparently reducing their power, responsibility, authority, status, or compensation— or even by terminating their association with the organization. The staff must share its knowledge of the reasons for the study; the way it will be conducted; and the improvements in performance the organization and its members can anticipate from successfully installing the changes. This is the staff's starting point for overcoming the natural resistance to change.

PARTICIPATION

Human nature is such that if one is asked to work on his own idea he will do so readily; if asked to work on some idea imposed on him from above, he will do so reluctantly. This alone would be sufficient reason for the organization planner to solicit the ideas of those he interviews in the fact-finding process. More important is the reason that the person who actually performs the work is more intimately familiar with his job than anyone else can possibly be, even his superior. This skill, coupled with the analytical techniques of the organization planner, brings to bear on the problem all the intellectual resources available. Nothing less is acceptable. This participation in no way relieves the staff of responsibility for the results of the study. The final reason is the excellent training in organization planning that each manager who participates in a study receives. This is management training in the best sense of the word and one of the most important results of the work of the organization planning staff.

RECOGNITION

Appreciation given directly to a participant in an organization survey is a courtesy. If it is expressed to his boss or to others, orally or in writing, it is recognition. This is a powerful tool in motivating the cooperation of others with the organization planning staff. We all want recognition and will do much to get it.

Using a person's help and ideas is a form of recognition. However, never pirate or even appear to pirate the ideas of others and use them as your own. Starting at the top and going down through the structure in obtaining authorization for an organization survey is also a form of recognition—recognition of position.

CONFIDENCE AND BELIEF IN THE STAFF

In order to earn confidence and belief in its work, the staff should:

1 . Establish a reputation for honesty and candor
2. Refuse to play corporate politics—avoid discussing an executive's personality or his performance; be impartial and rational in the formulation of organization change proposals and in evaluating jobs; attack problems, not individuals
3. Be conservative in making promises and keep those that are made

4. Be conservative in stating expected benefits of change proposals and in claiming sole credit for results if any others are involved

5. Establish a reputation for helpfulness; don't try to mastermind

6. Save face for others

7. Avoid the spectacular

8. Try to see things through others' eyes

9. Sell proposals from the bottom up

DEMONSTRATED RESULTS

The staff should get results on smaller projects before trying to take on major projects where the improved performance and results may not be apparent for years.

NOTE

1. Marvin Bower, *The Will to Manage* (New York: McGraw-Hill, 1966).

3

Managing the Organization Planning Staff

PLANNING THE ORGANIZATION IMPROVEMENT MASTER PROGRAM

Now we will discuss the methods used in managing a staff effectively and in making organization changes. A necessary tool in managing an organization planning staff is the organization improvement program. Exhibit 6.1 is an example of such a program developed for the Automobile Company. It was used as a guide in determining the priorities for the projects of the staff. The ultimate objective of a planned program should be to improve the organization structure falling within the scope of the staff's responsibility. Control should be exercised over (1) the work undertaken; (2) the progress on each project; and (3) the results achieved.

APPROVING INDIVIDUAL PROJECTS

The staff head, before he approves a project, must determine from a preliminary survey, that the expected benefits are greater than the probable costs of attaining them. Also, it should be possible for the staff to carry out the new project without undue delay in the projects already undertaken. Since a large part of the staff's work is requested by the chief executive and other key executives, the staff often is tempted to try to please everyone. However, unless strong project control is exercised, there is danger that the staff will spread itself too thin and become swamped with many uncompleted jobs that it can never bring to completion. In the final analysis, the chief executive must make the decision as to the priorities of the projects of his organization planning staff, using the long-range program as his guide.

REPORTING PROGRESS

The staff head should keep a card file on each project and make up a summary report of progress on each one at frequent regular periods for discussion with the chief executive.

CARRYING OUT THE PROJECT

There are many good books on techniques of conducting management improvement surveys, among them *Management Systems for Profit and Growth* by Richard F. Neuschel. These tools and techniques of systems analysis are sound and apply to all organizations. However, the following discussion is limited to the tools of analysis that are peculiar to the successful execution of organization surveys.

In discussing the application of these techniques and tools, we will use, as an illustration, the organization survey of the Art Association (see Chapter 11). This organization is small enough so that all of the elements of the survey are clearly evident in one survey report. We will largely limit ourselves to the discussion of the objectives of the organization and the organization of the work into positions and units in order to carry it out. What are the minimum facts? They are usually:

1. The structure of organization that includes the unit and position titles and descriptions of the positions.
2. The names and background of the people manning the organization.
3. The principal functions of each unit.

Getting the facts in the area of organization planning is not so easy as it sounds. Anyone who has had any experience in the analysis, description and evaluation of a management job can testify to this. Activities in the factory area are largely physical and repetitive. They can, therefore, be analyzed effectively by physical time-and-motion study. But time-and-motion study of a man writing, telephoning, smoking a pipe, and shifting papers from one stack to another would not be very revealing. If time study techniques are not helpful, then what techniques should be used in making an organization study?

Even though the activities connected with management jobs are primarily mental and creative, they are subject to analysis and description, even time study of a sort. As a specific example for analysis, let us take the position of the director of the Art Association. The analyst must ask himself these questions: What are the responsibilities of the job? How does it fit into the total plan of organization? What is the incumbent principally accountable for? What goals does he strive to attain? What duties will he normally perform himself? Which ones will he normally delegate to others? In other words, what does he personally try to contribute to the group effort? Sometimes this information, if given at all, is given verbally to the incumbent of the job when he is hired. Sometimes there is a position description prepared for the purpose of evaluation, recruiting, and performance appraisal. Sometimes duties of the job are set forth in an organization manual. During the fact-finding stage, all such documents should be compared with what the incumbent is actually doing. How does he actually perform his work? Getting the facts on this is not easy. First of all, the formal written data on the job and unit should be assembled. Such information may be obtained from manuals, organization charts, job descriptions, man specifications, policy and procedure instructions, and the like. They show how the job should be done. These should be reviewed with the appropriate executives to ensure their accuracy. Then the analyst must get the facts on how the job is being done.

THE WAY THE JOB IS BEING DONE

There is no easy way to accumulate this data. The most accurate method, of course, is to get the incumbent to maintain a daily work log similar to those kept by management consultants in order to charge their time to the appropriate project and client. By summarizing the man hours the executive spends on various types of work, the analyst can begin to get a better picture of how this work distribution compares to the way the job is supposed to be done. This information should then be summarized and presented on a work distribution or linear responsibility chart covering all the positions in the unit under study.

THE LINEAR OR WORK DISTRIBUTION CHART

In Exhibits 3.1 and 3.2 we see the use of linear responsibility charts, both present and proposed, in order to analyze the distribution of work at the Art Association. It is easy to see how these charts help identify the weaknesses in the present structure and work distribution of the organization. It is then possible to develop a new work distribution and plan of organization. Once this is done, it is a relatively simple matter to write the proposed job descriptions, performance standards, and man specifications for each job and even to determine the number of incumbents required. A performance standard for the job of director of the Art Association might read something like this.

Exhibit 3.1 Present Linear Responsibility Chart (Phase I): Art Association

Legend:
- ▨ Does Work
- ▨ Directly Supervises Work
- ▨ Generally Directs Work
- ▢ Functionally Directs Work
- ▨ Must Recommend Before Decision
- ⋮ May Exchange Views Before Decision
- ▨ Must Be Notified After Decision

Column headers (left to right): EXECUTIVE SECRETARY, DIRECTOR, ACCOUNTANT, REGISTRAR, REGISTRAR P/T, SEC'Y & PUBLICITY, PUBLICITY P/T, RECEPTIONIST, STOREKEEPER P/T, SALESMAN P/T, LIBRARIAN P/T, FACULTY, JANITOR/BLDG. MAINT., NIGHT JANITOR P/T, JANITOR P/T, TOTAL HOURS PER WEEK, COMMENTS

Task	TOTAL HOURS PER WEEK	COMMENTS
Plans Work of School	5	Should Spend More Time on This
Provides Services to Association	40	To Public Relations
Registers Students/Keeps Records	27	To Administrative Assistant
Keeps Books	35	To Accountant
Provides Secretarial Services	42	To Administrative Assistant
Provides Publicity to Media	14	To Public Relations
Provides Reception Services	9	To Part-time Worker
Maintains Library	15	To Part-time Worker
Maintains Building & Grounds	77	No Change
Publishes Bulletin	3	To Public Relations
Sells in Store	27	No Change
Purchases Supplies & Equipment	10	To Administrative Assistant
Prepares Financial Statements	11	No Change
Conducts Hiring Interviews	6	To Administrative Assistant
Receives Incoming Calls	22	To Part-time Worker
Opens and Distributes Mail	7	To Part-time Worker
Provides Pay Checks	3	To Accountant
Hires & Pays Models	3	To Accountant
Assigns Lockers/Receives Payment	2	To Accountant
Bills Association Members	3	To Accountant
Manages Cafeteria	26	Eliminate/Farm Out
Types, Files, Stuffs Envelopes	1	To Part-time Worker
TOTAL HOURS PER WEEK	388	

TOTAL HOURS PER WEEK by column: EXECUTIVE SECRETARY 40, DIRECTOR 40, ACCOUNTANT 40, REGISTRAR 12, REGISTRAR P/T 40, SEC'Y & PUBLICITY 12, PUBLICITY P/T 40, RECEPTIONIST 12, STOREKEEPER P/T 12, SALESMAN P/T 12, LIBRARIAN P/T 40, FACULTY 12, JANITOR/BLDG. MAINT. 12, NIGHT JANITOR P/T 12, JANITOR P/T 12

Exhibit 3.2 Proposed Linear Responsibility Chart (Phase I): Art Association

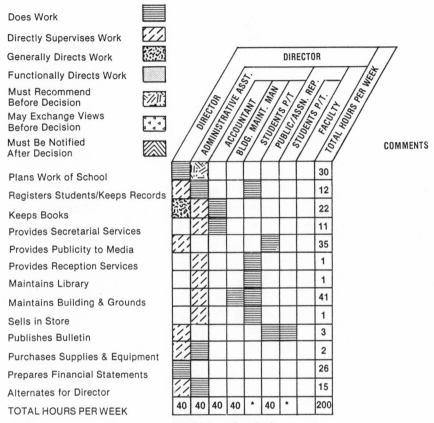

*Variable as Required

PRINCIPAL ACCOUNTABILITIES

A satisfactory standard of performance in this position will be achieved when:

1. The following objectives are realized in the community:

   —The museum and school of fine arts are properly maintained.

   —Outstanding exhibitions are provided for and conducted in these facilities to unite the membership in fellowship and promote the cultivation of the fine arts in the community.

2. These facilities are self-supporting and rely at a minimum upon grants or gifts from the members or from government agencies (local, federal, or state).

3. The reputation of the association and the caliber of art instruction received at the school are recognized by other similar organizations and the general public as being among the finest in the nation.

MAN SPECIFICATION

	Minimum	Desired
Age:	27	35
Education:	2 yrs. college	College degree in business administration.
Experience:	5 yrs. in managing a professional teaching staff	5 yrs. teaching art or producing it
Technical Skills:	Forms design Work simplification Accounting Art and archeology	

Supervision Received:
> Must operate successfully with only broad policy guidance from the executive committee

Management Skills Involved:
> Ability to develop objectives and the plans to carry them out
> To motivate subordinates and others
> To train subordinates
> To organize work

Personal Characteristics:
> Motivation to spend considerable personal time in self-development
> Rational and analytical thinker
> Emotional stability

Additional Factors:
> Must be satisfied with little possibility of advancement within the association

By making this kind of analysis of the jobs and present staff members, we can see which incumbents will have to be replaced and which ones can be transferred to other and perhaps necessarily lower rated jobs in the proposed structure. This anlaysis will also tell us how many new employees will have to be recruited from the outside. There is little doubt that the present art school director will have to be replaced with a man of considerably more experience in professional management, preferably in running a profitable art association or art school.

ACTIVITY STRENGTH ANALYSIS

What results are expected of the organization? What are the primary work processes required to get these results? What are the minimum activities required to manage and support the organization needed to carry out the essential work processes?

To answer these questions it is advisable to use the technique of activity strength analysis (see the activity strength analysis chart in Exhibit 3.3).

Exhibit 3.3 Activity Strength Analysis: Art Association

ORGANIZATION OBJECTIVES	POSITIONS AND FUNCTIONS REQUIRED	ACTION
To Teach Art To Provide Student Services	Faculty Library Service Registration Art Store Cafeteria	NC NC NC NC C
To Maintain School in Good Repair & Housekeeping	Building Maintenance Care of Building & Grounds Provide Receptionist	NC NC R
To Plan, Organize, Direct & Control Activities	Director Administrative Assistant Accountant	S N C
To Arrange Shows, to Promote Activities, to Raise Funds & to Market Services	Public & Art Association Representative Provide Secretarial Service	C-S NC

ACTION CODE

N-Create New Activity

C-Change Activity

R-Reduce or Eliminate Activity

NC-No Change

S-Strengthen Activity

On the left side of the chart, the analyst should list the major organizational purposes to be achieved by the essential work processes. These are followed by the leadership, identification, and other activities necessary to the execution of the essential work. Any voids or unessential activities should be carefully noted; any that should be changed or strengthened should also be noted and appropriately marked. Grouping of the activities should not be the subject of this analysis.

ACTIVITY GROUPING ANALYSIS

The purpose of this analytical technique is to achieve the most effective grouping for managerial purposes of the essential activities as determined above through the technique of grouping analysis (see Exhibit 3.4). Care must be taken to "pyramid" the objectives properly. In this way all the activities can be managed effectively without slighting any essential work. In addition, the supporting staffs must be properly positioned in relation to the activity or activities that they serve, i.e., the apples should be with the apples and the oranges with the oranges. Homogeneity of goals is most important to the effective functioning of an organization. If a person's goals do not support those of his boss, regardless of the type of

Exhibit 3.4 Grouping Analysis: Art Association

POSITIONS AND RESERVED FUNCTIONS	PROPOSED GROUPING OF POSITIONS AND FUNCTIONS
Chief Executive Officer •Association Relations •External Relations	**Director** *Public and Art Assn. Representative* •Editing Bulletin •Issuing Press Releases •Conducting Fund Drives
•Planning, Organizing, Directing & Controlling School Activities	**Administrative Asst.** *Accountant/Clerk* •Purchasing Supplies & Equipment •Library Services •Cafeteria Services •Receptionist Service •Janitorial & Maint. •Registration & Files •Typing •Finance
•Providing Teaching Services	**Faculty** •Teaching Art

activity, there is certain to be trouble in implementing them. The recent trend toward result-oriented performance appraisal has forcefully demonstrated the importance of this principle. Peter F. Drucker in *Management: Tasks, Responsibilities, Practices* (pages 542-46), discusses the importance of these techniques of organization analysis and job design.

DECISIONS ANALYSIS

The technique of decisions analysis (see Exhibit 3.5) is used to determine the lowest practical level to which a class of decisions should be delegated in the proposed structure. Down the left of the chart are listed various classes of decisions. Along the top of the chart from left to right are the factors determining the strategic value of the decision category. "Futurity" refers to the length of time after the decision is made before the result of the decision can be evaluated. "Reversibility" indicates the ease with which the decision can be reversed. Some decisions are virtually irreversible. Other decisions can be reversed only at great cost; while some can be reversed at minimum cost. "Scope" means the extent of the organization affected by the decision. "Human impact" indicates the degree of the impact on the people affected by the decision. Termination can have a devastating effect. Taking away a company car could have a

Exhibit 3.5 Decisions Analysis: Art Association

DELEGATION LEVEL

Executive Comm.	—E
Director	—D
Admin. Asst.	—A
Publ. Rel. Rep.	—P
Accountant	—AC

STRATEGIC VALUE

PTS.	DEGREE
40-50	I
30-39	II
20-29	III
10-19	IV

DECISION TYPE	FUTURITY		REVERSIBILITY		SCOPE		HUMAN IMPACT		FREQUENCY		STRATEGIC VALUE	TOTAL POINTS	LOWEST DELEGATION: FACTS AVAILABLE	COMPETENCE	ADVICE AVAILABLE	STATUTORY LIMIT	PRESENT	PROPOSED
Capital Expenditure—Major	FU-1	10	R-1	10	SC-1	10	HU-4	4	FR-1	10	I	44	A	A	A	E	E	E
Capital Expenditure—Minor	FU-5	2	R-3	6	SC-3	6	HU-4	4	FR-4	4	III	22	A	A	A	D	D	A
Operating Expenditure—Budgeted	FU-5	2	R-3	6	SC-3	6	HU-4	4	FR-4	4	III	22	A	A	A	D	D	A
Operating Expenditure—Not Budgeted	FU-5	2	R-3	6	SC-3	6	HU-4	4	FR-4	4	III	22	A	A	A	E	E	A
Execution of Contracts—Not Specified	FU-1	10	R-1	10	SC-1	10	HU-4	4	FR-1	10	I	44	A	A	A	E	E	E
Sale of Assets	FU-1	10	R-1	10	SC-1	10	HU-4	4	FR-1	10	I	44	A	A	A	E	E	E
Scholarship Grants	FU-1	10	R-1	10	SC-2	8	HU-1	10	FR-4	4	I	42	D	D	D	D	D	D
Approving Expenses—Director	FU-5	2	R-1	10	SC-4	4	HU-4	4	FR-4	4	III	24	E	E	A	E	E	E
Approving Expenses—Others	FU-5	2	R-5	2	SC-4	4	HU-3	6	FR-4	4	IV	18	D	D	A	D	D	A
Selecting Banks	FU-1	10	R-5	2	SC-1	10	HU-4	4	FR-1	10	II	36	A	A	A	D	D	A
Approving Position Guide—Director	FU-1	10	R-5	2	SC-1	10	HU-1	10	FR-1	10	I	42	E	E	D	E	E	E
Approving Position Descriptions—Others	FU-5	2	R-5	2	SC-4	4	HU-1	10	FR-1	10	III	28	A	A	A	D	D	D
Approving Status Changes—Director	FU-1	10	R-1	10	SC-1	10	HU-1	10	FR-3	6	I	46	E	E	E	E	E	E
Approving Status Changes—Others	FU-1	10	R-1	10	SC-4	4	HU-1	10	FR-3	6	I	40	D	D	D	D	D	D

FUTURITY		SCOPE		FREQUENCY		REVERSIBILITY (LOSS $s)		HUMAN IMPACT		TOTAL PTS.
FU-1	Continuing	SC-1	Entire Org.	FR-1	Once in 4 Yrs.	R-1	Irreversible	HU-1	Hire/Terminate	10
FU-2	5–10 Years	SC-2	One Division	FR-2	Once in 2 Yrs.	R-2	100M-500M	HU-2	Demotion/Trans.	8
FU-3	3–4 Years	SC-3	Large Unit	FR-3	Once in 1 Yr.	R-3	50M-100M	HU-3	Benefit Reduction	6
FU-4	1–2 Years	SC-4	Small Unit	FR-4	More Than Once	R-4	1M-50M	HU-4	Perquisite Red.	4
FU-5	Under One Year					R-%	Under 1M			2

lesser impact. "Frequency" indicates how often the decision would normally be made. Approving major capital expenditures is made rarely, while approving minor travel expenses is made frequently. The analyst must determine the degree according to the degrees listed in the code, enter the point value in the appropriate column, and total the points for each decision class. The strategic value is determined by the total points. The remainder of the chart is used to determine the maximum delegation level feasible. "Delegation levels" in the structure are coded as shown. The "facts available" column indicates the lowest level where the facts are available to make the decision. The "competence" column indicates the lowest level where the competence is available to make the decision. "Advice available" indicates the lowest level where the specialized staff advice is available. "Statutory limit" indicates the lowest level where mandatory policy or bylaws permit the decision to be made. "Present" indicates the level where the decision is currently being made and "proposed" indicates the level where the analyst believes the decision should be made.

In applying the technique of decisions analysis in the Art Association example, the analyst should immediately question why the executive committee must authorize routine grounds and billing maintenance expenses even though such expenses have been included in a previously approved expense budget. It would appear that these expense decisions have a low strategic value and there is no reason that they could not effectively be delegated to the administrative assistant if the statutory restrictions on the delegation could be lifted.

Use of these three techniques in Exhibits 3.3, 3.4, and 3.5 becomes much more complex and time-consuming when applied to organizations larger than the Art Association, but the principles and concepts are the same. Since certain specialized staffs exist only for the purpose of helping the line executives make better decisions, it is easy to see that sound decisions analysis must precede the final determinations on the positioning of the staffs and the grouping of the supporting work processes. Some management authorities contend that almost all of the corporate organization structure, work, and human resources are devoted to some phase of the information flow, problem-solving, and decision-making process. For this reason, we believe that study of the decision-making process is a particularly fruitful area for future research in the interest of improving the performance and results of large problem-solving organizations.

ALTERNATIVE ORGANIZATION PLAN EVALUATION

Application of organization principles and criteria is illustrated in the evaluation of alternative organization plans as shown in the Organization Plan Evaluation Chart (see Exhibit 3.6). The various plans are listed down the left hand side of the chart. From left to right across the top of the

Exhibit 3.6 Organization Plan Evaluation: Art Association

	OBJECTIVES	GROUPING	LEVELS	SPAN OF MANAGEMENT	DEFINITION	STAFFABILITY	OTHER	TOTAL PTS.
WEIGHTING	2	1	1	1	1	1	1	
PLAN A	20	10	10	10	10	10	5	75
PLAN B	20	10	10	10	10	10	5	75
PLAN C	20	10	10	8	10	10	3	71
PLAN D	20	10	10	9	10	10	10	79

chart are listed the organization planning principles and criteria that the analyst believes are important. In order to evaluate the alternatives, these decision-making criteria are appropriately weighted. Here the organization planner should take into consideration the chief executive's viewpoint and value system. In Exhibit 3.7 are two alternative plans that were not in the original report. In Plan A, the position of administrative assistant has been eliminated to illustrate what impact this would have on the point value of this organization plan. Clearly, elimination of this one position has destroyed, or at least impaired, the balance and span of control of the structure, since now the part-time workers and the maintenance man report straight to the director. On the other hand, if the director is a skilled manager and he has capable men in the subordinate positions, the span should be something he could reasonably handle. We suspect, however, that the director is not a skilled manager, but a former art teacher promoted beyond his abilities, and this new administrative assistant position is designed to shore up this weakness in staffing. Another more effective and less drastic alternative (Plan B) would be to make the maintenance man a service manager with supervision over the store, the cafeteria, the receptionist, and other services. This plan would provide for the separation of routine services from administrative planning and control activities. In such a plan the administrative assistant would have more time to devote to the installation of the proposals in the report without the interruptions incident to the line supervision of the routine services of the Art Association. Plan C is Exhibit 11.2. Plan D is Exhibit 11.3.

MANAGEMENT-BY-OBJECTIVES PERFORMANCE APPRAISAL

This is the only major organization analysis technique not covered in this survey. Specific result goals should have been recommended to the

Exhibit 3.7 Alternative Organization Plans: Art Association

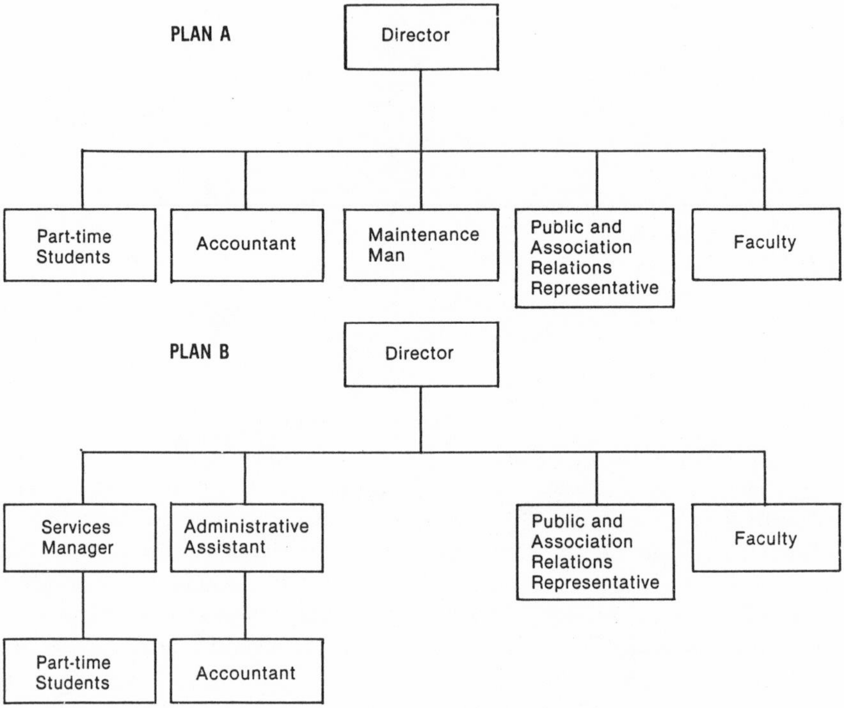

director in carrying out the approved proposals in the report, that is, for example, making an economic study as a basis for the expansion of the enrollment. Perhaps it would also be wise for the analyst to recommend in the report that the director or his administrative assistant investigate the possibility of obtaining government or foundation funds to help cover the Art Association's operating deficit. Why was consideration apparently not given to the feasibility of having an annual fund-raising campaign among alumni and association members, or sponsoring a bazaar, dance, or some other fund-raising activity of the type so common among other non-profit educational and cultural associations? Few non-profit organizations with paid staff are self-sustaining. The report, therefore, may offer an unrealistic strategy for the association and its director. In the next chapter we will discuss what we have learned from experiences in the specific case studies in Part II on how to develop, control, and maintain a sound organization structure.

4

How to Develop a Sound Organization Structure

This book has been written primarily for the manager of an organization, no matter what its size or its purpose. He may head the entire organization or a component. After applying the recommended analytical methodology, discussed in the previous chapter, to his subordinate organization, he should be able to decide whether or not the work of his organization should be restructured, how to draw up a more rational plan of organization, and how to implement it. In this chapter we do more than that. We give the reasons for using the techniques by means of evaluating the case experiences—both successful and unsuccessful—in enough detail and time dimension to explain exactly how, when, and why to approach the problem and apply the analytical techniques.

The expert bridge player is not the one who has memorized the rules and follows them blindly. The real expert is the one who knows from practical experience the reason behind the rules. As a result, he knows when to deviate from the rules to solve a specific problem. This is particularly important in analyzing organization structure. Any major structural change in one component may have an important impact on the functioning of the organization as a whole or some part of it—and such a change is almost irreversible. For this reason, no major organization change should be undertaken without assembling minimum facts, and without thinking through the possible impact of the change on the entire operation in the most professional manner possible, using the most refined techniques of analysis available. In this way a manager will be able to appraise the potential results of an organization change more fully, more sharply, and more penetratingly. In addition, we attempt to give fundamental suggestions from this experience that will be of practical assistance to the practicing manager in the development and maintenance of a sound organization structure as follows:

1. *Conduct a broad management survey.* It is surprising how many managers of very large companies have never participated in a management survey. Even in such a small organization as the Art Association (see Chapter 11), failure to conduct such a survey proved to be the major obstacle to the design of a workable plan of organization. As skilled as were the men on the organization survey task force, they apparently had neither the time nor the expertise to make a broad business study. An advertising executive conducted such a survey in the case of the reorganization of the Church Diocese (see Chapter 9). This survey took one year to complete and cost the diocese $10,000. The results of the survey, however, proved to be essential in restructuring the organization.

2. *Prepare a management philosophy.* Almost every businessman has seen a survey report prepared by a management consultant, even if he has never had one prepared for his organization. Most are also familiar with a brief corporate creed. Few, however, have seen a complete written statement of corporate philosophy from which such a creed, policies and procedures, and a strategic plan can and should be derived. Such a corporate philosophy should state in specific terms just what the organization would like to become and what services it would like to render to the public. If properly done, it should provide guidance and stability in management decision-making. It is a basis for the development of a strategic plan for the organization. The staff prepared a philosophy at the Recreation Company and it proved vital in developing the strategy and structure.

3. *Develop a strategic plan.* Next, the chief executive should develop a strategic plan in writing. George Steiner describes such a plan in his book *Strategic Planning: What Every Manager Must Know.* The Stanford Research Institute (SRI) Long-Range Planning Service issues reports that should be read by an executive who wants specific guidance in the methodology of preparing such a plan. Unless his organization is of such a size that he can afford a staff specialist in strategic planning, an executive should attend the SRI long-range planning seminars and acquire some technical competence in this field. However, care must be taken to institute the formal strategic planning process concurrently in order that the plan may be periodically reviewed and updated. In the absence of a formal strategic plan, a specific statement of corporate objectives should be prepared. The staff prepared a strategic plan at the Recreation Company and used it in developing the profit center organization plan (see Chapter 8).

4. *Analyze and define the present organization structure.* This should be the easiest step for a company that has an organizational manual or job evaluation program containing up-to-date position descriptions and man specifications. An audit of these descriptions, using linear responsibility and authority flow charting techniques, will usually disclose voids, over-

laps, and inaccuracies in the wording of these descriptions. This step usually requires a thorough analysis and revision of the present position descriptions and man specifications, if they exist, or their preparation and approval, if they do not. A qualified compensation specialist or job analyst with a little training in the techniques of linear responsibility charting can help perform this time-consuming but essential job using the evaluation job descriptions as a base. The staff used this technique very successfully at the Hard Rubber Company (see Chapter 5).

5. *Evaluate the qualifications of the key men against the man specifications.* This is the most distasteful of all the steps and also perhaps the most important. Unfortunately, man specifications and a skill inventory were not prepared for the key positions and personnel in the Art Association survey report (see Chapter 11). If this had been done, no doubt the report would have focused on the need to replace the director with a man more qualified in managerial skills as well as skills in the art education field. Failure to take this step and failure to see that a broad management survey was first made were the two key deficiencies in this case.

6. *Design long- and short-range plans of organization.* Using the techniques of linear responsibility charting, activity strength analysis, grouping analysis, decisions analysis, and organization plan evaluation charting, the manager should identify the weaknesses and strengths of his present organization structure in carrying out his strategic plan. Note how the staff used these techniques in Chapter 3. As a result of this analysis, the organization analyst should be able to identify the present activities and positons that should be eliminated or reduced in the interests of real economy. He should also be able to identify the activities that are not positioned properly within the structure. In carrying out this analysis, the intelligent application of the principles of organization is essential. There are five principal ways to organize: (1) function; (2) area; (3) product; (4) clientele; and (5) skill.

First identify the critical statement of purpose in the strategic plan. Identify the important goals the organization wishes to achieve and how it plans to accomplish them. This analysis permits the analyst to determine what key activities will be required to achieve these goals. These are the key workflow processes. They are the line functions. The analyst can then design the management structure and decide where in that structure the supporting staff services should be positioned. Once the basic functions and structure are designed, then he can consider the very important subject of designing the authority flow and the strategic decision-making processes within the structure. This analysis can be simplified by using the techniques of linear responsibility charting and decisions analysis charting (see Chapter 3). The objective of this analysis is to assure that final decision-making authority in each strategic decision category is delegated to the lowest practical level in the structure where these particular decisions can be made with qualified staff support. This authority flow, of course, should be made within the constraints of established policy controls and systems and may require a revision of these constraints.

7. *Document the organization structure and systems of control.* This step requires the analysis and documentation of the present organization structure policies, procedures, and principles as well as the processes for making changes in these documents. Formalization of administrative constraints is essential in large, rapid-growth companies, although more and more of the smaller companies also have written documents, job descriptions, charts, policies, procedures, and organization manuals. The staff of the Automobile Company prepared and issued such documents in an organization manual and a corporate policy guide.

Out-of-date management documents of this kind, however, are worse than useless because they misdirect. For this reason, the decision to formalize should be accompanied by a decision to provide the money, time, and effort to keep the organization documents current. Formalization makes the managerial task easier, but it does not replace the manager. In defining the structure, keep the documents simple but adequate to accomplish organization analysis and job evaluation purposes.

8. *Establish a sound management performance appraisal system.* Many organizations have formal systems for appraising the performance of their management executives—many are trait-oriented; a few are position description-oriented. In increasing numbers, they are becoming objectives-oriented also. The Recreation Company had MBO, but it was not so effective as it might have been due to lack of support for the program by the chief executive officer. Executives interested in results-oriented performance appraisal should read *How to Manage by Results,* by Dale D. McConkey.

9. *Establish fair and competitive compensation structures and incentives.* Establish an effective system of management job evaluation and compensation. A manager in a key job, who performs in an outstanding fashion, should be rewarded in an outstanding way both financially and non-financially, if he is to be effectively motivated. An executive who performs in less than outstanding fashion should not receive supplementary incentive compensation even though he may threaten to leave. Except in a scarce-talent job, he can be replaced through internal promotion or outside hire. Formal management job evaluation, if it does not already exist, should be established concurrently with the preparation of job descriptions and man specifications for the key positions. This was the first step taken by the staff at the Automobile Company (see Chapter 6).

Descriptions for other than key management positions should be used for evaluation and performance appraisal only; they should not be formalized, manualized and distributed. The benefit does not usually warrant the cost. Supplementary management incentive compensation plans should not be established until performance standards and appraisal techniques are reasonably sound; otherwise, there is a likely possibility that the wrong executive and the wrong performance will be rewarded. This practice can cause serious operating, cost, and executive performance problems.

10. *Continuously control, audit, and refine the structure and techniques.* In too many organizations the chief executive regards organization planning as a one-shot, emergency project rather than a continuing refining and adjusting process. The *Principle of Continuity* (see Exhibit 1.1) seeks to emphasize the fact that it is not the former. Frequently, the chief executive retains interest in organization planning only as long as a major reorganization of the top structure is underway. After it is completed, the maintenance of the job descriptions and evaluations is sometimes delegated to the systems or personnel staff. This change took place at both the Recreation Company and the Automobile Company. Such a staff may not be equipped either through interest, training, or level in the organization structure to recommend to the chief executive major changes in the organization structure, functions, and positions of the top corporate executives. For this reason, changes that should be made in the structure from time to time are not called to the attention of the chief executive. Before long, a survival crisis requires another major and traumatic reorganization.

A chief executive should never cease to be actively interested in the state of his organization structure, and should personally audit the accuracy of the job descriptions, policies, and procedures annually, or see that this is done accurately by his staff. At the same time he should consider recommended changes in the structure that may be required to carry out effectively the strategic plan and goals of the organization. He must always remember that no goal can be achieved except through the work structure and functions of his organization. For this reason management consultants, when they are called on to diagnose the cause of poor performance in some aspect of a business, most frequently look first at the organization structure and functions in the appropriate area. Here again, the techniques of organization and work analysis discussed in Chapter 3 can be effectively used for purposes of diagnosis, just as they can be used in improving the plan of organization. The need for change in structure may result from: (1) changes in the company's strategic plan, creed, policies, or procedures; (2) personnel changes; (3) changes in federal, state, or local government legislation; (4) problems in organizational functioning effectiveness or costs; and (5) problems in executive effectiveness together with unusually high failure and turnover rates. Even if there is no periodic audit planned, improvement studies should be initiated at any time when evidence of overlap in duties, unneeded levels, narrow spans of control, overstaffing, staff duplication, or jurisdictional friction is observed by the chief executive.

11. *Effectively control and stabilize the organization structure.* Responsibility for authorizing organizational changes should be fixed by policy, just as for any other major management decision seriously affecting the profitability or survival of the organization. The chief executive should never permit an off-the-cuff or expedient organization change or even a commitment that one will be made without a thorough study and a written proposal after minimum facts have been assembled, analyzed, and reviewed by all the affected executives. This approval process should be outlined in a mandatory corporate policy directive (see Exhibit 1.2). In none of the cases in Part II did the staff develop and issue such an organization planning policy.

BENEFITS OF ACHIEVING A SOUND STRUCTURE

The following are some of the benefits a chief executive may expect to achieve through developing and maintaining a sound organization structure:

1. More important decision-making delegation to lower levels in the structure providing more time for the chief executive to plan for the external and long-range needs of the business.
2. Better utilization of executive time.
3. Discontinuance of one-man rule.
4. Greater emphasis on organization and systems improvement.
5. Better use of management information systems and computers.
6. Quicker and more effective decision-making.
7. Fewer levels of staff and less staff overlap and duplication.
8. More effective use of highly paid staff and technical specialists.
9. Better communications throughout the structure.
10. Greater application of the principle of management by exception.
11. More accurate and less biased performance appraisals and performance improvement motivation.
12. Improved manager development and training.
13. Clearer understanding by executives of how to operate effectively under the present plan of organization.
14. Simplified work processes and systems.
15. Fewer unqualified men in key jobs.
16. Less misunderstanding, pulling and hauling, and cancelling of instructions.

In general, a sound organization structure means much better organizational performance, results, and profits.

EVALUATION OF THE CASE EXPERIENCES IN DIVISIONALIZATION

Next, we will evaluate the two examples of divisionalization, Chapters 6 and 7, in the light of the organizational problems—discussed in *Effecting Change in Large Organizations*, by Eli Ginzberg and Ewing W. Reilley—as follows:

1. Changing the work of the chief executive.
2. Changing the work of the top staff executives.
3. Changing the work of the product division heads.
4. Deciding to change the organization structure.
5. Psychological factors affecting the change.
6. Preparing the objective organization plans, both long- and short-term.
7. The initial stage of implementation.
8. New work patterns.
9. The process of achieving directed change in organizations.

In doing so we shall attempt to reappraise and refine their findings.

It must be remembered, however, that this study of organization change is limited to diversified business enterprises of large size in transition from functionalized to divisionalized structures (see *Strategy and Structure*, by Alfred D. Chandler, Jr.). In the strictest sense, only the Automobile and Recreation Company cases qualify within this criterion. Therefore, we will discuss these two examples as they confirm or raise questions about the findings in this study.

CHANGING THE WORK OF THE CHIEF EXECUTIVE

The proposition was stated that the chief executive is generally a self-made entrepreneur who has built up the business in an authoritarian way, and it is difficult, if not impossible, for him to change his way of managing to a more professional, fact-based, scientific approach, as required by a divisionalized organization structure.

This finding applied more to the chief executive of the Recreation Company than to the chief executive of the Automobile Company, although neither were actually the founders of their enterprises; in the former, the grandfather of the chief executive was the founder of the company, in the latter, the chief executive was twice removed from the founder and no one held a large share of the stock. More to the point, neither one of the men was an analytical, experienced, professional manager like Alfred P. Sloan[1] of General Motors, Ralph J. Cordiner[2] of General Electric, or Ernest R. Breech[3] of Ford. Neither knew what was involved in running a large divisionalized company. They knew even less about piloting a company through the difficult transition from a functionalized structure to a divisionalized one or how to select a top team who could.

We do, however, agree that the professional management ability of the chief executive is crucial to the success of a reorganization particularly during the initial stages of implementation. This skill deficiency can be minimized if the chief executive is willing to visit and learn from chief executives who have successfully divisionalized their companies. Reading professional literature by other presidents, while essential, is not enough. On-the-spot analytical observation of the president of a successful divisionalized company in action is a must. None of these chief executives recognized their lack of management skill as a problem.

Lack of management skill also caused difficulties for the chief executives in the other cases studied, with the exception of the president of the Management Association Chapter. In this one instance, the chief executive had no trouble adjusting to the change in the work associated with the change in the structure of his organization. He was even instrumental in bringing about the change in his own job. He was fully equal to the unpleasant tasks essential to the implementation of a major organization change.

These two cases fully support the finding that the chief executive must be able to plan and operate as a team member rather than as a "one-man band." Moreover, he must have the will to manage by policy rather than by expedient, and must be willing not only to enforce policy but, more important, to comply with it himself. This is a most difficult learning process for an entrepreneur who has achieved the position of chief executive of a large business enterprise.

CHANGE IN THE WORK OF KEY STAFF EXECUTIVES

Ginzberg and Reilley found that the change from *providing functional service to* operating executives to *exercising functional control and guidance over* the same operating executives was a difficult one for a long-service staff executive to make. Our cases show that there was little reluctance on the part of top management in the case of the Automobile Company or the Recreation Company to bring in professional staff men who knew how to exercise functional control. We observed considerable resistance, however, on the part of the long-service top product division executives when asked to submit to the exercise of this functional control. Much line and staff misunderstanding and conflict resulted. There also was a lack of direct personal contact with and support of the specialized staff men by the chief executive. More important, the CEO did not know how important it was for him to live by and enforce his own mandatory management directives and policies.

CHANGING WORK OF THE DIVISION HEADS

Ginzberg and Reilley point out that management generalists are not to be found in a functionalized company in sufficient numbers to provide all of the experienced division general managers required by divisionalization. This problem was particularly acute at the Recreation Company. At the Automobile Company, even though the car division heads had all the "core" profit center functions in their divisions, they had little real profit accountability. There were no divisional profit-and-loss statements and no division head had any accurate knowledge of the real profitability of his operations or where the money was being made or lost. Consequently, his decisions could not really be based on their impact on the profitability of division operations. In short, the profit-center boundaries and charters of their divisions were not accurately defined and there was no integrated profitability accounting system as such.

DECIDING TO CHANGE THE ORGANIZATION STRUCTURE

Ginzberg and Reilley stress the fact that, even though the acceptance of change is a requirement of modern life, there is much inertia and resistance to change in companies that have not gone through frequent organizational changes. Alfred D. Chandler, Jr., in his book *Strategy and Structure*, notes the fact that Du Pont, Sears, Standard Oil of New Jersey, and General Motors nearly went out of business before their chief executives became willing to divisionalize. General Electric alone acted on the basis of an opportunity rather than in response to a survival threat. Both the Automobile Company and the Recreation Company were faced with survival threats. Even the small non-profit Art Association was facing a serious financial problem before submitting to an organization survey. The Management Association Chapter and the Church Diocese were the only organizations that clearly were not responding to a crisis of survival before a major reorganization was decided upon. It is clear, therefore, as stated in the *Principle of Continuity* that each organization must have a built-in mechanism to assure that organization planning takes place by making it a continuing responsibility of an executive inside the company. The question of deciding to change or not to change the structure in response to a survival threat is not so much the problem of deciding whether or not to reorganize, but how to do it successfully with minimum economic loss during the transition period. Where action is taken to realize an opportunity rather than to face a survival threat, then a balance sheet approach—weighing the pros and cons—is a more appropriate technique to use in deciding to change. Also, in the absence of a crisis, there is more opportunity to select the appropriate timing for the change if the decision to change has been made. A patient dying of cancer does not decide, using the balance sheet approach, if he has the money to have the operation, or whether the benefits will outweigh the costs, inconveniences, and disadvantages. If he waits too long the problem will be solved for him. He will not survive. He must borrow enough to have the operation and do it in a hurry if cancer is the diagnosis of a reputable physician.

The seriousness of the financial problems of a business enterprise can usually be found in the market share and the annual report to the shareholders. The root causes, if organizational in nature, are difficult to determine without considerable organization analysis. It is also unpalatable for the chief executive to admit that it is necessary to recruit trained staff executives and division general managers from successful divisionalized companies. Failure to do this was one of the Automobile Company's major divisionalization errors. It was some time before a professional manager who could run a divisionalized corporation was made chief executive.

PSYCHOLOGICAL FACTORS AFFECTING THE CHANGE

According to Ginzberg and Reilley, top management should understand the psychological factors motivating the resistance to change in order to minimize their adverse affect. Ginzberg and Reilley suggested three ways this could be done:

1. Effective communications.
2. Control of anxiety and avoidance reactions.
3. Using effective teaching techniques.

Communication of the proposed organization change by the original chief executive of the Automobile Company was ineffective. This was not because the plan was not clearly thought through by the staff, but because the chief executive was a lawyer by training. He was not a trained professional manager who could understand and communicate the new organization plan personally and enforce discipline with it among his key division heads. He was also unable to allay their fears that they would not be able to adjust successfully to the change by teaching them their new job responsibilities and skills. These methods were also not used effectively at the Recreation Company or in any of the other organizations undergoing major change, except where the chief executive was an experienced professional manager, as at the Management Association Chapter. In this case the change was effectively, consistently, and persistently implemented until the anticipated results were achieved. In all cases where failure or unsatisfactory results ensued, the cause was primarily due to the lack of professional management skills or the motivation to acquire them on the part of the chief executive.

PREPARING THE PLAN

Ginzberg and Reilley observed that the key to the development and implementation of a new plan of organization is the active participation of the chief executive himself. He must recognize the need for organization change and be willing to devote considerable personal time to the problem. The first chief executive of the Automobile Company, owing to the skillful efforts of his vice president-finance, who was a professional manager, finally recognized the need for divisionalization. However, he delegated, almost to the point of abdication, the development and execution of the plan to his vice president-finance, and vice president-organization. For this reason, he was unable to communicate the basic concepts of the divisionalization program effectively to his key division heads.

This critical limitation resulted in ineffectiveness and vacillation in carrying out the reorganization program. With the advent of a professional manager as chief executive, execution of the divisionalization program was resumed. A fully divisionalized structure, however, with integrated car divisions—as at General Motors—has never been achieved. The automobile activities are still functionalized just as they are at Ford Motor Company.

The first chief executive of the Automobile Company was never willing to work on a close personal basis with his organization staff in the execution of the plan. He made no effort to learn about professional management. He never visited the offices of his organization staff as Breech frequently did at Ford. This was also true of the chief executive of the Recreation Company, although he did some reading in management and was active in management associations. The last chief executive of the Automobile Company, although he was more skilled in finance than in professional management, occasionally visited the organization department. In neither case were the working relationships of the staff with the chief executive nearly so close as they should have been for the effective preparation, communication, and implementation of the divisionalization program. This lack of support by the chief executive also reflected itself in less than satisfactory working relationships among the organization staff and the key staff and operating division executives.

In the Management Association Chapter alone, there was a close working relationship between the chief executive and the staff officer developing the organization plan.

THE INITIAL STAGE OF IMPLEMENTATION

Ginzberg and Reilley stress the importance of announcing the organization change in both written announcements and a general meeting of executives and employees. This they believe tends to clarify many uncertainties, contradictions, and potential conflicts as well as to minimize fear reactions.

At the Automobile Company there were meetings announcing the change that were different from the management meetings at Ford as outlined in *Ford: Decline and Rebirth*, by Allan Nevins and Frank Ernest Hill. There were no question-and-answer sessions at which the executives and employees could ask frank and technical questions of the top executives. Management meetings with question-and-answer sessions were started at the Automobile Company, but were quickly discontinued at the request of staff heads. Allegedly, they objected to being asked questions that they could not answer by the audience.

Management meetings among the top executives were held at the Recreation Company also, but here, too, the question-and-answer sessions were limited. The presentations were too generalized and they were prepared by training specialists rather than by the technical staffs. On the whole, a reasonably good job of communicating the divisionalization program was accomplished at initial meetings, but the continuing communications, follow-up, and participation by staff and division heads were wholly inadequate.

NEW WORK PATTERNS

Ginzberg and Reilley also stress the many actions that management should take to ensure effective continuing follow-through after initial efforts at organization change implementation have been instituted. They believe management should make adjustments in reinforcing personnel policies so that they support the new organization structure. These include adjustments in executive compensation, promotion, and discipline policies. In moving authority down to the divisions, top management should simultaneously develop effective measures of control so that it can know accurately how well the division heads are performing their market and profit responsibilities. Management will also find it necessary to validate the plan when a reasonable period after installation is completed—perhaps two years—to be sure the changes have actually taken place as planned. With regard to the implementation process itself, management should establish methods of feedback so that it can, if necessary, take quick corrective action.

At the Automobile Company, follow-up was inadequate. After about two years into the implementation period, a nationally known management consulting firm made an audit of the program progress. This study, while helpful in some ways, in general added to the vacillation of the first chief executive in his divisionalization policy. It resulted finally in failure to establish the integrated car divisions. This fact substantially limited the achievement of potential results.

The MBO performance appraisal system, although sound in design, has never been installed in all departments of the Automobile Company on a mandatory basis. To our knowledge, the management incentive plan has never yet been tied to the MBO performance appraisal system as it is at General Motors. Goals have never been made personal and operational. For this reason, promotions could not be made on a company-wide basis founded on fact-oriented performance appraisals. An audit and renewal of the divisionalization program would seem to be very much in order at the Automobile Company in spite of the improved market and profit results achieved to date. For a company successfully to compete with General Motors, nothing less than a fully divisionalized organization structure and controls would be effective.

THE IMPORTANCE OF TIME

Ginzberg and Reilley conclude by emphasizing the importance of the length of time required to realize results from a directed organization change. Our cases thoroughly confirm this conclusion. Seven years were required at the Automobile Company before costs began to be controlled—even longer before the market share began to improve. The Recreation Company—ten years after divisionalization—is beginning to realize increased earnings per share and reduction in long-term debt. For seven years after reorganization, the Hard Rubber Company showed little real growth, diversification, or profit increase. Even the Management Association Chapter took over seven years to show any substantial improvement in the active participation of its membership.

THE UNIQUENESS OF THE ORGANIZATION

Case studies confirm the finding of Ginzberg and Reilley that a thorough exploration of the unique history of the development of the organization and the reasons for changes in the structure are of vital importance in preparing for any organization survey and in making any specific major organizational change proposals. That is why we have given so much time in the cases to a discussion of the unique history of the organization as well as to its functions and structure. It is also helpful to make a similar historical study of the development of organizations of the same general type and purpose as illustrated in Chapter 6. In studying the Automobile Company organization, the staff made exhaustive studies of the Ford and General Motors structures in particular and large divisionalized companies in other industries in general. Since *Strategy and Structure* has been written by Chandler, divisionalization change has been made immeasurably easier both to plan and carry out in growing, diversified manufacturing companies. It is hoped that the same kind of structural studies will be made of hospitals, churches, colleges, and other large special purpose service organizations. Such studies help to highlight both the uniqueness and the similarities of the structural patterns of successful organizations.

CRUCIAL ROLE OF THE CHIEF EXECUTIVE

The case studies confirm this finding of Ginzberg and Reilley as most important. Wherever the implementation of a major reorganization has not been successful, it has been a result of the failure of the chief executive to prepare himself properly or to take the time to play his crucial role. We found this problem at both the Automobile Company and the Recreation Company. To a lesser degree, this situation existed at the Hard Rubber Company, because the original chief executive was replaced by another entrepreneur. There is no substitute for a strong, well-read, thoughtful, analytical, professional manager with a will to manage as a chief executive. Without this kind of a chief executive, there is not much of an organization planning staff, no matter how professional and capable, can do to develop and maintain a sound structure. For an excellent discusison of this concept see *The Will to Manage*, by Marvin Bower.

THE CONTROL OF ANXIETY

Ginzberg and Reilley concluded that control of anxiety was crucial to successful organization change. There will be some anxiety during any organization change no matter how minor. The possibility of having a new boss causes fear in the most emotionally stable executive. This fear is not always without justification. We have seen capable professional managers summarily dismissed by a new boss without a trial period to make way for a previous associate in which he had more confidence. If the management has, in the past, established a reputation for treating its experienced and capable managers well during management changes, reductions in force, or organization changes, then this anxiety will be minimized. If not, it is fully justified. To minimize anxiety, the changes should be fact-based and the reasons for it should be clearly understood and generally supported by key executives affected before the changes are approved, staffed, and announced. This was effectively done in the cases of the Automobile Company and the Recreation Company.

LEARNING NEW SKILLS

If the chief executive plays his crucial role properly, he will learn enough about operating under the new organization plan to change his own work behavior properly and to teach his key subordinates to change their work behavior also. He is the only one who can do this effectively. Organization planners, no matter how proficient, cannot.

RESEARCH ON PLANNED CHANGE IN ORGANIZATION

Ginzberg and Reilley state that their work and conclusions should be considered only an initial exploratory study of the process of directed change in large industrial organizations. It was hoped that it also would encourage further research in the following directions:

1. The systematic collection of organization planning tools and materials
2. Comparative analysis of organizations that have undergone major change
3. The design of controlled experimental studies, particularly in connection with problems of implementation
4. Borrowing from the theoretical and methodological advances in the social sciences and psychology and applying findings to the study of change

It is hoped that this book will add to what is currently known about the tools and materials that have proven successful in carrying out planned organization change. Part I of the book has been concerned with the discussion of these tools and how they should be applied, using the case experiences in Part II for purposes of illustration.

COMPARATIVE ANALYSIS OF ORGANIZATIONS THAT HAVE UNDERGONE DIRECTED CHANGE

This has been the subject of the cases in Part II. We have also used these case experiences to reappraise and refine the findings of Ginzberg and Reilley. We have generally evaluated these experiences in Part I of this book. Further, we have made suggestions on the organization and management of the organization planning staff itself.

DESIGN OF CONTROLLED EXPERIMENTS IN CONNECTION WITH THE PROBLEMS OF IMPLEMENTATION

Although controlled experiments with planned change in large organizations might prove helpful, they are almost impossible to carry out under laboratory conditions. Employing techniques and practices that have proven successful has demonstrated the fact that much can be done to eliminate problems of implementation. For example, we have suggested that the chief executive make a serious and continuing effort to improve his organization planning skills; that he establish close and effective working relationships with his organization planning staff members; and that he meet with them regularly in their quarters or in a convenient location away from the interruptions of the office to develop organization plans and make implementational decisions.

BORROWING FROM THE THEORETICAL FINDINGS IN THE BEHAVIORAL SCIENCES

We have attempted to establish a communications bridge between practicing managers and behavioral scientists by analyzing the organization structures in Part II against E. Wight Bakke's Bonds of Organization (see Exhibit 4.1 at end of Chapter 4) as outlined in his *Concept of the Social Organization*. The results of this analysis have been used as a basis for suggesting methods of improving the techniques of organization planning, both by the chief executive and by his staff.

FUTURE DIRECTIONS FOR RESEARCH

Having been actively engaged for many years in helping to bring about planned organizational change, the author has acquired knowledge of both the successful processes of organizational change and the proven techniques of planning for and implementing it. One major objective of this book has been to systematize, with the help of the social sciences and a framework of theory, much of the empirical knowledge of the subject, at least in preliminary fashion. As a consequence, it should now be somewhat easier to differentiate between what is known and what is not known about successful practice, and, therefore, easier to recognize where additional effort must be made if greater understanding and control over the process of planned organizational change is to be achieved. The following is a comparative evaluation of case experiences.

HOW THE MEMBERS RESPONDED TO CHANGE

1. *The Hard Rubber Company.* Here we found a rigid organization that, like the Church Diocese, had been unaccustomed to change. It had remained about the same size and had been engaged in the same kind of work with the same tools for about one hundred years. The administrative tools and techniques were similarly antiquated. Turnover among the salaried personnel was extremely low. They had learned to do their jobs well over a long period of time and were unwilling to change their work behavior. Discipline was poor. They firmly believed no one would ever be fired for refusal to change their ways. So they resisted the changes, confident that the outsiders who were bringing in modern management improvements and practices would no doubt leave before they did. Resistance to change was strong.

2. *The Automobile Company.* This also was an organization, like the Hard Rubber Company, that had imported few outsiders and even fewer modern admnistrative methods since its inception fifty years ago. Without the survival motivation, changing a very large organization like this one that had not been accustomed to change would have been almost impossible.

3. *The Recreation Company.* The Recreation Company was also, like the Hard Rubber Company, an old organization that had changed little during its long existence and, though the chief executive was more interested in and knowledgeable about modern management methods than the chief executive of the Automobile Company, he did not believe in living by his own mandatory policies. It was "do as I say, not as I do" that caused the problem of policy enforcement there.

4. *The Management Association Chapter.* The duties of the officials in this organization were unpaid and extracurricular in nature and the financial reinforcements were weak or non-existent. For this reason the difficulty in this organization was not a resistance to change in the work, but in getting the non-paid members to become active at all in advancing the work and goals of the organization.

5. *The Church Diocese.* This was the oldest of all the organizations in going without change or modernization of management methods. Consequently, work habits were far more ingrained and difficult to change. Discipline and motivation were also weak because the bishop was unwilling to discipline the members of the clergy in his immediate official family who were afraid they could not learn their new work patterns. There was no crisis of survival to motivate the change. The executive secretary of the diocese was a prime factor in the resistance movement and he was quite successful. As a result of his rigidity, many essential elements of the approved change did not take place until the bishop retired. The new bishop instituted strategic planning and improved personnel policies, compensation, and benefits.

CONCLUSION: RESPONSE TO CHANGE

This comparative evaluation shows considerable variance in the strength of the resistance to change found in these cases.

If we are to generalize from these experiences at all, we would conclude that the organizations that had least experience with structural change; had poor reinforcements; had the weakest discipline; were not in a survival crisis; and had the least professional chief executives encountered the greatest difficulty overcoming resistance to change. All these factors had a bearing where there was inadequate work change. The most important factor was the role of the chief executive and his willingness (or lack of it) to carry out the changes in spite of resistance by his key executives.

The bishop gave the new organization plan lip service but, when the chips were down, he went along with those in his immediate office that resisted the changes. We might further postulate that, the more likely that there would be resistance to change, the more crucial would be the role of the chief executive. Even though the staff anticipated this problem in the Church Diocese well in advance and tried everything possible to enlist the firm commitment of the bishop in the execution of the change, its efforts were unsuccessful. In these cases the effectiveness, rather than the outright survival, of the organization was at stake. For this reason realizing major performance improvement did not provide sufficient motivation for the bishop to enforce implementation and take the unpleasant disciplinary actions required. Indeed, the bishop himself found it difficult to change from a "one-man band" to a "team player" as required by the structure. He never really used the studies and the services of the planning director except when the recommendations coincided with his preconceived ideas and required him to do nothing very unpleasant or costly. His will to manage was not sufficient to the task.

STRENGTH AND WEAKNESS OF THE VARIOUS COMMUNICATIONS AND LEARNING DEVICES

1. *The Hard Rubber Company.* Changes in organization were effectuated through formal job evaluation change procedures and revisions in the organization manual. This was followed by an annual desk audit of all the salaried positions. These proved to be effective teaching devices.

2. *The Automobile Company.* The organization department had very effective documents and manual systems for communicating changes in organization and policy. There was little effort, however, except in the personnel division, to use the documents as tools in the formal training of executives and non-management employees.

3. *The Recreation Company.* The Recreation Company had a policy and procedures manual that included an organization section. The company newsletter was used to announce changes frequently before the organization and compensation planning staff knew of the change. Formal presentations before small groups of executives were used very effectively to acquaint the top group with the reason for the changes.

4. *The Management Association Chapter.* A newsletter, an operations manual, and a chapter organization chart and long-range plan were used to communicate the changes to the membership. They were quite effective.

5. *The Church Diocese.* A group meeting with the executive council of the diocese and the diocesan newspaper were used to communicate the change. There never was an organization and policy manual issued, although one was recommended to the bishop and approved. An accurate

and complete article on the change was published in a well-known business publication. There was little formal training, however, in the new policies and organization requirements.

CONCLUSION: COMMUNICATIONS DEVICES

As a result of this comparative analysis, we see considerable variation in the media of communication and methods used to train the members of the organization in new work practices and policies. The staffs found it most effective to use many methods for communicating the changes, including internal notices followed by changes in the organization and policy manuals and executive directories. These, in turn, were followed by general management meetings and small training conferences, which completed the training job. We have concluded that the type of media used for communication was not important so long as some written method was used. Media and methods were generally effective and communicating the change generally presented no problem.

INTERPLAY BETWEEN THE CHIEF EXECUTIVE, THE ORGANIZATION PLANNING STAFF, AND THE SENIOR EXECUTIVES

1. *The Hard Rubber Company.* The supervisor of organization planning, an individual contributor, reported to the manager of administrative planning, who reported to the vice president and controller. The controller, in turn, reported to the chief executive officer. The communications problem was not so bad as it might appear from the number of management levels between the organization planner and the chief executive. Both superiors were professional management analysts and gave the organization planner excellent support. Contacts with the chief executive were primarily limited to writing up his job description for the organization manual and evaluating the positions of the key executives under him. The staff specialist had direct access to the chief executive whenever he wished. He also enjoyed a close personal working relationship with his superior, the controller, and with the other senior executives.

2. *The Automobile Company.* When the organization staff was first established, the corporate controller was promoted to the position of vice president-organization, reporting directly to the chief executive officer. He had three functions under his direction: (1) organization planning, (2) strategic planning, and (3) administrative committee secretariat. The vice president-organization was also on the board of directors. His working relationships with the finance vice president, the chief executive officer, and with the other officers and senior executives were very close and

effective. He had everything he needed but the knowledgeable and active participation of the chief executive in planning the strategy and the organization structure. As we have seen, the participation and support of the chief executive is a crucial factor when a divisionalization reorganization is required and resistance to change is anticipated. When the vice president-finance died, he was replaced by the vice president-organization, who was replaced by the corporate secretary as director of organization. The latter was not vice president and member of the board as his predecessor had been. He did, however, report to the chief executive officer and continued to have a close working relationship with him. He had been trained as a lawyer but was interested in and knowledgeable about professional management. He was shortly replaced by a long-service purchasing executive and one of the original internally appointed senior organization planning specialists. When the position of administrative vice president was established in charge of directing the entire corporation in a one-over-one relationship with the chief executive officer, the secretary of the administrative committee was made the director of the organization. The function of administrative committee secretariat was transferred to the corporate secretary's office, and the long-range planning function was transferred to the finance vice president.

In all of these staff head changes no trained member of the organization planning staff had been promoted to organization planning director. These long-service executives were, however, well-respected top managers greatly interested in and well read in professional management. More important, they all had warm, close working relationships with the chief executive officer.

The last mentioned organization staff director had been a lawyer in the legal department and had no previous experience in organization planning; however, he freely admitted his limitations in this regard to the administrative vice president, his superior, and asked that he not be expected to make any major decisions for at least six months, his training period. During this time he went to seminars and read a number of practical organization and management books. He was a thoughtful and analytical executive who achieved excellent performance as staff head.

The organization director in his previous capacity as secretary of the administrative committee had, for some time before his appointment, been spending about two hours a day every day with the administrative vice president reviewing the administrative committee agenda and following up on the execution of the decisions of the committee. In this way he had developed, in spite of his youth, an in-depth knowledge of corporate affairs and enjoyed a very close personal working relationship with the administrative vice president. In addition, he had earned the latter's respect and confidence. In his new role as director of organization, he continued this close working relationship with his superior, and under his direction the staff reached its highest level of effectiveness. It carried out important recommendations of the outside management consulting firm, conducted major organization survey projects of its own, reviewed organization proposals from the divisions and corporate staffs, and installed the organization manual and the corporate policy manual. This was accomplished with a staff of only four professionals.

When the vice president-administration retired, he was replaced by a long-service executive groomed in advance to be the next chief executive officer. The latter placed the organization department under the general direction of his administrative assistant, a highly respected corporate vice president. They were both engineers by training and they selected for the first time an organization analyst—also an engineer—to head the staff. The company had been going through a very austere period with a top-heavy staff and the administrative vice president used the organization planners to give him suggestions where overlap and duplication could be eliminated with corresponding reductions in personnel. He had only just begun this staff reduction program when he resigned because of a well-publicized conflict of interest scandal. His predecessor returned from his retirement and again filled the job of administrative vice president until another successor could be found.

Finally, a financially trained group executive-international and formerly a member of the company's accounting firm was appointed administrative vice president. In spite of the efforts of the organization planning staff to avoid politics and be thoroughly professional in its work, the staff head was never able to develop the same personal and confidential working relationship with the new administrative vice president that he had enjoyed with his predecessor. As a result the staff was ineffective. Almost immediately his superior accelerated the lay-off program by cutting the staff of all departments across the board, both in heads and salaries, from 25 percent to 40 percent; 7,000 exercutives were laid off in two weeks. Because it was primarily a cost-cutting move, the experienced, highly paid, and generally more skilled staff professionals were the first ones to be laid off. In this case, we see the decline of the organization planning staff head in status, authority, effectiveness, and in his close working relationships with the chief executive officer from the time when the first incumbent was vice president-organization reporting to the CEO and who was a member of the board of directors with an annual base salary of over $350,000, plus incentive compensation of a like amount, to the last incumbent, who had been a former staff member and who now reported to an administrative vice president. He received a salary of only about $35,000.

3. *The Recreation Company.* Originally, the staff consisted of one long-service employee reporting to the vice president-employee/public relations and organization planning who, in turn, reported to the chief

executive officer. This staff man's primary function was to administer a rather depressed and outmoded salary program. His superior, however, enjoyed a very close and confidential working relationship with the chief executive. The staff specialist was a bright but inexperienced and abrasive young man who did not get along well with the senior executives. His superior could see the need for a major reorganization of the company and knew this would require a professional staff. He hired a seasoned professional manager and former management consultant as director of organization planning, compensation planning, and building services. The new staff head immediately began recruiting mature, experienced specialists in general management, organization planning, and compensation. One was a management consultant.

The chief executive had used his consulting firm to conduct an organization survey of the company. In the files, the staff had this survey as well as the reports of several other management consultants. This material proved most helpful as background for their organization surveys. The staff's first priority was to up-date the salary program and structure. The next target was the establishment of a policy and procedures manual. The staff men worked largely as free internal consultants primarily on division organization and compensation projects. One man was in charge of planning the move of the company to a new building and he also directed office and building services.

With his superior's backing, the organization planning head had no trouble making presentations to the chief executive officer and getting decisions.

The vice president-in-charge made an enlarged policy program and the reissuance of the policy and procedures manual a high-priority objective. In carrying out this step, the staff found certain policies could not be prepared because there were no corporate staffs in critical functional areas to develop and administer the policies. The staff then began to design a strengthened top-management organization structure for the corporation.

During this period the vice president worked very closely with the chief executive officer and gained top line acceptance and support for the staff.

In spite of this fact, the chief executive made major organization changes and announced them in "Chalk-Talk," the employee publication, without consulting the staff head unless salary changes were involved, which required his approval. It was a standing joke in the department that the staff had to read the company newspaper to find out what organization changes had taken place. There was no organization control policy. Title inflation was rampant. The staff director thought of himself as a captive internal consultant who could carry out a management project better and cheaper than an outside consultant. He did not see himself as the director of an internal control staff. For this reason he spent much of his time in competition for assignments with outside consultants, largely at the division head level. He thought—perhaps too optimistically —that, if his staff achieved a reputation for making sound organization surveys for the division heads, ultimately the chief executive officer would ask him to make a top-management organization survey of the corporation.

When the staff made its policy presentation, the chief executive officer said that he did not know whether or not there should be any group executives in his organization structure. He then asked the staff to make a study and tell him whether he should have any group executives or not. This was the opening they wanted to conduct a study and to recommend a stronger top-management organization structure. They made this study, which included a proposal for a strong central structure rather than the weak "holding company" structure that existed at that time. They gave the organization proposal to the chief executive officer in a color slide presentation, which lasted over two hours. Much to their surprise he accepted it without change. They had anticipated considerable opposition.

One of the most important elements of the proposal was the establishment of several new staff head positions as well as a chief operating officer and four group executives. Filling the position of chief operating officer meant—at least to the chief executive—appointing his successor. The staff was reasonably sure that he had not yet trained anyone inside the company that he felt could take his place as chief executive. He admitted to the staff, however, that he was extremely anxious to turn his job over to a qualified man from the outside, and this new chief operating officer position would provide the ideal way for him to do that. However, he wanted this fact kept confidential until he had cleared the proposal for the new organization structure with the board of directors. He asked the staff to prepare a brief fifteen minute version of the presentation and give it to the board of directors. After the proposal's approval by the board, the staff gave it to all the key executives in small groups.

After this change was approved by the board, the chief executive showed a new respect for the staff. He began, for the first time, to consult the staff head in advance on changes he planned to make in the organization structure. Immediately he began to fill the four new group executive positions by promoting his division heads. Without the aid of an executive search firm, he began to travel in the company plane to interview prospective candidates for the new position of chief operating officer. Finally he hired a former glass company division head. This executive had obtained excellent background in running a division of a basic materials processing company. He had no experience, however, in managing a large divisionalized, highly diversified, conglomerate like the Recreation Company.

If the new chief operating officer had taken a more thoughtful fact-oriented approach to his new assignment and used the available staffs, he might not have experienced so much difficulty in implementing the program. He did not, however, welcome organizational concepts that differed from his own experience in the glass business. Since an integrated process manufacturing company, like a glass plant, normally does not need group executives, he decided that highly diversified recreation companies did not need them either. For this reason, he demoted the newly appointed group executives back to their former division head positions. He decided that organization planning was not so difficult as the staff made it appear in order to ensure job tenure, and he could make organization changes very well without their help. He looked at about five minutes of the top organization presentation and decided that the staff was overcomplicating the problem.

The vice president and the staff head both resigned to head their own companies. The director of industrial relations was made vice president-industrial relations by the chief operating officer and was also given direction over both management development and organization planning. He appointed one of the staff as the new director of compensation and organization planning. The new staff head then reported to the vice president-industrial relations, who reported to the chief operating officer. He, in turn, reported to the chief executive officer. The chief executive obviously thought he had carried out the staff's organizational recommendations and that he no longer needed to be concerned with major top-management organization problems. The chief operating officer did follow the staff's proposal for the establishment of a new corporate marketing staff by appointing a former division head from a large diversified electrical manufacturing company as vice president of marketing. He was the only one of the key executives recruited from the outside who had general management experience in a successful divisionalized company. It is interesting to speculate on what would have happened if the chief executive had gone to a sophisticated divisionalized company like General Motors for his key men as Henry Ford II had done in 1945.

The chief operating officer next centralized research and development as the staff had recommended. The chief executive reestablished a public relations staff reporting to him—also as recommended. Finally, with the appointment of a corporate manufacturing-staff director, all of the staff's major organization change proposals, except putting the corporate controller under the vice president-finance and reestablishing the group executives, were carried out.

There are several levels of management between the chief executive and the director of organization planning. The staff is now again largely concerned with compensation matters and maintaining the policy and procedures manual. It rarely reviews or recommends on major top organization changes.

4. *Professional Management Association Chapter.* In this case there was a continuing and close personal working relationship between the organization specialist and the chief executive. This made it very easy for

him to get his organizational recommendations approved. This was the only case, except for the Automobile Company and Church Diocese where the organization specialist reported directly to and worked closely with the chief executive officer. In this example, the CEO was himself a professional manager and the arrangement worked very effectively. The staff man wrote the chapter organization manual. All his organization recommendations were approved and as vice president-membership he recommended staffing. The chapter ultimately achieved excellent results in the increased activity of the members. Later the activity declined and the chapter was abolished.

5. *The Church Diocese.* The working relationship of the planning director and the bishop was not close even though the planning director reported to the bishop directly. The staff man was a layman and an outsider in comparison to the long-time personal relationship that existed between the bishop and the executive secretary of the diocese. The bishop frequently accused the planning director of tinkering too much with the machinery of the automobile and not spending enough time finding out where it ought to be driven. This was clearly a rationalization that the bishop used to avoid giving support to the planning director, who was a highly qualified management professional. Even though the planning director did report directly to the bishop, the bishop was not a professional manager and was not experienced in the techniques of supporting a planning staff. For this reason, the working relationship was anything but satisfactory. It would appear from this case that reporting directly to the chief executive is but one step toward establishing a proper reciprocal support relationship. However, the qualifications, interests, and the will to manage of the chief executive are also vital. It was not until the bishop retired and was replaced that planning was given the proper attention.

CONCLUSION: INTERPLAY BETWEEN THE CEO, THE OP STAFF, AND THE SENIOR EXECUTIVES

From this experience we can conclude that—particularly in a major reorganization—it is highly desirable to give the director of organization planning equal stature with the other key corporate officers whom he must counsel by making him a corporate officer himself and by putting him on the board of directors. This, in itself, may not guarantee the staff an effective working relationship if the chief executive is not a professional manager, but it will help. The cases clearly demonstrate that the less contact the staff head has with the chief executive, the more ineffective becomes the organization planning function.

This principle also applies at the division level, although there are a few divisions large enough to warrant a full-time organization planning specialist; if not, the division general manager must make his own organization surveys without staff assistance.

The more time the chief executive spends on organization planning problems the better. The more he keeps up with the field, the more able he is to perform his crucial role. A close working relation among the chief executive, his organization planners, and senior executives in the successful conduct of organization surveys and execution of approved recommendations is essential to the successful execution of major directed organization change.

SUMMARY OF CONCLUSIONS

Organization of Organization Planning

In summary, from the case experiences we have found that the chief executive's will to manage and his professional management expertise (including analytical ability, organization planning skill, and emotional stability) are essential prerequisites to effective planned organization change. As is suggested in *Strategy and Structure*, by Chandler, a man in the position of chief executive with the skills of the entrepreneur usually must be replaced by a man with the skills and the emotional make-up of an engineer if a major reorganization is to be successfully carried out. He should be a thoughtful analyst and problem-solver rather than an emotional, risk-taking entrepreneur.

This is not to diminish the importance of the risk-taking skills during the initial phase of the organization building process. It takes an entrepreneur to put together a large knowledge organization. However, the success of an entrepreneur depends largely on the intuitive mental processes and skills of a horse-trader.

The chief executive should have such skills also but basically he must bring to the job the trained, logical, and analytical mind of an engineer. If not, it is impossible for him to develop the required skills on the job through training in analytical techniques only. Also, if he does not bring to the job a high degree of emotional stability, integrity, and self-control, these factors, too, cannot be developed on the job through training. Given these basic recruiting prerequisites, however, a chief executive can learn to do his own organization planning through reading "how-to-do-it" books; by approving and enforcing an organization control policy; by perfecting his organization planning techniques through on-the-job experience; by conducting his own organization studies; and by maintaining his own organization manual.

If his organization grows large enough, he should acquire the services of a full-time organization planner to help him conduct his organization studies.

He should never completely delegate these studies to his organization planner, however, and above all he should not have him report through another top executive who heads a major business function, i.e., industrial relations, finance, and the like. This would raise a question about his real or apparent interfunctional objectivity and block communications. Even if he has an organization planner, the chief executive must actively provide the environment in which control of the organization structure can be continuously and effectively maintained. He must always make his assignments to his key subordinates in line with the approved plan of organization. Organizational discipline cannot be enforced by a staff man no matter how skilled he may be in the techniques of organization planning. This is an authority only the chief executive has. If the chief executive does not know enough about the practical application of the concepts embodied in the plan of organization to delegate assignments properly and train his key executives to carry out their proper roles, then no matter how sound the plan of organization is, the management team will not function effectively under it.

Not only must the chief executive actively participate in the organization planning function, so must his key division and corporate staff heads. The organization planner then becomes a resource to the chief executive through providing functional guidance and control over the activities of the staff directors and division heads in carrying out their reserved organizing responsibilities. He maintains the organization and policy manual as well as the organization survey guide, which set forth the best and most perfected techniques for conducting organization surveys and for proposing organizational changes. He reviews organization changes proposed by product division and staff heads for the chief executive officer and recommends action from a corporate-wide, interfunctional perspective and viewpoint. He and his staff normally should not conduct free organization studies as a service for the corporate staff and product division heads. If any such studies are conducted by the organization planning staff, the cost should be charged back to the divisions and staffs concerned on a fee basis. The staff head should provide advice only to division and staff department heads on the techniques to be used in conducting their organization studies, and he should review the organization change proposals resulting from such studies to see if the organization planning principles and techniques have been properly applied in making the proposal. The organization planner should keep informed of the most perfected organization planning principles and techniques available that can usefully be applied by these executives or by his divisional counterparts. If, as in the early stages of the Automobile Company and the Recreation Company organization planning programs, the corporate staff tries to provide a free internal organization consulting service to the divisions, the size of this staff rapidly expands as a result of their futile efforts to provide a free service to all who want it. In doing so, their activities weaken the ability of the division heads to perform their own reserved organization planning responsibilities. At some point the economic nonsense of trying to provide a free internal management consulting service will become obvious as it did at the Automobile Company. Then the overexpanded staff must go through a painful period of contraction. As the organization planning staff finally achieves the role of a small functional guidance and control staff, it gradually begins on an economical basis to perform the full range of responsibilities outlined in Chapter 1. In this role, the maximum staff performance and results can be achieved with a minimum of effort and cost.

THE MOST USEFUL TOOLS AND TECHNIQUES OF ORGANIZATION PLANNING

What can we learn from the case experiences as to the best and most perfected tools and techniques for conducting organization surveys? Any business executive who would like to have information on the various techniques for conducting management surveys should read *Management Systems for Profit and Growth*, by Richard Neuschel. Since this book is concerned primarily with the techniques of organization planning, we will limit our discussion to these tools only. In any reasonably large organization, the organization and policy manual should be on top of the tool kit; next should be the organization survey guide. In the organization manual there should be four key policies: the policy on planning the organization structure, the titling policy, the staffing policy, and the announcements policy. If the organization planner also has the responsibility for exempt job evaluation—and he should—there also will be an exempt salary administration policy and procedure manual.

As exhibited in the Art Association case, the organization survey report should not only include position descriptions for the new or changed management positions, but should also contain man specifications for these same positions. These specifications will help ensure that the men in the key positions have the proper managerial as well as product business and technical skills to meet the minimum job requirements. The specifications should clearly indicate not only the desired, but the minimum skills required. If the incumbent does not have the minimum management skills or the emotional stability and intelligence to acquire these skills in a reasonable length of time, he should be replaced by the most outstanding professional manager available. Minimum skills in key jobs are not enough if an organization is in a crisis of survival.

In conducting a well-planned organization survey, the organization planner—whether a line manager or a staff specialist—should spend considerable time both finding out how the organization developed and exploring its strengths and weaknesses. If a broad business study has been made, he should use it; if not, he should have one made. He should review the job specifications, if any, for the key jobs in the present structure, and should obtain a complete inventory of the work history and management and technical skills of the men filling these positions. If there are any men in these jobs that do not have—and have made no attempt to acquire—the needed skills, any apparent effort to "organize away" from these men should be identified for corrective action. This problem is illustrated by the experience of the Hard Rubber Company where the top marketing research staff was positioned under the controller instead of under an unqualified vice president-sales. On the other hand, any tendency to organize toward the skills of a particularly aggressive and capable individual should be identified. A treasurer, who has purchasing skills and, therefore, has been given the corporate purchasing department for this reason only, is an example. One of the most prevalent problem areas was found where a single incumbent was filling two, and sometimes even three, key positions in the structure. At the Recreation Company two division heads were also group executives. A division head's position is so demanding that it would be impossible for him concurrently to perform a group executive's position properly and objectively. This is equivalent in baseball to having one man play first base and second base at the same time. It should be clear why such an organization finds it hard to compete with another organization that has full-time qualified professionals in each key position. Such a competitor may even have two or three backup men in lower rated positions ready and trained in advance to step into a sudden vacancy if the circumstances require it.

When the chief executive is in any doubt whether the candidate meets the minimum requirements of the position for which he is being considered, he should ask the advice of the organization planner who conducted the survey and prepared the position specification. A design engineer cannot be held accountable for the performance of the product if it has been made with materials that do not meet the minimum specifications he has established. Similarly, the organization planner should not be held accountable for performance limitations if the plan has been staffed with men who do not meet the minimum skill requirements of the key position specifications he has prepared. Even if a soundly designed structure is capably staffed, it may not perform effectively. Much depends also on the leadership skills of the manager in charge.

The organizational planner should only be held accountable for the fact that the organization could perform effectively if capably staffed, managed, and motivated.

Other analytical tools are of course job descriptions, organization charts (structural and functional), linear responsiblity charts, workflow charts, activity strength analysis charts, grouping charts, decisions analysis charts, organization plan evaluation charts, and the like. The use of these tools is described in detail in Chapters 3, 8, and 11. In the Hard Rubber Company, the key tools were the master functional organization chart, the organization and policy manual, and the compensation job descriptions. In the Automobile Company, the most useful tools were the organization manual, the corporate policy guide, the organization survey guide, the master program, the corporate management philosophy, and the organization plan evaluation charts. At the Recreation Company, the tools were the corporate policy and procedures manual, evaluation job descriptions, the top-management organization survey, the corporate management philosophy, activity strength analysis charts, grouping analysis charts, decisions analysis charts, plan evaluation analysis charts, replacement charts, and the manager manpower trial balance. At the Church Diocese, the organization survey, structural organization charts, and the plan evaluation charts were most useful. At the Management Association Chapter, the structural organization chart, the organization and policy manual, the corporate management philosophy, and the long-range plan were the tools most frequently used. At the Art Association we see illustrated the use of the top-management organization survey, the structural organization chart, the organization manual position description, the linear responsibility chart, the activity strength analysis chart, the grouping chart, decisions analysis chart, and the plan evaluation chart. These simple but very powerful fact-gathering and analytical tools were used for solving organizational problems. In each case we have also illustrated how the dynamics of an organizational problem can be analyzed using the Bonds of Organization.

USEFULNESS OF THE PRINCIPLES
OF ORGANIZATION

The Principle of Definition. This principle has proved, in the cases outlined in Part II, to be an important one in solving organization, structural, and control problems in all sizes and types of organizations. Even a poorly designed organization will perform much better if the structure and functions of the key positions and components are clearly defined, documented, and communicated to all key executives and employees who must operate within the structure. Documentation of the present structure is an essential first step in management job evaluation. Titles that are accurate are more important to effective management than many businessmen realize, since it is only through titles that much of the organizational information is communicated both internally and externally. We hear much about giving men overblown non-descriptive corporate titles instead of raises. This practice is particularly prevalent in large banks. In manufacturing companies, the common practice of calling unincorporated division general managers "presidents" is fundamentally unsound for the same reason. A corporate president has a very different job; he has stockholders to worry about; he attends board meetings, and the like. An unincorporated division president has no such duties. To imply that he does is dangerously misleading not only internally but externally. Accurate duty communications through descriptive functional titles is the very essence of good management. Anything that intentionally or unintentionally misleads in this respect is a violation of this principle. Some titles convey no functional information at all. "Division A" is an example of such a title. This is an opportunity to communicate where the opportunity has been completely wasted. A title is shorthand for a position description. Obviously all outside persons wishing to know the content of a person's position and duties have only his title or that of his unit to give them that information. Such information is essential also to many inside persons, particularly secretaries who must route mail by title. Too random a selection of unit and position titles is confusing.

Principle of the Objective. This principle has proven important when the organization planner is trying to decide whether all the activities are present in the structure to permit attainment of the common objective. This leads, of course, to the need for a broad business study and a written corporate management philosophy as a basis for determining the strategy and objectives of the organization. Even in the absence of such a study, the organization planner must define objectives for the unit. Sometimes he may effectively do this as a result of discussions with the top executives who have done considerable thinking on this subject and by reviewing their speeches or articles. Sometimes he must make such a business study himself. Ideally, he should then write a formal management report to the chief executive (which will include a management philosophy) to clarify his thinking. Because of its confidentiality, the report may never be read by anyone except the staff head's immediate superior. Application of this principle leads to a thorough activity strength analysis (see Exhibit 3.3). Unneeded activities and positions are also identified for elimination in this process.

Principle of Specialization. This principle is not being properly applied when, as at the Recreation Company, a vice president was in charge of several unrelated functions, i.e., Public Relations, Personnel and Organization Planning. Having the one incumbent fill two unrelated positions has the same result. His objectives do not "pyramid" properly. The application of this principle is important no matter what type of organization is being analyzed.

Principle of Coordination. The failure to apply this principle is illustrated most clearly in the Recreation Company structure, where the vice president of finance reported to the chief executive officer and the controller reported to the chief operating officer. Proper managerial coordination of two such closely related staff functions becomes impossible in such a structural arrangement.

Principle of Responsibility and Authority. Failure properly to apply this principle can be most clearly observed in reviewing the structures of the Recreation Company and the Automobile Company. Many of the division heads recognized no accountability to the head of the organization of which they were a part. For example, the president of the outboard motors division of the Recreation Company would not permit the corporate internal auditors to visit his division for the purpose of auditing the books of account.

Principle of Accountability. There was no experience in the cases in Part II where the violation of this principle caused a major problem. The chief executives and other managers, to their credit, took full accountability for the acts of their subordinates.

Principle of Correspondence. There were also no cases in Part II where failure to apply this principle caused an organizational dysfunction.

Principle of Span of Management Control. The failure to apply this principle is most clearly illustrated wherever you have an excessively layered structure. This condition was evident in the structures of the Automobile Company and the Recreation Company. Broad spans and minimum levels are key principles in designing any large organization to facilitate communications.

Principle of Balance. Wherever we find a violation of either the Principle of the Span of Management Control or the Principle Specialization, we usually find loads out of balance. The principle of the heaviest overload most often falls on the shoulders of the chief executive or some aggressive subordinate. This was illustrated in the Automobile Company and the Recreation Company and the Church Diocese structures. Even in the Management Association Chapter we find an overload resting on the shoulders of the chief executive. Organizational planning can be most effective when this principle is used to relieve the workload on the chief executive or others by developing a more balanced work structure.

Principle of Continuity. Applying this principle is extremely important in maintaining a sound organization. There is no such thing as a structure that stays well designed forever. Strategy and objectives are necessarily dynamic and in a state of continuous change. There is always an aggressive and capable individual eager to take over functions that do not logically belong within his jurisdiction. Since strategy and objectives can only be achieved through the work structure of the present organization, it must continually be adjusted in order to carry out the objectives effectively. For this reason, it is no accident that a management consultant must analyze the structure when he is asked to advise on why the organization is not functioning properly. This is also the reason why the continuing design and control of the structure is so vital to the effective functioning, economy, and profitability of any organization, whatever may be its purpose.

Principle of Minimum Levels. This principle is applied when an unnecessary management level is eliminated, such as the position of the vice president-employee/public relations and organization planning at the

Recreation Company. Staff group executive positions have rarely been found to be essential, except possibly in the largest functionalized organizations such as petroleum companies. Staffs should have the broadest practical spans of control, not only to eliminate unnecessary positions, but to improve communication between the staff specialists and the chief executive and other general executives they are advising. The organization planning staff structure at the Recreation Company had three levels of management while the General Electric structure has been limited only to eight.

Principle of Functional Growth. This principle illustrates the need for divisionalizing the structure to improve the economic performance of large functional organizations. The complexity of the original Automobile Company organization is illustrative of this principle.

Principle of Centralization. The application of this principle requires establishing strong top- and divisional management structures. This principle was applied in the divisionalization program at the Automobile Company. The staff also found weak top-management organization structure at the Recreation Company and in the Church diocese as well as in some of the smaller divisions of the Recreation Company.

Principle of Delegation. This principle is the last to be considered when analyzing an organization structure (see Exhibit 3.5). Once the overall structure has been designed, the unnecessary activities eliminated, and the necessary control activities and systems strengthened or created, then a detailed "decisions analysis" should be conducted to be sure this principle has been properly applied. The definition of the limits of authority delegation may be spelled out to some extent in the position descriptions. It is left, however, to the policy framework to assure that this principle has been employed effectively. Decisions analysis is the tool to be used for this purpose. Linear responsibility charting is also a practical analytical tool to assure maximum decision-making delegation and a minimum of authority drift back to the top of the organization structure. In the absence of any formal policy framework, almost all of the decisions are made at the top of the organizational pyramid. That is why a policy manual is so essential as a tool of the organization planner. Sometimes an organizational audit is necessary to ensure that decisions are being made at the level provided for in written corporate policies and procedures.

Principle of Separating Long-Range Work from Short-Range Work. This principle is being applied when we design a "split-staff" structure by having the chief executive officer concentrate on long-range planning activities while the chief operating officer concentrates on the day-to-day operating problems. When there is only one general executive officer, he must deal with both types of work, thus violating this principle. Long-range planning, although vital, receives too little of his time and attention. The chief executive in the structures of the Recreation Company, the

Automobile Company, and the Church Diocese suffered from this common problem. Proper design of the organization structure is one means to relieve the chief executive from operating problems so he can devote enough time to long-range planning work. Then it is essential to identify the staffs that are devoting a large part of their time to longer range and external relations problems so they can report directly to the chief executive officer.

NOTES

1. Alfred P. Sloan, *My Years with General Motors* (New York: Doubleday, 1964).

2. Ralph J. Cordiner, *New Frontiers for Professional Managers* (New York: McGraw-Hill, 1956).

3. Allan Nevins and Frank Ernest Hill, *Ford: Decline and Rebirth* (New York: Scribner's, 1963).

Exhibit 4.1
The Bonds of Organization

Research studies of behavioral scientists highlight the fact that an organization is not just a strategy or even a structure, important though they are, but a kind of open bio- or living system—a multi-institutional system of response. It connotes people responding to problems, events, situations, policies, plans, and to other people. Up to this point, this book has been concerned with the mechanics, statics, and structural aspects of organization. Now we will discuss the dynamics or behavioral aspects of organization.

In describing this multi-institutional system of response, we will use the "Bonds of Organization" as outlined by E. Wight Bakke in his *Concept of the Social Organization*. Knowledge of how to apply this conceptual framework in the analysis of organization problems should make the dynamics of organization performance more understandable to the reader. Although the idea of an organization as a system refers to the functional whole, Wilbur M. McFeely in *Organization Change: Perceptions and Realities* says it is clear that the vitality or effectiveness of the system is dependent on a series of highly interpendent variables. For purposes of analysis, he identifies seven of these as follows:

1. *Linkage.*

    This refers to the essential network of group and interpersonal relationships that are the very foundation of an organization.

    The vertical line of responsibility and authority as previously discussed in the Principles of Organization (see Exhibit 1.1) is perhaps the most important of these linkages. There are also many other functional and lateral linkages. Existence of sound linkages is indicated by the responsiveness of those in power. Mutual support stems from mutual influence.

2. *Balanced emphasis.*

    In the context of an organizational system, balanced emphasis refers primarily to the relative weight given to the long versus the short term; to the relative attention given various functions of an organization.

    One of the principles of organization previously discussed is the Principle of Balance. Mr. McFeely contends, however, that it is not only important to maintain balanced emphasis among the functions of an organization, but also between the long-term and the short-term objectives and work.

3. *Paths of decision-making.*

    The key point of this element of an organizational system is the effectiveness of the delegation of authority; and organizational analysts are quick to point out that delegation of authority goes beyond organization structure—it seems to be equated with a particular philosophy of management—it is a basic ingredient of management style. In this context, the extent to which authority is delegated appears to be an index of the degree of trust or confidence key managers have in those who report to them. And this "confidence factor" is far more important than the authority that is theoretically vested in a position as spelled out by the organization manual.

Decision-making has been previously discussed in the Principle of Delegation. Although decision-making normally follows the formal structure, the informal system either facilitates or becomes a bottleneck to this process.

4. *The reward system.*

The ostensible purpose of the reward system is to reinforce all elements of expected behavior; this encompasses both tangible and intangible rewards. Thus, in a system of response, the system of rewards is clearly a prime element.

This is the reason job evaluation should be such an integral part of organization planning.

5. *Administrative Constraints.*

Every objective, plan, or policy of an organization is, in a sense, a constraint that affects the speed with which the system can respond to threats, problems, and opportunities.

Administrative constraints should not necessarily have negative connotations. They are organization mechanisms that are generally accepted by managers as essential in order to transform random behavior into organizational performance.

6. *Cultural constraints.*

To distinguish between administrative constraints and cultural constraints is, admittedly, a bit academic. They flow from each other. But, in this context, where administrative constraints refer to the creedal or common law of the organization, cultural refers to the habits, attitudes, traditions, outlooks, and patterns of interaction that either develop internally, or are part of the behavior pattern that people bring with them to their roles.

Every repetitive informal practice of an organization is a cultural constraint. The way an organization responds to a problem seems particularly conditioned by its cultural heritage. Habits and attitudes that have proven successful in the past seem to be enshrined in the present. For this reason an organization in trouble tends to resort to past remedies even though the current basic cause of the problem may be quite different. This tends to freeze the array of coping responses.

7. *Self-correcting mechanisms.*

This element of the system underscores the need for individuals, groups, and the entire organization to be self-correcting—to adjust to the realities of the organization's experience and environment in ways that preserve its forward momentum. Acts of self-correction, of course, also find expression in the other elements of the organizational system. But, here, the emphasis is directed toward various activities or mechanisms that seem to support, encourage, and define paths for self-correction.

A primary mechanism is the quality of the continuing exploration into the organization's role and aspirations. This is the essence of strategic planning as well as the Principle of Continuity.

And now let us turn to a discussion of the Bonds of Organization, from *Concept of the Social Organization,* by E. Wight Bakke, from which the extracts in the following outline are taken.

BONDS OF ORGANIZATION
The Basic Work Requirements of an Organization
(A Biological Model)

According to Bakke, the following is a definition of an organization:

A social organization is a continuing system of differentiated and coordinated human activities utilizing, transforming, and welding together a specific set of human, material, capital, ideational, and natural resources into a unique problem-solving whole whose function is to satisfy particular human needs in interaction with other systems of human activities and resources in its particular environment.

The following types of activities would appear to be essential in order to attain these objectives in the sense that attainment is imperiled if such activities are poorly performed; impossible, if not done at all. In the following, these bonds of organization have been described in words commonly used in business to facilitate understanding.

Identification Activities

In many relationships of participants and outsiders to a social organization it is essential that those involved have an adequate image of the uniqueness and wholeness of the organization. It is essential that the organization as a whole mean something definite, and that the name of the organization shall call to mind unique identifying features.

These activities are required to define and symbolize the uniqueness of the organization, including its goals and the main features that distinguish it from other organizations.

Example: Public Relations, Public Affairs, and the like.

If effectively performed, there is a clear image in the minds of the general public; if not, the image does not exist, or it is blurred and inaccurate.

Perpetuation Activities

The basic resources essential to the operation of an organization are those human, material, capital, ideational, and natural elements in the world that are employed by the agents of the organization in its activities. The nature of these resources, their quality, their quantity, and their specific attributes are of a high level of importance in determining the structure of the organization, for they necessarily dictate the kinds of activities that are appropriate to their acquisition, maintenance, transformation, and their employment, and they determine certain limits with which the Organizational Charter can be actualized.

These activities are needed to acquire, maintain, transform, develop, and renew the basic resources used by agents of the organization in the performance of their work.

If properly carried out, resources of the quantity and quality are always available to carry out the organizational operations. These resources perpetuation activities include:

1. *Personnel Activities*

>The people who are participants in the organization and their biological equipment, their abilities (thinking, doing, feeling), their predispositions (attitudes, habits, sentiments), and their self-conceptions are the most prominent of the organization's basic resources.

>These activities perpetuate people and their qualities.
>Example: Human Resources Department.

2. *Service Activities*

>The material resources are those of raw materials, equipment, and plant currently owned by the organization and employed in operations of the organization, or those that are potentally available for ownership or employment. These are distinguished from natural resources by the fact that they have been processed through human activity.

>These activities perpetuate materials, equipment, and plant.
>Example: Purchasing Department.

3. *Finance Activities*

>Capital resources are the wealth or symbols of wealth owned and utilized or available for ownershp and utilization in acquiring, transforming, and welding together the other resources of the organization.

>These activities perpetuate capital.
>Example: Finance Department.

4. *Thoughtways Activities*

>The ideational resources are the ideas used or available for use by agents or members of the organization, and by those outside the organization whose behavior affects the operations of the organization, and the language in which these are expressed and communicated.

>These activities perpetuate ideas.
>Example: Product Planning Department.

5. *Conservation Activities*

>Natural resources are the products of nature (not processed through human activity), owned and/or utilized, or available for ownership and/or utilization by the organization. Note that what may be called material, organic, animal, and spiritual kingdoms of nature are included.

>These activities perpetuate natural resources and access to them.
>Example: Real Estate Department.

A major symptom of inefficiency in the performance of these activities would be reports of quantitative shortages and qualitative inadequacies in people, materials, equipment, capital, ideas, or natural resources.

Workflow Activities

>If effectively carried out, these activities result in Work and an Output of a quantity and quality adequate to sustain the continued contributions to,

and support for, organizational operations by participants and recipients of the output.

These are the line activities. They constitute the core of operations or flow of work without which the helper or support activities are meaningless. To aid them is the principal function of all the other activities. The two major subclasses are:

1. *Production Activities.* These activities create or make the output, i.e., the product or service for which the organization exists.

   Example: The Manufacturing Department.

2. *Distribution Activities.* These activities distribute the product or service to or toward the ultimate user.

   Example: Sales Department.

A major symptom of ineffectiveness in these activities is an inconsistency between the quantity and quality of the output and the quantity and quality acceptable to the customers. Other symptoms are the interruptions in the flow of work, less than optimum use of basic resources, and incurring total costs for the output that cannot be recovered through income resulting from distribution.

Control Activities.

These activities are those that unify all the other differentiated activities in the performance of the organizational mission with a minimum of leakages (irrelevant or negative activities). Characteristics of basic resources (especially people) are that they are multi-directional and are not necessarily oriented toward the performance of the organization's function. Subclasses are:

1. *Directive Activities.* These are the activities that initiate action and the type and direction of action for people and other resources. They are those that:
   a. Determine the target for performance.
   b. Make known to agents from whom performance is desired the details of that performance and the results expected.
   c. Order (or request), authorize, and sanction the performance.
   d. Obtain acceptance for or compliance with this order (or request).

2. *Motivation Activities.* These activities reward or penalize or promise rewards or penalties for behavior in the interest of making it conform to the type desired by the person or persons administering the rewards and penalties.

   Ineffectiveness in these activities results in work varying from the type desired.

3. *Evaluation Activities.* Important among these activities are the following:
   a. Supervise performance.
   b. Review, appraise, and rate performance, performers, and results according to standards established.
   c. Assign people (as well as other resources) to positions on scales pertaining to a number of dimensions (such as prestige, importance, power, ability, acceptability, etc.).
   d. Assess the significance of other people, groups, and organizations, and events for the self realization of the people, groups, or organizations doing the rating.

  e. Compare the relative advantages and costs of alternative courses of action.
  f. Predict probable consequences of alternative courses of action.
  g. Assess the impact of changes in one part of the organization on other parts and the whole.
  h. Assess periodically the state of the whole organization internally and in relation to its environment.

  A symptom of ineffectiveness is the occurrence of results disadvantageous to the organization traceable to mistaken judgment or failure to make a timely judgment.

4. *Communications Activities.* These activities are those which supply the participants with the premises and data that they need to perform other activities.

  They include statements of objectives; position descriptions; policies, plans, rules, standards and time requirements; and the nature and potential of the resources to be used.

  Example: The controller distributes approved budgets and force authorizations.

  A symptom of ineffectiveness is a necessity for participants to make decisions or take action without knowing what is expected of them or arrival too late of information that would affect the decision. The communications system tries to furnish the right participant with adequate, authentic, and authoritative data and premises at the right time and the right place to make possible the activity and results expected of them.

A general symptom of ineffectiveness of control activities is the occurrence of results disadvantageous, irrelevant, or negative to the performance of the organization function.

Homeostatic Activities. These are activities that stabilize and vitalize the organization as a whole in an evolving state of dynamic equilibrium.

  They are not differentiated or special-purpose activities as are those previously discussed, but are combinations of other activities. They are synergic in character in that they add no new work elements to the concept. External conditions can cause stresses and strains within an organization that can threaten the stability, integrity and viability—even the existence—of an organization in relation to its external environment. Three processes are:

1. *The Fusion Process.* The need for this process arises from the fact that groups and individuals have expectancies and goals that are not always compatible with those of the organization as a whole. This process attempts to reconcile or fuse the expectancies of the individuals with those of the organization as a whole. Ineffectiveness in carrying out this process results in the persistence (not necessarily the occurrence) of factionalism, rebellious acts, insubordination, indifference, or apathy of participants toward the needs of the organization and lack of interest in defending the organization and its image.

2. *Problem-Solving Process.* The need for the Problem-Solving Process is so obvious as to need little elaboration. Whether the problem is in the form of a disturbance to, or difficulty in, operations and achievement of results, or in the form of an opportunity for activity which, if adequately exploited, promises ad-

vantageous and desirable results, and whether the threat or promise is directed at one or more resources, or at one or more systems of activity, or at the organization as a whole, it calls for the marshalling of the organization's resources and activities and their coordinated combination in a more or less systematic problem-solving process.

Assuming that a stimulus situation has occurred that has a potential impact on the operations and structure of the organization, then follows:

a. *Awareness.* Were those responsible aware of the problem?

b. *Exploration.* Were adequate and relevant facts gathered on the following:

    (1) *The Cause.* Who is accountable? What are their objectives? What situational factors are accountable? Can they be modified?

    (2) *The Character.* Does the situation present a threat or a promise? How long has the situation existed? Who else is affected? What are they likely to do about it?

    (3) *The Impact.* What will failure to solve the problem cost the organization? What will solving the problem gain? The quantity and quality of what basic resources are likely to be affected? What activity is likely to be affected? Will it affect the integrity of the organization—immediate or long-range?

    (4) *Involvements.* Who has a contribution to make to the solution?

    (5) *Placement.* In what activities is action likely to be required to meet the situation?

c. *Simplification.* Was the problem, as revealed, reduced to terms amenable to practical and effective action?

d. *Search and Cue.* Were sufficient alternative solutions suggested?

e. *Appraisal of Alternatives.* Were the alternatives carefully appraised as to their probable effectiveness and efficiency in the light of the facts, the function to be performed, the resources required, capability of agents, their readiness and counter-strategy?

f. *Choice and Decision.* Was the most efficient alternative chosen? Was the decision made in time? Was it clear?

g. *Mobilization.* Were the objectives defined and justified? Were the plans for implementation carefully drawn up and clearly communicated to the agents involved? Was their understanding assured? Were adequate resources made available?

h. *Response and Action.* Were the necessary activities carried out and controlled so as to accomplish the objectives in the plan? Were effective modifications made in the activities in light of evolving experience in the process of implementation?

i. *Experience and Judgment.* Were the results of the effort reviewed and appraised as to the neutralization of the threat or the realization of the opportunity? What was the margin of gain over cost?

j. *Closure or Renewal.* Was the problem considered solved or was a decision made to restructure the problem and renew efforts to solve it? Was a decision made to tackle new problems revealed by the experience in solving this one?

The most obvious symptom of ineffectiveness in the problem-solving process is the accumulation of recognized but unsolved problems, particularly those that are weakening the ability of the organization to perform its function and survive.

3. *Leadership Activities.* This process provides vision, initiative, and guidance in respect to preservation of the organization's integrity and functional effectiveness. It incorporates a number of activities and focuses them on achieving homeostasis in the face of the opportunity and necessity for development and growth.

The planned organization changes in Part II, in addition to being analyzed from a structural viewpoint, have also been analyzed in their dynamic aspects using the above Bonds of Organization as a guide.

Part II

Cases in Organization Planning and Control

5

Rebuilding a Small Industrial Enterprise: The Hard Rubber Company

HISTORY OF THE ORGANIZATION

Forty years ago, the Hard Rubber Company was an old organization of about 2,600 employees, of whom 700 or so were salaried. For over one hundred years the company had been a pioneer in the field of molding a large variety of hard rubber products. The company was comprised of a head office and two plants. It also boasted a wholly owned reclaim rubber manufacturing subsidiary. Its annual sales volume was $15 million. The products included:

1. Vessels for transporting acids and other corrosive materials
2. Hard rubber lining for storage tanks
3. Hard rubber lined pipe
4. Caster wheels
5. Water meter parts
6. Refrigeration parts
7. Photo developing trays and tanks
8. Molded cutlery handles
9. Butt plates for guns
10. Chair arm pads for metal furniture

In addition, the company manufactured standard consumer products like bowling balls and combs. It also produced a small volume of extruded plastic products.

At one plant, battery cases were molded in large volume for many brand names. An organization chart of the company, as it existed in the early fifties, is shown in Exhibit 5.1.

REBUILDING AND DOCUMENTING THE STRUCTURE

An administrative modernization program was initiated by the controller when he came with the company in the forties. The first step of his staff was to analyze, define, document, and evaluate the exempt salaried positions and the organization structure. As a result of this analysis, the need for many new functions such as organization planning, management development, market research, public relations, budgeting, salary administration, internal auditing, methods and procedures, and the like, was identified, and these activities were created. In spite of the new functions, as shown on the chart, the total number of salaried employees was reduced by structural simplification from 640 to 550. In three years, the organizational planner then prepared a manual of organization and policy—one of the first such manuals—to document and communicate what was essentially a small functionalized organization structure. The manual index contained the following:

1. Purpose and Use of the Manual
2. Position Description Content
3. Position and Unit Titles
4. General Responsibilities and Authorities of All Positions
5. Company Line and Staff Organization
6. Definitions
7. Administration, Organization, and Other Basic Company Policies
8. Top-Management Position Descriptions

GROUPING OF FUNCTIONS

Functions were also transferred from one unit to another to provide for more effective grouping to facilitate management coordination and control. One example of such a change was the transfer of shipping from manufacturing to production planning at the two plants.

BENEFITS

The following were generally recognized benefits of this reorganization:

1. Unnecessary activities and jobs were eliminated. The number of salaried employees was reduced by over 14 percent with a corresponding reduction in salaries and related costs.

Exhibit 5.1 Organization Plan (Phase I): Hard Rubber Company

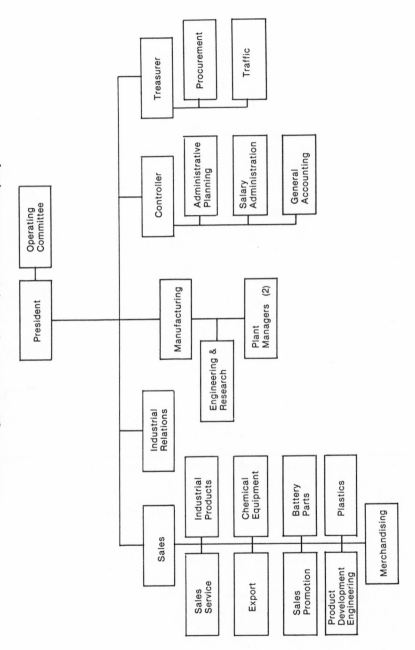

2. The documented organization structure and exempt job evaluation program provided a sound basis for salary administration, performance standards and appraisal, systems analysis, training, cost control, and other major management improvement programs.

3. Teamwork and coordination between departments was improved. There was much less friction and misunderstanding.

4. Necessary new functions were inaugurated to carry out the strategic objectives of the company.

5. Existing functions were realigned for ease of management coordination.

6. Individual and group performance and effectiveness were greatly improved.

STRATEGY AND STRUCTURE OF THE COMPANY UP TO THE PRESENT

In retrospect, the company has realized a benefit that was not apparent at the time the organization rebuilding program was undertaken. Eight years later the company was acquired by a group of acquisition-minded entrepreneurs. Since that time, the company has undergone explosive diversification and growth through acquisition. This growth could not have been achieved without destroying profits as the company had been organized at first.

By 1970 the original company had become the molded products division and only one of thirteen product divisions. A new plant had been built. At this location consumer products—bowling balls and combs—were manufactured in two profit-center divisions. The overall company was now highly diversified in technology as well as products. A Chemical Division made industrial chemicals called silicas and silicates in a new plant. The Electrical Products Division produced a variety of items in two plants from a new heat resistant, non-inflammable plastic. The Cables Division manufactured cables for computers, printed circuit assemblies for missiles, and machine control equipment and communication wires for air force flying suits. Another acquired single plant division manufactured garden hoses and is one of the nation's largest suppliers of them. Of the thirteen divisions headed by presidents, two reported directly to the chief executive officer; the others reported to the chief executive through two senior vice presidents who acted as group executives. A vice president-administration was also the controller, and he supervised an assistant vice president-compensation and benefits—among others—who now had the organization planning responsibility.

Sales volume had increased from about $15 million to over $162 million. Annual net earnings were $7.5 million. Employees had increased from 2,600 to 6,300. The stock value had increased from about $6 per share to $23 per share during the same period. The title "president" was used for the heads of the profit-center divisions no doubt because they were incorporated entities headed by presidents when they were acquired.

By 1979, the company had grown in sales volume to $336 million with annual net earnings of $12.4 million. However, in 1980 the trend was reversed. Sales went down to $326 million, profits to $10 million, and return on shareholders equity from 11.2 percent to 8.7 percent. This downturn was caused by reduced demand in several major markets and by increased interest rates. These markets were automotive, construction, and agricultural equipment. According to the CEO, the variety of divisions and products made it difficult for him to communicate progress to the stockholders and the investment community. Divisions were then organized into three groups: Fluid Power and Metal Components, Electrical, and Consumer and Safety Products.

In 1984 a group of investors bought the company in leveraged buyout and changed it to a privately held corporation. Many of the divisions were sold, including all those manufacturing hard rubber products. There are only three divisions left as shown on the organization chart in Exhibit 5.2, excluding two foreign divisions. Since the company is now privately held and financial statements are not available, we have no information on current sales and profits. However, we understand sales in 1987 are down to about $80 million and profits to about $2 million. The company grew rapidly through highly diverse acquisitions and it contracted just as rapidly after going private through divestitures. Its future is uncertain. What is certain is that it is no longer a hard rubber company. The hard rubber comb is made by another company.

ANALYSIS AGAINST THE BONDS OF ORGANIZATION

Identification

Originally, there was no public relations activity. This function was created during the initial phase in the development of the organization. Since it was structurally a part of the advertising activity in the sales department, it was too oriented toward product advertising and not enough toward institutional identification. Today public relations has been recently created as a communications function reporting directly to the chief executive officer.

Perpetuation

Human resources perpetuation activities were split at the corporate level between "organized" and "non-organized" employee services. The industrial relations manager handled the former while the controller handled the latter through a supervisor of salary administration and a supervisor of organization planning. This split no longer exists in the current structure; both are under a director-human resources, reporting directly to the CEO.

**Exhibit 5.2 Organization Plan (Phase II), 1988:
Hard Rubber Company**

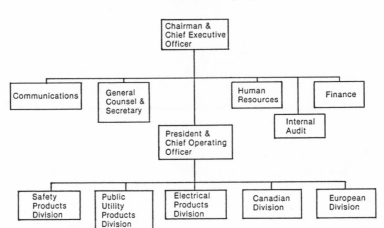

Workflow

Workflow activities were originally organized on a functional basis. Currently, we find them organized on a profit-center product division basis.

Control

Control activities—except for custodial accounting—were all but non-existent originally. The administrative planning department was created to perform these activities. Now there is a vice president-finance.

HOMEOSTATIC ACTIVITIES

Fusion Process

For many years there was little commitment to the organization on the part of organized employees. Discipline was weak because the chief executive officer tended to give in too easily to union and other outside pressures. As a result, after World War II, the "will to manage" was absent. Work standards were loose. With the change in management, this weakness in discipline was corrected. This strengthening of discipline did not involve a change in the organization structure. However, the tools were used more effectively as a result.

The fusion of salaried employee goals with those of the company was a different matter. Most of them were long-service, well-paid, committed, and reasonably capable employees. The turnover was very low (about one-half of 1 percent per year). The performance appraisal system was trait- rather than goal-oriented, and salaries rapidly moved high into the very competitive rate ranges after the job evaluation program had been in place only a short time. This fostered good repetitive performance, but did not encourage innovative performance. Salary costs were unnecessarily high. A modern "management-by-objectives" program reinforced by substantial rewards would, no doubt, have improved both work and self-development performance.

Problem-Solving Process

The problem-solving process, thanks to the influence of the original controller, was rational and fact-oriented. The staff in the newly created administrative planning department provided a good example of improvement-oriented professional administrative staff work to everyone in the organization. However, poor discipline and failure to diversify were limiting profits and threatening the long-term survival of the organization.

Leadership Activities

The lack of diversification and attendant risks were clear. The one major technology of the company was the job-shop manufacture of hard rubber products. This technology was firmly implanted, not only in the name of the company, but in the skills and abilities of its long-service employees. It had edged into the plastics business on a limited basis, because the carbon black associated with hard rubber production made it entirely impractical to manufacture plastics in large volume at the same location without disastrous contamination. The old management had been reluctant to strike out boldly through acquisition in the easy-entry field of extruded plastics, in which there was such fierce fly-by-night competition. The new management on the other hand, not only brought in better discipline, tighter work standards, and greater profits in the hard rubber end of the business, but it also had greater access to the outside capital resources so essential in carrying out an acquisition program. Most of the new fields that the company entered—with the exception of the worsted textile business—have proved to be successful and profitable. Diversification was largely achieved through outside acquisition and not through internal new product development. In this way the company not only obtained new products and plants, but also the talent to run them profitably. In time, the Hard Rubber Company became less and less at the mercy of obsolescence in the hard rubber technology. Today hard rubber products are not manufactured at all.

WHEN IS REORGANIZATION NECESSARY?

The need for new functions and functional realignments became clear during the analysis and evaluation of the exempt positions as required by the installation of the salary administration program. Because the controller saw the need for new functions, he established them in his own area of jurisdiction—finance—instead of where they logically belonged organizationally. No doubt he believed that these functions would ultimately gravitate to their logical place in the structure after they had proven their usefulness and effectiveness. If they had been incubated in the proper structural position, however, without the controller's informed and skillful leadership, performance would no doubt have been unsatisfactory, due to inept supervision. They might, therefore, have been abolished after a short trial period. Skillful and sophisticated top-management general executives in every functional area would no doubt have obviated the need for this strategy. We believe this staffing inadequacy was the reason all the realignments necessary to achieve a rational grouping of functions were not carried out.

ORGANIZATION OF ORGANIZATION PLANNING

There was one organization planning specialist who reported directly to the manager of administrative planning. The manager-administrative planning, in turn, reported to the controller, who reported to the chief executive officer. In a company of this size, he not only had the full range of organization planning functions, he also was accountable for management development and training, salaried job evaluation, and head office personnel. Here there were many levels of management between the staff man and the chief executive and there was little direct communication between them. Fortunately, however, the controller was a very skilled professional generalist in management. He was not only one of the most progressive executives in the Controller's Institute, he had been very active for many years in the Society for Advancement of Management. In many ways he had achieved the same kind of close relationship and trust on the part of the chief executive officer as had the vice president of finance of the Automobile Company (see Chaper 6). However, when the chief executive lost control of the company, the new managers, being financiers and entrepreneurs, demonstrated little interest in professional management. Consequently, the organization planning function received minimal top-management understanding and support. It was soon subordinated to the management systems function. There it rapidly lost its effectiveness and impact on the corporate organization structure.

TOOLS AND TECHNIQUES OF ORGANIZATION PLANNING

Fortunately, for seven years the organization planning specialist had been encouraged to develop and use the most sophisticated tools and techniques of organization planning that could profitably be employed in a company of such small size. The organization and policy manual was generally thought to be one of the most advanced for its time. The organization planner also exercised staff control over the number of salaried positions authorized in the budget through the authority of the controller. Such manpower controls are generally found to be very difficult to administer when the organization planning staff is not under the controller. The tools of organization analysis used at that time were not very refined. Techniques of activity strength analysis, grouping analysis, and decisions analysis, as outlined in Chapter 3, had not yet been developed. Work distribution analysis and linear responsibility charting were also in their infancy. However, through the analytical use of the master functional organization chart, it was possible to eliminate many unnecessary positions, levels, and functions in the structure. It was also possible to see where voids existed and new functions were needed to carry out the goals and strategy of the company.

PRINCIPLES OF ORGANIZATION PLANNING

There was no formal strategic plan or long-range planning process in the corporation except in the form of a sales budget, which was developed and administered by the budget manager in the administrative planning department. No thought was given to diversification through acquisition, which came into such prominence with the advent of the new management. However, the integration and profitable management of these highly diversified acquisitions by divisionalizing the structure would not have been possible if the modern tools of management had not been developed by the previous regime. Application of the *Principle of the Objective* was important initially as were the *Principle of Coordination*, the *Principle of Specialization* and the *Principle of Definition*. In documenting and controlling the organization structure, first for evaluation and later for organization planning, the staff found several instances where the *Principle of Correspondence* had been violated.

As the organization planning function lost the support of the chief executive officer, however, the *Principle of Continuity* was not appropriately applied. The new management thought there was no need to maintain an organization planner at a high salary to deal with continuing organization changes. Of course, as a result of violating this principle, many off-the-cuff organization changes have occurred over the intervening years, until there are now apparent weaknesses in the structure that can only be dealt with through major changes in organization. Obviously, many months of fact-finding and analysis would be required before a staff analyst could reach any final conclusions. These apparent weaknesses in design, however, would be the place to start.

6

Divisionalizing a Large Corporation: The Automobile Company

HISTORY OF THE AUTOMOBILE COMPANY ORGANIZATION

In the twenties, at the time the Automobile Company was founded by a former GM executive, it was much easier than at present for a new automobile with a clear superiority to be successful. This company had such a product. The original automotive engineers had spent some time in designing the new car. The high compression engine gave it a getaway that beat the other cars of its time. In an era when breakdowns were common, the products of this company had a built-in durability that other cars did not have. The springing was outstanding and the car boasted many other engineering "firsts." The founder of the company, in his autobiography, said his little company had a hard time weathering the Depression of the thirties and every part of the organization was cut to the bone except the engineering department. As a result, the organization became engineering-oriented. The research director of General Motors was the founder's idol. The founder was also people-oriented and management-oriented, in part as a result of his work experience as head of one of the divisions of General Motors, where he enjoyed a close working relationship with Alfred Sloan, the organization genius.

Early in the career of the founder, he developed an intuitive respect for organization. The following is a quotation from the autobiography:

The Mental Equipment of a Business

In the development of the great modern business corporations as servants of mankind, men have devised a creative force that transcends themselves. None of these corporations are [*sic*] perfect yet, of course, but before you condemn their crudities remember how young they are and then ask yourself what other time in history can show anything to compare with these teams of men, in their capacity to enrich mankind and in their capacity to extend human powers in almost any direction we may wish to go.

Kettering had become a great scientist; then he was an inventor and we wanted him because of his vision, because through him there probably will be revealed greater tasks for the force we represented.

Nourished by such a mind, a great corporation's departmentalized intelligence becomes still greater; but to support a research mind there must be other kinds of minds, those of production men, of merchants, of mechanics, of advertising men and countless others. When all these minds *through organization* are made to function as a single intelligence each member of which is a special, gifted part, why, then you can expect to produce magic. Nowhere in the world is there a people with wealth so widespread as in America; nowhere is there a people who have so much. It seems to me quite obvious that we do not owe this difference to a few outstanding men; we owe it to a scheme of working together whereby lots of varied intelligences in a great business organization pool their most effective parts.

This eloquent statement demonstrates an unusually clear understanding of the importance of organization structure that would do credit to a professional manager of today. Nevertheless, in spite of his intuitive understanding of the benefits of organization, he was not so skilled in this field as was Alfred Sloan of General Motors.

Early in this century General Motors began to capitalize on Sloan's philosophy, his scheme of organization, and his acquisition and development of men of talent. Because GM's major competitors did not give the importance to a philosophy of management that it deserved, they almost went out of business after World War II. The Ford Motor Company, under Henry Ford II and Ernest R. Breech, modernized and divisionalized the organization in the late forties as outlined in detail in *Ford: Decline and Rebirth,* by Allan Nevins and Frank Ernest Hill.

By mid-century, the Automobile Company was still being run by the founder's associates, much as the founder himself had managed it. There were no organization charts. Cost controls were rudimentary. There was no organization and policy manual. It was run on a personal, informal basis just as Henry Ford, the elder, had run the Ford Motor Company. When the "buyers' market" returned and a squeeze on profits began shortly after World War II, the vice president-finance began to cut costs by paring down the staffs just in the way the founder and he had successfully weathered the Great Depression. There was, however a professional controller in the company who was to become his successor. In sharp contrast to the original vice president-finance, this man was a trained professional manager. He had been brought in from the company's auditing firm to modernize the financial control system. He saw the danger of across-the-board staff cuts to meet the crisis. This would only hasten the demise of the company in the face of strong competition from two well-managed and capably staffed companies like GM and Ford. By that time two men had in succession replaced the founder as chief executive. The last was a lawyer who had been brought into the company at the suggestion of the head of the original law firm, who was a close friend of the founder. He had achieved an outstanding reputation for running the Automobile Company's tank plant during World War II and had caught the chief executive's eye as a good, hard driving, production man. An engineer in the same plant was also marked as a "comer." The former was made corporation chief executive and the latter was made president of one of the car divisions. Neither of these men was market-oriented or a professionally trained manager. Essentially, one was a lawyer and the other was an engineer. It is hardly surprising then that neither one recognized the importance of the gradual but drastic change in issue values that determined whether or not the customer bought one make of automobile instead of another. No longer was it critical that the car be durable. By the end of the thirties all cars were durable. Customers were beginning to be more wealthy. This year's automobile was beginning to be a status symbol in an affluent society. Styling became the issue value. Not only did the customer want the car to be big and low and beautiful; its styling should change substantially each year so the neighbors could see that he could afford the latest model. Henry Ford's preoccupation with the Model T, a cheap car in one color for the masses, and the founder's interest in the durable car prevented both from seeing the gradual but substantial change in the automobile customer's tastes, issue values, and interests. General Motors had become, on the other hand, professionally managed and marketing-oriented. GM had almost gone out of business in the early twenties because of poor management and a lack of market sensitivity. As a result, the top executives, by necessity, became experts in the field of professional management and marketing.

The new vice president-finance sold the chief executive on the importance of reorganizing the corporation on the same GM divisionalization concepts that Henry Ford II[1] and Ernest Breech had previously applied in reorganizing Ford. He told the chief executive that a major reorganization of this kind would be costly. While no money should be wasted on unnecessary staff, "head chopping" was not the answer to the loss of market share. Considerable money would be required to tide the company over the period of reorganization until an improvement in market share and profits could be realized from the change.

The vice president anticipated that the reorganization would be more difficult than was the one at Ford. After all, Ford had reorganized during a "seller's market" after the war, when the basic problem was to make the car at a reasonable price. There was no problem in selling it. Furthermore, one of the strongest assets Ford had at that time was a strong dealer body.

The "bread-and-butter car" was the small car, Car D. Of the four car divisions, the small car division was the only one without its own dealer body. Car Division A, Car Division B, and Car Division C often sold Car D as a cheap come-on for their higher priced product. This may have been a good strategy during the Depression, but it was not geared to the affluent markets of the fifties. A real profit-center division for Car D should, above all, have direct access to its market. The small car division did not have this vital asset through its own dealer body.

Immediately after World War II, Ford executives recognized the need for professional management and made a comeback under the capable direction of Henry Ford II, Ernest Breech, and the "whiz-kids." General Motors first began to apply professional management principles in the twenties when the Du Pont influence began to take effect under the leadership of Pierre Du Pont as president.

The Automobile Company, on the other hand, continued to be an engineering- rather than a management-oriented organization even after durability ceased to be an issue with new car purchasers. Many of the engineers in the company subscribed to the "mouse trap" philosophy, i.e., if you could build a better engineered car, then the public would beat a path to your door. They underestimated the importance of management, organization, and marketing. Styling was a part of, and entirely dominated by, the engineering division. The job of the stylist was to make the engineering package look as beautiful as possible. There was no professional marketing research staff in the company to alert the engineers to the error of their ways. Their ideas were just as outmoded from a marketing viewpoint as the Model T concept of Henry Ford.

THE AUTOMOBILE COMPANY AT MID-CENTURY

When the "buyer's market" hit the Automobile Company after World War II, the company was behind the times not only in the styling of its cars, but more important in its management methods and organization structure. There was no real understanding of the GM philosophy of management by the line executives. There were no job descriptions, job evaluation, or policy documents. As a result, there was little discipline of the system. There was a vigorous resistance by line managers to any management control devices or policies generated by staffs. Any effort of the staff to install such needed administrative constraints was met by the charge that the staffs were trying to "run the company." They did not appreciate the real role of a strong staff, which should be getting facts, making recommendations, and coordinating policy administration. Suddenly, in a little over three months, the company's market share plunged from 18 percent to 13 percent.

The director of divisional records development in the control division wrote a memo to the vice president-finance outlining in some detail the principles of "divisionalization" as had been successfully applied at the two larger competitors, General Motors and Ford. *Concept of the Corporation* by Peter Drucker was cited as the authority for information on the General Motors concept of organization. Speeches by the Ford executive vice president and the vice president-finance were given as the authority for the comments on the Ford organization and the changes made to achieve a divisionalized organization structure. The divisional records development staff prepared a summary of this report for presentation to the board of directors. The board subsequently approved this program and announced it to the shareholders.

The controller was promoted to the position of vice president-organization, reporting directly to the chief executive officer in order to carry out the reorganization program. He then appointed the director of divisional records development as director of organization to recruit the men for his staff. Two men were recruited from the outside. One was an experienced organization planner from a small company; the other had been assistant to the president of a large steel corporation. He was an expert in the specialized field of supplementary management compensation, and was brought in primarily to revise the company management incentive plan. Over the years, bonus payments had been automatically granted under the plan and were considered by a participant to be almost like part of his base salary.

Internally, men were promoted to the organization staff from every major functional area; one was the assistant to the vice president of engineering; one was head of materials control in central production; one was an assistant controller; two came from the legal department; and one had been vice president-manufacturing for one of the car divisions. These were the senior staff specialists. Later, one more senior man was brought in from the outside. He had been corporate secretary of an electric products manufacturing company. All the other staff men—and there were about twenty—were the so-called junior organization planning specialists. Since none of these men had any experience in conducting organization surveys, the first job of the experienced organization planner was to develop an organization survey guide, setting forth standard techniques for conducting organization surveys, analyzing facts, preparing reports, and carrying out approved recommendations. The organization planner developed a master schedule for carrying out the reorganization studies in all functional areas of the corporation (see Exhibit 6.1). In addition, he directed organization surveys of the critically weak sales and service functions on a company-wide basis.

THE ORIGINAL ORGANIZATION STRUCTURE
BEFORE DIVISIONALIZATION

The chief executive officer reported to the chairman of the board. Everyone else reported to the chief executive officer.

Exhibit 6.1 Divisionalization Program: Automobile Company

ACTION STEPS	1970	1971	1972	1973	1974	1975	1976	1977	1978
I. Define Existing Positions and Organization Structure									
II. Prepare Organization Survey Report									
III. Conduct Study of Committee Structure									
A. Establish Interim Scheduling Committee									
B. Establish Product Planning Committee									
C. Establish Administrative Council									
D. Establish Salaried Personnel Committee									
IV. Obtain Approval of Short-term Organization Plan and Plant Realignment									
V. Develop Objectives/Program									
VI. Conduct Functional Organization Surveys									
A. Sales and Service									
B. Manufacturing/Traffic/Purchasing									
C. Engineering									
D. Finance									
E. Industrial Relations									
F. Advertising and Public Relations									
G. Business Research									
VII. Install Divisionalization Policies and Procedures									
A. Finance									
B. Sales									
C. Manufacturing									
D. Engineering									
E. Industrial Relations									
F. Public Relations									
G. Business Research									
H. Product and Volume Planning									
VIII. Establish Organization and Policy Manuals									
IX. Prepare Evaluation Position Descriptions									
X. Establish Management Position Evaluation Program									
XI. Establish Management Development Program									
XII. Establish Monthly Management Meeting Program									
XIII. Separate Operating From Functional Divisions									
A. Defense Operations									
B. Axle and Transmission									
C. Forge and Foundry									
XIV. Establish Integrated Product Divisions									
A. Car A Division									
B. Car B Division									
C. Car C Division									
D. Car D Division									
E. Air Conditioning Division									
F. Marine and Industrial Engine Division									
G. Powdered Metal Products Division									
H. Chemical Products Division									
XV. Audit Results at All Product Divisions									

The structure comprised an operating span of control of eleven executives and a staff span of control of nine. This obviously placed a heavy load on the chief executive officer and there was no chief operating officer.

The chief executive officer was assisted in the management of the company by an informal committee of the key staff heads and the car division heads called the president's council. There was no agenda and no recording of decisions. A member could bring up for discussion in the meeting itself any subject on which he wanted a decision without prior staff work, fact-finding, or analysis. There was also a broader communications committee of more than thirty-five executives, who met to discuss operating problems. This was called the operations committee.

One of the staff men from the legal division was given the job of developing a report with recommendations on the top-management organization of the company. The two staff men who had been brought in from outside the company were given the assignment to assist him so he could benefit from their organization planning experience.

The following suggestions were made in his report:

I. Creation of a general management group.
   A. Creation of an executive committee of the board—this would require a change in the bylaws to shift most of the responsibility for the general management of the corporation from the president's council to an executive committee.
   B. Separation of general management vice presidents from service and operating activities to permit their participation in general management. To do this, these vice presidents must shape their functional organizations so as to permit themselves to have more time to concentrate on general management.
II. The realignment of operations (plants and products) so as to permit the most effective operation of the company followed by corresponding division of operating management and designation of profit centers.
III. The development of the operating units as integrated businesses.
IV. The allocation of individual functions both as between general functional areas and as between central and operating management; e.g., should procurement be part of the manufacturing function and, if so, how much should it be divisionalized; who should handle advertising; what should be the functions of central sales and central manufacturing, where the functions are divisionalized? Through this allocation we will reduce overlaps, highlight voids, and make desirable realignments.
V. The developing of the necessary supporting groups and procedures necessary for operation of the two management levels—
   A. Revision of the appropriations procedures.
   B. Long-range planning procedure for formulating, integrating, and approving objectives and supporting programs.
   C. Areas in which we will establish standards for division performance and measure results.

VI. The clear statement in writing of the functions, responsibilities, and relationships of the various parts of the organization in organization charts, manuals, and the like.

Concurrently, this legal division's staff man's two associates prepared an unofficial internal consulting report on the same subject. The following were their findings:

1. Lines of authority, particularly in top management, are not clearly defined. Responsibilities and authorities from the president to each employee should be clarified and understood by all responsible executives.

2. The heads of too many large operating components (eleven) report directly to the president. The president should be given executive vice presidents and/or group vice presidents to assist him in the job of directing the operating components of the corporation.

3. The president and major division and staff department heads do not have the internal administrative staff assistance (in personnel, budget, and the like) to perform their executive responsibilities. There should be a decentralization of these administrative services to the divisions within the necessary centralized controls.

4. The top committees are not properly staffed and organized to advise effectively the president and major operating division heads. The composition and functions of these committees should be revised and defined accordingly.

5. Functions of the central staff divisions are not properly grouped according to their major purposes. Appropriate transfers of functions should be made and new staff divisions should be established where advisable.

6. The corporation has not taken positive steps to identify and develop men with unusual management ability in key management positions. This should be done as soon as possible.

7. Administrative instructions, accounting procedures, and other central management controls are not properly set up to provide effective management of divisionalized organization components.

8. More authority should be delegated to the heads of operating components to run their operations independently on a day-to-day basis within the necessary corporate programs and policy coordination.

9. Certain major staff components need to institute new functions to provide more effective coordination of the operating components, particularly in the coordination and improvement of regional sales and manufacturing research activities.

10. There is evidence of ineffectiveness and confusion in the relations with dealer organizations in the field. This has been a contributing factor to a weakening of distribution outlets. Responsibilities and authority for dealer contacts and relationships should be defined. An effective organization should be developed for building up and maintaining strong, well-guided, and profitable outlets for the products of the corporation so necessary to the improvement of its competitive position.

Exhibit 6.2 Organization Plan (Phase I): Automobile Company

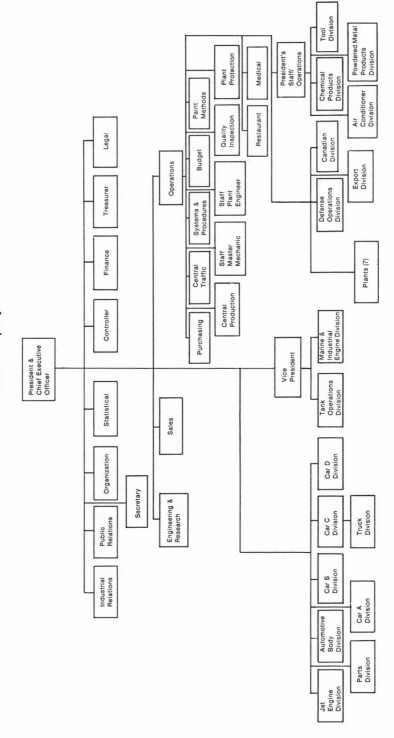

Exhibit 6.3 Organization Plan (Phase II), 1988: Automobile Company

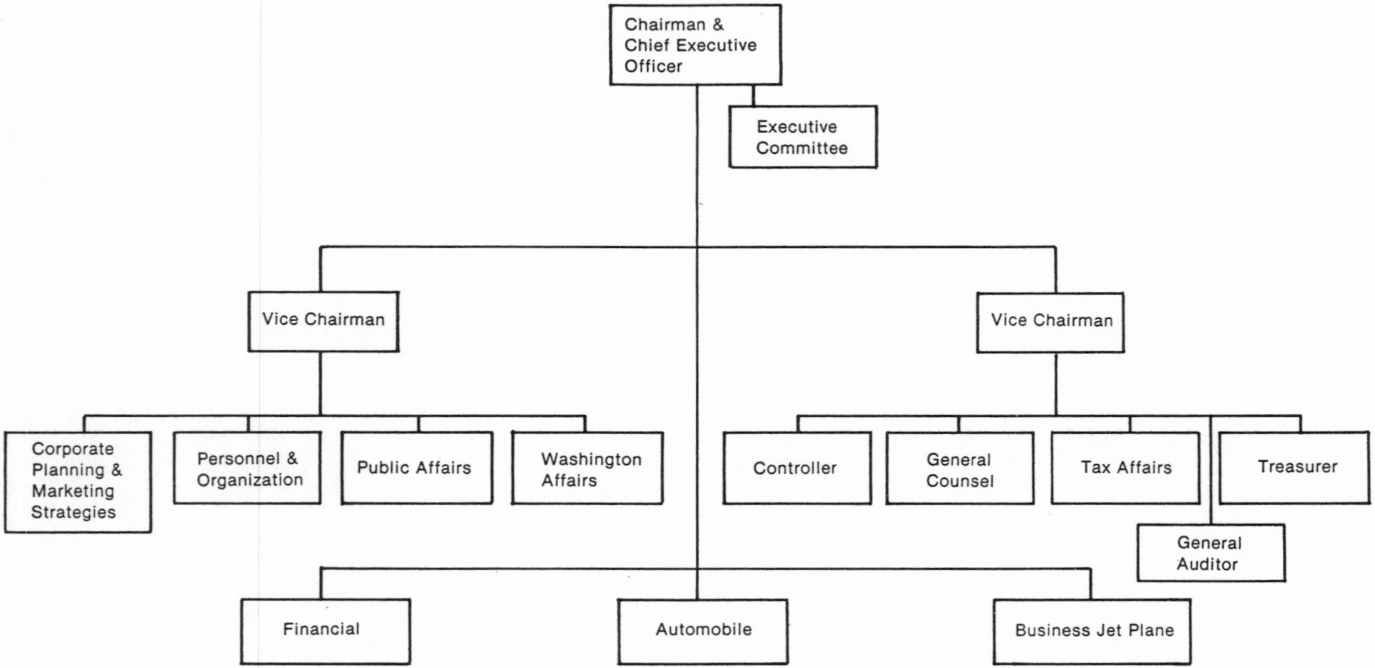

In addition to these recommendations, the report pointed out that functional organization surveys were underway in the following areas:

1. Staff manufacturing
2. Sales functions and regional organization
3. Product service
4. Engineering and research
5. Purchasing and traffic
6. General office services
7. Personnel
8. Styling
9. Plant realignment and divisional management
10. Advertising and sales promotion

In addition to these surveys, a long-range planning task force was established under the corporate secretary to make an overall business study of the automobile business and the competitive position of the company in the industry. This study was made available to the organization department.

Suddenly, two years after the reorganization began, the vice president-finance and father of the divisionalization program died of a brain tumor. There was no one else in top management with his professional management experience and authority to assume the leadership of the program. The program had only just begun and already the car division heads were complaining that there were no demonstrated results in increased share of the market and profits. Of course, this was an unwarranted criticism, since Ford's divisionalization program had required six years before there were any substantial results. This was the case in spite of the fact that their program had been carried out in a seller's market. Furthermore, Ford had been run by an experienced team of top executives from General Motors, under the leadership of Ernest Breech. They managed the company, implemented the program, and enforced discipline.

With the death of the vice president-finance, the critics of the program, who naturally resisted the mandatory administrative constraints required by divisionalization, became more and more vocal. In order to silence them, the new vice president-finance (who had been the vice president-organization) agreed to have management consultants come in and validate the divisionalizaiton program and the work of the organization department.

It was the conclusion of the consultants' report that:

1. The company had tried to divisionalize in a shorter time than had Ford.
2. The organization department had taken the "organization planning" approach and had not made a real business study before designing the top structure.

3. Top management had parcelled out functions to the divisions before establishing controls to ensure effective performance of the delegations.

4. The small car division could not be a profit center because it had no direct control over its dealer body.

5. There was no clear understanding of the philosophy of "divisionalization" by the key division executives.

6. Deviations from the concept and program were permitted by the chief executive officer without exercising real discipline of the system.

7. The divisionalization reorganization was carried out in a "gossipy" atmosphere, where any deviation from the plan was considered a reversal in strategy, particularly by the outside financial analysts and those in the company who were not completely sold on the program.

8. There was a natural resistance to any mandatory control mechanisms developed by corporate staffs among the line operating executives in the divisions, who accused the corporate staffs of trying to take over line authority. They did not understand the important functional control role of the staff in a divisionalized company.

The crux of the problem was, of course, the lack of modern professional management experience on the part of the car division heads, and their reluctance to learn new and complex concepts and techniques from the trained professional staff men brought in from the outside.

At that time a decision was made to bring in a controller, an executive from the auditing firm retained by the company. Although young, he was a trained professional accountant and began to get profit results from using the systems developed previously. He was next promoted to group executive of international operations, and finally to chief executive officer.

Profit performance has been improving—with occasional downswings—ever since. Market share, however, has not exceeded the level of the early sixties.

ANALYSIS AGAINST THE BONDS OF ORGANIZATION

Identification Activities

The organization charter is basically contained in the bylaws. When the company's share of the market declined so rapidly after World War II, many blamed the problem on outmoded styling. An outstanding automobile stylist was brought in to modernize the entire product line. Concurrently, the vice president-public relations created a new company logo, with a related corporate identity program to help create the image of a forward-looking, progressive organization fighting to make a comeback against two larger and more profitable competitors. This program was launched to publicize the completely redesigned line of cars. Sales spurted upward again and the new insigne became the symbol of the organization. Employees wore them in the form of tie clasps, cuff links, lockets, and the like. It did much to rebuild the morale of the employees and the confidence of the general public, who were concerned that the Automobile Company might follow the path of many of its predecessors out of the automobile business.

PERPETUATION ACTIVITIES

People

The human resources of the company were primarily highly skilled in the technical fields of automobile engineering and production. Because of the founder's emphasis on product excellence and durability, this was understandable. However, in the field of professional management they were much less proficient. They displayed the same lack of skill in using organization charts, position descriptions, and other modern management tools as had the executives at Ford during the regime of Henry Ford, Senior. Fortunately, the goon squads were absent and so the morale was much better at the Automobile Company than at Ford when young Henry Ford II took over. The major difference was that Henry Ford II imported trained professional managers from General Motors and put them in key line positions, and the Automobile Company tried the more humane but less effective method of importing trained professional managers and putting them in staff positions with the hope that they would train the long-service corporate officers and division presidents. As the vice president-organization put it, this was an "evolutionary" rather than a "revolutionary" approach to divisionalization.

It was not until the advent of the financially trained chief executive that professional management men from the outside were put in top line positions as division heads and group executives.

Capital

Originally, the company had insufficient capital to weather a divisionalization program. It did, however, have the borrowing power because of the relatively high equity in facilities and equipment. This was extremely important to the company's ultimate survival. Thus, the vice president-finance had no trouble in borrowing $260 million from an insurance company to finance the tremendous cost of the divisionalization program.

Ideas

The creedal philosophy of the corporation was based on the values held to be important by the founder. He placed a high value on product innovation, durability, and service. For this reason the organization was said in the industry to be engineering-oriented. Although the engineers were relatively few in number, it was generally agreed that, man-for-man, they were technically more competent than their counterparts at either Ford or General Motors. Their mission was important in the eyes of the founder of the company and they knew it. For this reason cars of the company were credited with having many engineering firsts. On the other hand, the company had few management innovations to their credit, as did GM.

After World War II there were, for example, no flexible budgets; there was no salaried job evaluation system; and there were no organization charts and job descriptions. These were professional management tools that were common in many smaller companies outside the automobile business. Further, there was no understanding of the management language in which these tools were communicated. This made the training job, as it had been in Ford, a tremendous one. The organization department tried to accomplish it as quickly as possible through the issuance of an organization survey guide and organization manual. The long-service executives generally thought of themselves as automobile production experts or engineers rather than as professional managers.

This value system consequently had its impact on the structure of the organization. The stylist, when first brought in from the outside, was made a vice president of the corporation, but he reported to the vice president-engineering. Only recently has this function become differentiated from engineering as it has been for some time at both Ford and General Motors. Since the company was not professionally managed, it was not one that valued strategy and sound organization structure so much as it valued personalities. Consequently, the company was not managed through a discipline of the system, as at GM or Ford. There were no written administrative constraints. There were a few outmoded operating procedures that the top executives disregarded whenever it suited their purposes to do so. A manual of mandatory policies was not issued until four years after the divisionalization program began. Violation of the conflict of interest policy by the president, which resulted in his resignation, was symptomatic of the attitude of the top executives toward written policies and the importance of managing "by policy." The control activities were weak as well.

WORKFLOW ACTIVITIES

Production

These activities were initially carried out in the production plants under the operating vice president and in the operating divisions of the corporation. They were concerned with the production and assembly of parts for the cars, trucks, and other products.

Distribution

These were also carried out in the operating divisions, except for Car D. Distribution and warehousing of replacement parts were the responsibility of the parts division. The weakness in the distribution organization lay in the fact that the small car division had no control over its dealer body. In general, the dealers also were poorly positoned in the market place, poorly capitalized and poorly managed in comparison to the dealers of its two major competitors, Ford and GM.

CONTROL ACTIVITIES

Directive

There were many signs in the corporation that the control activities were weak. They were performed on a personal and verbal, rather than on a systematic and mandatory, basis in accord with written policy.

Motivation

The company had become too large to be run on a personal basis and the management incentive plan was not used to reward and reinforce outstanding performance. There was no incentive for salaried personnel to perform in an outstanding manner. With no written policy, each manager tended to run his own show on a personal basis without any check and balance on his authority. On the other hand, he had no real final authority, since any of his decisions might be subject to reversal at a later date by higher authority up to and including the chief executive officer and the board of directors.

Evaluation

Performance was largely evaluated on a trait-oriented rather than a position description or objectives-oriented basis. Supervisors tended to be biased in favor of a no-complaints yes-man rather than toward a professional with strong opinions who tended to disturb the status quo. The staff's proposal to revise the management incentive plan was an important step. However, immediately after approval of the plan, financial results were so poor that no bonuses were awarded. For this reason, there was no opportunity to find out whether they would be awarded on the basis of performance and results.

Communication

Written management directives and other similar information were communicated to supervisors through the management personnel mailing list. The staff maintained this list on an organizational basis and controlled its use for the issuance of all organization and policy manual documents and notices. The primary difficulty in maintianing this list resulted from the rapid changes in structure and duties, particularly those of the informal kind. These changes were not approved and announced on an official basis. Reports and other upward communications did not go through these same channels, but were communicated by the specialized staff concerned.

HOMEOSTATIC ACTIVITIES

Fusion Process

From the beginning of the rapid decline in market share, the company was blessed with a great many committed salaried employees who had many years of faithful service to their credit. Further, there was not a great deal of opportunity for mobility open to professional and managerial personnel in Detroit, a city dominated by only three large employers, of which the Automobile Company was the largest. At one point these talented executives endured payless paydays, which were borne without a grumble. It was to maintain this high morale that it was decided not to import talent for top managerial positions from the other two larger competitors. So, fusion was no real problem.

THE PROBLEM-SOLVING PROCESS

Awareness

The original vice president-finance was aware of the survival problem, but he was one of the few inside the corporation with sufficient professional management background to have a real comprehension of the basic cause. His speeches showed a remarkably penetrating insight into the root-causes of the difficulty.

Exploration

The company remained engineering- and production-oriented long after GM had become professional management-oriented. Although GM had many good production men, they also had Alfred Sloan, a thoughtful professional manager, as their chief executive officer.

Failure to solve the management problem could rapidly put the company out of the automobile business as had happened in the case of Studebaker-Packard Corporation, and as is happening, in more recent times, in the case of American Motors Corporation.

The interests of all the groups dependent on the economic survival of the corporation would be adversely affected by its demise; for example: the shareholders; the consumers; the suppliers; the employees; and even the competitors were being accused of monopolistic practices by the federal government.

The Identification Activities, the Perpetuation Activities, and the Control Activities were the most important of the work processes. The provision of adequate capital resources was critically involved, as was the provision of the thoughtways resources in the management field.

Choice and Decision

The divisionalization decision was the proper one, it was made in time and it was clear-cut and unequivocal. All executives who were required to carry out this decision, particularly the car division presidents, appeared to concur. In reality, however, they had their reservations. They were not trained enough in the field of professional management really to grasp the concepts they said they understood. This resulted in the near sabotage of the program during the crisis period after the death of the vice president-finance. If management talent had been brought in from the outside, as it was in the case of the Ford divisionalization program, and put in top-management positions, this risk would have been minimized.

Mobilization

The objectives of the divisionalization program were clearly defined, the plans for operations were carefully prepared, and the specifications and standards for implementation were clearly drafted by management professionals recruited from the outside and put in staff positions. They were not, however, clearly communicated by the chief executive officer to the long-service corporate staffs and key division heads, who were to carry them out. At least, the communication was not accepted. The delegation of authority was eagerly accepted but not the establishment of central staff controls in each functional area. Sufficient time was not given to the corporate staffs to develop and install the necessary policies and systems of control required by the delegation.

As a result of this lack of proper program communication and training, there was little response and action at the operating division level.

Results of the divisionalization program were thoroughly reviewed by the management consulting firm in their studies made over a two year period, starting two years after the program began. As a result of their recommendations, vitally needed administrative constraints were established in the form of a body of written policy issued in a policy manual. This manual was expanded during the next two years and is still in use today.

Closure or Renewal

As a result of two years of experience with divisionalization, the problem was not considered closed but redirected toward the creation of a strong top-management structure that would permit the delegation of real authority to the division heads without undue risk to the survival of the corporation.

LEADERSHIP ACTIVITIES

There is a serious question, because of the refusal of the original chief executive to accept the organization accountability, that there was any personal and conscious involvement on his part or on the part of the other top executives in the divisionalization program. They did not properly communicate divisionalization concepts to the car division heads or enforce discipline in the execution of these concepts. This leadership did not actually take place until the advent of a professional accountant as chief executive six years after the divisionalization program was initiated.

ORGANIZATION OF ORGANIZATION PLANNING

Initially, the organization planning function was ideally organized. The vice president-organization had formerly been the controller under the vice president-finance when he first sold the chief executive on the critical need for the divisionalization program to save the company. This program was similar to the one the "whiz-kids" at Ford carried out immediately after World War II under Ernest Breech, the chief operating officer.

The vice president-organization reported directly to the chief executive. He was paid a salary of about $150,000 per year plus an equal amount in bonus. He was also a member of the board of directors. He had the full range of organization planning functions except exempt job evaluation, which remained in industrial relations; in addition, he had the long-range planning function as well as the secretariat of the administrative committee during its incubative stages. Next, the administrative committee secretariat was transferred to the corporate secretary and the long-range planning function was transferred to the vice president-finance.

Later, when the organization planning director was no longer an elected corporate officer, he then reported to the vice president and administrative assistant to the chief executive officer. Under this organizational arrangement no effort was made to prevent the organization staff from having direct access to the chief executive officer. The administrative assistant did try to ensure that the staff was using the chief executive's time well and did not bother him with comparatively unimportant problems. The administrative assistant had a very close working relationship with the chief executive, which had been developed over the years. There is little doubt that the staff received better understanding and support from the chief executive through the administrative assistant than it would have had it reported to him directly. The chief executive, an engineer, was by no means a professional manager like Breech of Ford or Cordiner of General Electric; neither was he so firm a believer in the practical benefits of professional management practices as had been his immediate predecessor.

However, undoubtedly the most effective management of the organization staff took place when one of the organization specialists from the legal department became director of organization reporting directly to the administrative vice president. The latter was, in effect, the chief executive officer, since all staff and line units of the company reported directly to him. The director of organization had been the secretary of the administrative committee before his appointment and had, in this capacity, developed a very close working relationship with the administrative vice president. This close working relationship continued when he assumed his role as director of organization.

As a lawyer he proved to be a rapid learner and he quickly acquired an unusual in-depth knowledge about professional management and organization. He and the administrative vice president used the staff effectively. Currently, the staff has been combined with personnel and reports to the chief executive officer. Here we find a violation of the Principle of Continuity. Once the corporation had completed major reorganization and profits began improving, the chief executive could no longer see the critical importance of having a strong organization staff reporting directly to him to counsel on structural changes, and thus prevent the need for another major and traumatic reorganization.

TOOLS AND TECHNIQUES OF ORGANIZATION PLANNING

The staff recognized the importance of making an overall business survey for its own use prior to making any organizational recommendations. This proved to be a valuable technique that has since been successfully employed in many companies. An organization survey guide was also issued outlining the accepted methods of making organization surveys. This manual was used as the primary tool for training the organization staff as well as the line managers in proper methods of conducting an organization survey and in implementing approved proposals. It also provided the staff with standardized methods of preparing organization charts, work distribution charts, procedural flow charts, and the like. The staff also prepared and issued an organization manual and a corporate policy guide, which are still in use today. The former contained descriptions of the functions of the major units, similar to the format of the

Ford organization manual. This manual, in addition to statements of functions, included a titling policy, terminology, organization principles, and a procedure for changing the manual in line with changes in structure. An organizational planning policy, similar to the one in Exhibit 1.2, was prepared but never issued. Consequently, many organization changes were made, particularly at the division level, without adequate study and review before commitments were made to staff the changed structure.

PRINCIPLES OF ORGANIZATION PLANNING

The *Principle of Definition* was the first to be applied since, before divisionalization, there were no organization charts or job descriptions to define the organization structure. When the first master chart was prepared, the staff could identify violations of the *Principle of Span of Management Control* as well as the *Principle of Balance*, the *Principle of Responsibility and Authority*, the *Principle of Coordination*, and the *Principle of Specialization*. The staff saw the need to relieve the heavy overload on the position of the chief executive officer resulting from the broad operating span of control. To accomplish this result, the staff recommended use of group executives and moved to strengthen the top policy committee structure. Unfortunately, as mentioned previously, the chief executive did not effectively communicate and enforce the concepts of divisionalization or mandatory policies with respect to decisions of his strong division heads, who acted as though divisionalization meant decentralization of decision-making authority without any central control. Not enough time, effort, and staff were given to the problem of developing central policies, procedures, and controls before profit-making authority and accountability were delegated by the CEO to the product division heads. As a result, serious mistakes were made, which tended to discredit the entire divisionalization program. This vital weakness in the program was not corrected until the corporate policy guide was prepared, and the new chief executive officer began to use the controls and enforce policy discipline. His predecessor did not even want a copy of the corporate policy guide; he could see no need for management by policy. In short, he did not have "the will to manage." This was the important difference between the General Motors management and the management of the Automobile Company.

STRATEGY AND STRUCTURE OF THE AUTOMOBILE COMPANY UP THE PRESENT

There have been no changes of similar magnitude in the organization structure or strategy of the Automobile Company since divisionalization. Strategy has been focused on improving the profits and share of the market of the product divisions. The company further diversified into the field of small boats and outboard motors.

In 1974 the retail sales in the United States reached 16.7 percent of the market. The number of employees worldwide was 245,000. Sales reached a record $9.8 billion. Net earnings were $220 million; the earnings, however, were still subject to major swings. In 1970, earnings were $303 million on sales of $7.4 billion. In 1972 there was a loss of $8 million on sales of $7 billion.

In 1979 came the gasoline shortage created by OPEC. Gasoline prices soared to $1.50 a gallon. The public demanded small fuel-efficient cars and began buying the Japanese imports. The company's profits plummeted to a loss of $1.7 billion in 1980. Only a Guaranteed Loan Program of $1.5 billion from the federal government saved the company from bankruptcy. The company began a crash program to downsize the entire car line. This included the introduction of an entirely new trans-axle front wheel drive engine. To conserve cash the company sold its foreign manufacturing subsidiaries, the tank plant, and the other non-automotive divisions. The operations were then limited largely to automobile production in the United States, Mexico, and Canada. This action proved successful and the guaranteed loans were repaid in full in advance. In 1986 sales were up to $22.6 billion and profits were at $1.4 billion. Share of the market was 11.9 percent. In 1985 the company acquired a corporation manufacturing business jet planes. In 1984 it was the only company to achieve the government mandated gas economy standard of 27 mpg. Although gas prices are down, the company plans to retain this competitive advantage.

The organization manual and the corporate policy guide are still maintained and the latter has been considerably expanded in the number of policies it contains. It still contains no organization planning policy, however, such as the one in Exhibit 1.2. The corporate organization and personnel office report to the chief executive officer. For this reason the staff is now more concerned with the control of salaries as an operating cost than with the design, review, and control of the top-management organization structure as required effectively to carry out strategy.

SUCCESS PATTERNS IN DIVISIONALIZED STRUCTURES

In preparing to divisionalize the Automobile Company, the organization staff made a study of the structures of successful divisionalized companies to see if a common pattern could be identified. This study was used to prepare the visual presentation on divisionalization given to the chief executive of the Recreation Company. Charts and concepts in this chapter were taken from this presentation (see Exhibits 6.4, 6.5, 6.6, 6.7, 6.8, 6.9, 6.10, and 6.11). In making this study, the staff was not trying to find a

Exhibit 6.4 Small Functional Structure

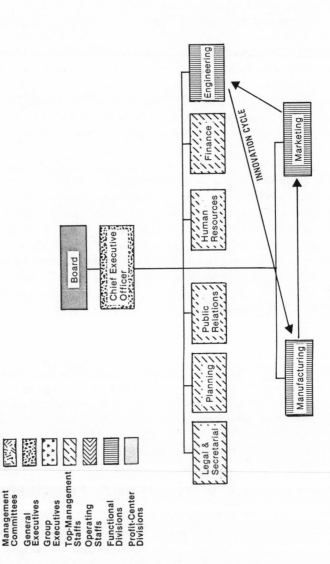

Board & Committees
Management Committees
General Executives
Group Executives
Top-Management Staffs
Operating Staffs
Functional Divisions
Profit-Center Divisions

Board

Chief Executive Officer

Legal & Secretarial

Planning

Public Relations

Human Resources

Finance

Engineering

INNOVATION CYCLE

Marketing

Manufacturing

pattern that could be copied exactly; it did believe, however, that large successful divisionalized organizations had discovered most of the essential functions that make for success in their particular product business or businesses. Whatever strategic plans they were achieving so successfully should be reflected in the design of their organizational structures and grouping of functions. An organization structure of a company that has been a leader in its industry over many years provides an excellent inventory of activities for the organizational planner to review in analyzing a similar structure. Both the structure and grouping of functions and nomenclature should be given careful attention to identify a success pattern, if one exists.

The staff analyzed the structures of successful business conglomerates so these designs could be compared with the structural pattern of the Automobile Company in various stages of divisionalization. The staff found two forces had strong impact on these structures; they were growth and diversification. These patterns in the development of a divisionalized structure originated both from a functional structure (see Exhibit 6.5) and from a holding company structure (see Exhibit 6.6). It will be noted that both of these structures have a relatively weak center. As a result of this study the staff concluded that the key problem in creating a well-designed structure for a large, diversified, divisionalized company was basically creating a strong center. Some of the organizational means for strengthening the center are the following:

1. Creating one or more general executive officers
2. Creating one or more levels of group executives
3. Changing the role of corporate staffs from a service-orientation to a policy and functional-control-orientation
4. Elaboration of general management and operations staffs, particularly in key control areas, i.e., organization planning
5. Realignment of corporate staffs
6. Establishment of staff group executives
7. Establishment of a strong policy framework and system of control
8. Strengthening the management policy committee structure

CODING ORGANIZATION CHARTS

An organization analyst will find the technique of coding an organization chart (see Exhibits 6.4, 6.5, 6.6, 6.7, and 6.8) very helpful in identifying structural weaknesses. Color coding may also be used. For example, in the coded chart of the Large Automobile Company (Exhibit 6.8), we see two profit center divisions—the Credit Corporation and the Data Sys-

Exhibit 6.5 Large Functional Structure

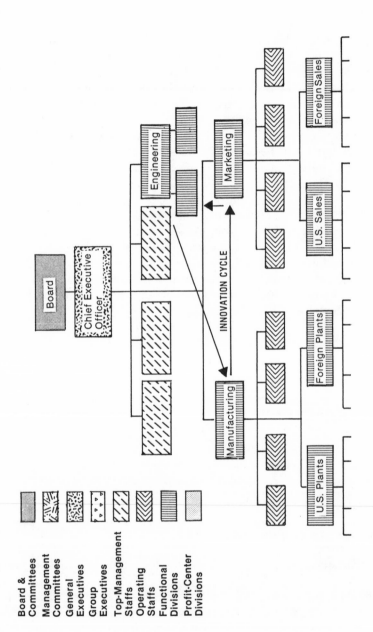

Board

Chief Executive Officer

Engineering

Manufacturing

Marketing

INNOVATION CYCLE

U.S. Plants

Foreign Plants

U.S. Sales

Foreign Sales

Board & Committees
Management Committees
General Executives
Group Executives
Top-Management Staffs
Operating Staffs
Functional Divisions
Profit-Center Divisions

Exhibit 6.6 Holding Company Structure

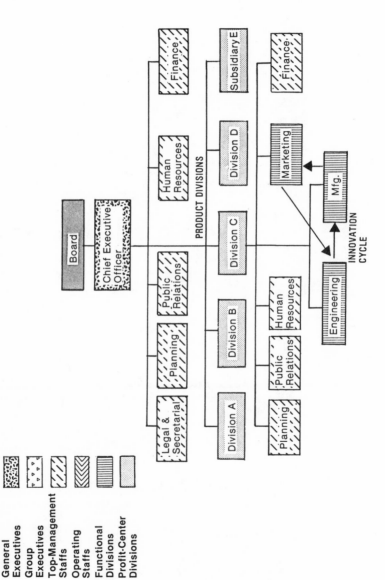

Exhibit 6.7 Structure after Divisionalization

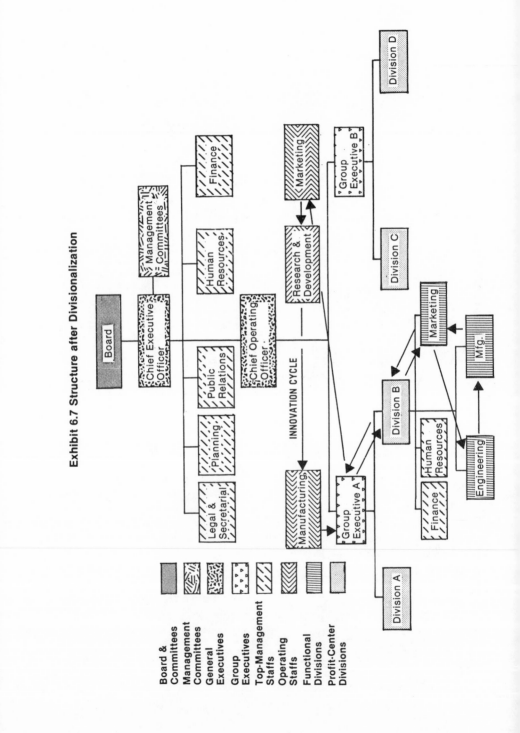

Exhibit 6.8 Coded Organization Plan, 1988: Large Automobile Company

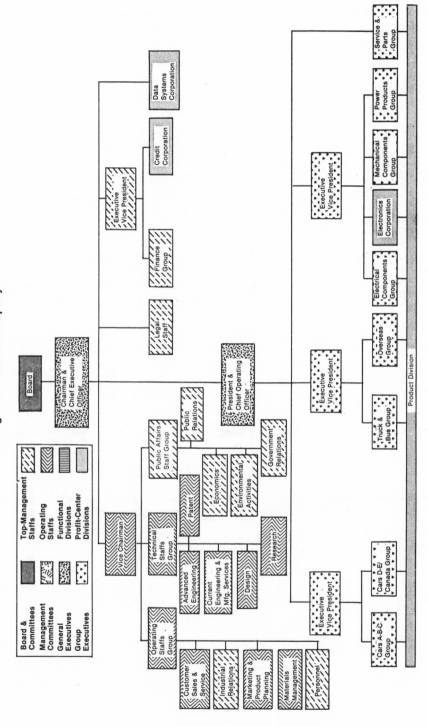

tems Corporation—positioned much higher in the structure than the other product divisions. Also the long-range top management staffs report to the same superior as the short-range operating staffs. Whenever the analyst observes such pattern deviations, he should investigate further to see if generally accepted organization design principles have been violated.

ANALYSIS OF THE AUTOMOBILE COMPANY ORGANIZATION

If the reader will refer to the Phase I organization of the Automobile Company (see Exhibit 6.2) he will notice the one-man general executive, the broad span of control under the chief executive officer, the weak management committee structure, the service-oriented staffs, the limited use of group executives and a manufacturing staff with line responsibilities. In the present divisionalization Phase II organization (see Exhibit 6.3), the reader will note the span of control has been drastically reduced and key control staffs have been established. The top structure has been strengthened by several of the above organizational means (see also Exhibit 6.7 and 6.8).

Exhibit 6.9 Indicators of Growth

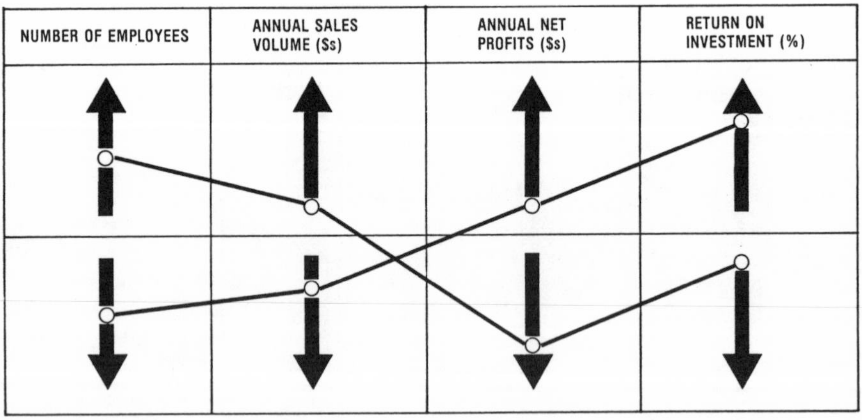

Exhibit 6.10 Impacts of Growth

TYPE OF GROWTH		IMPACT ON ORGANIZATION STRUCTURE	IMPACT ON CONCEPTS OF MANAGEMENT
Acquisition-Oriented	Acquisition of Integrated Companies	Strengthen Top Structure	Strengthen Policy Framework
Sales-Oriented	Growth in Sales Volume—Product A	Strengthen Advertising/Promotion-Field Sales Organization	Willing to Spend to Maintain Market Share—Product A
Research-Oriented	Development of New Products B-C-D-E	Strengthen Engineering Organization	Willing to Invest in Research & Development
Finance-Oriented	Growth in Net Profit & Return on Investment	Strengthen Financial Organization	Strengthen Financial Policies & Systems
Investor-Oriented	Increase in Stock Values & Dividend Payments	Strengthen Public/Shareholder–Relations Staff	Willing to Invest in Annual Reports, Shareholder Meetings, & Services

Exhibit 6.11 Division of Staff Work: Divisionalized Structure

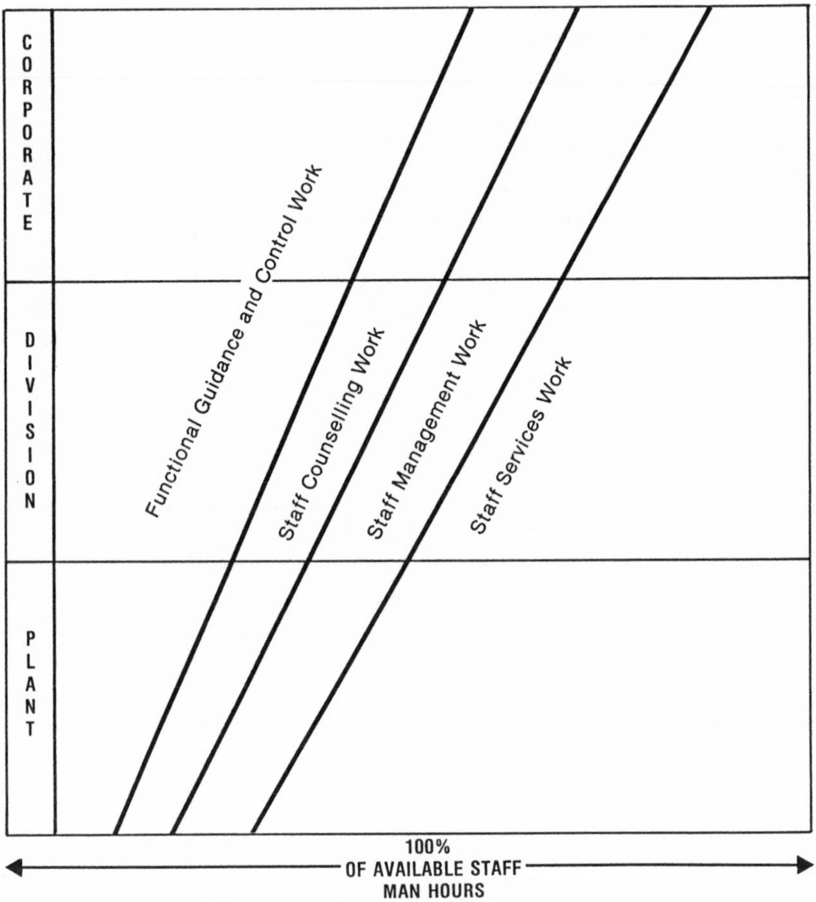

100%
OF AVAILABLE STAFF
MAN HOURS

ANALYSIS OF THE RECREATION COMPANY ORGANIZATION-DIVISIONALIZATION PHASE I

In Exhibit 7.1 we will see some of the same weaknesses: the one-man chief executive, the broad operating span of control, the weak management committee structure, service-oriented staffs, limited use of group executives, a weak policy framework, and no control staffs in critical functional areas. In Chapter 7 we will discuss this case in detail.

NOTE

1. Allan Nevins, and Frank Ernest Hill, *Ford: Decline and Rebirth* (New York: Scribner's, 1963).

7

Divisionalizing a Medium-Sized Corporation: The Recreation Company

HISTORY OF THE ORGANIZATION

In the fifties the Recreation Company (see Exhibit 7.1) was a small, functionally organized company with three plants. The executive offices were in an old building, which it owned in a large midwestern city. The company had been family-owned for many years. It was founded by the man who developed and marketed the first pool table in America. As a result, the technical skills of the first employees were woodworking and cabinet-making and their work was of high quality. Later the company diversified into the school equipment and bowling equipment field and, to a limited extent, into defense products. Its bonanza was the first mechanical pinsetter, which their engineers developed shortly after World War II. This innovation was closely followed by a major competitor with a pinspotter. The competitor leased its pinspotter while the recreation company sold the pinsetter on a long-term contract. The equipment cost about $15,000 per lane. Thus, a twenty lane bowling center would require an investment of $300,000. Many times the owner would lease the building. As a result, the initial down payment on the equipment was his only investment. His wholly owned capital was limited and his management ability and ethics were unknown quantities. It is hardly surprising that, as the number of bowling establishments and competition increased, more and more of the bowling center managers began to experience financial difficulties. The company was faced with the unfortunate alternative of repossessing the equipment and warehousing it indefinitely or selling it as used equipment on the open market. The latter

Exhibit 7.1 Organization Plan (Phase I): Recreation Company

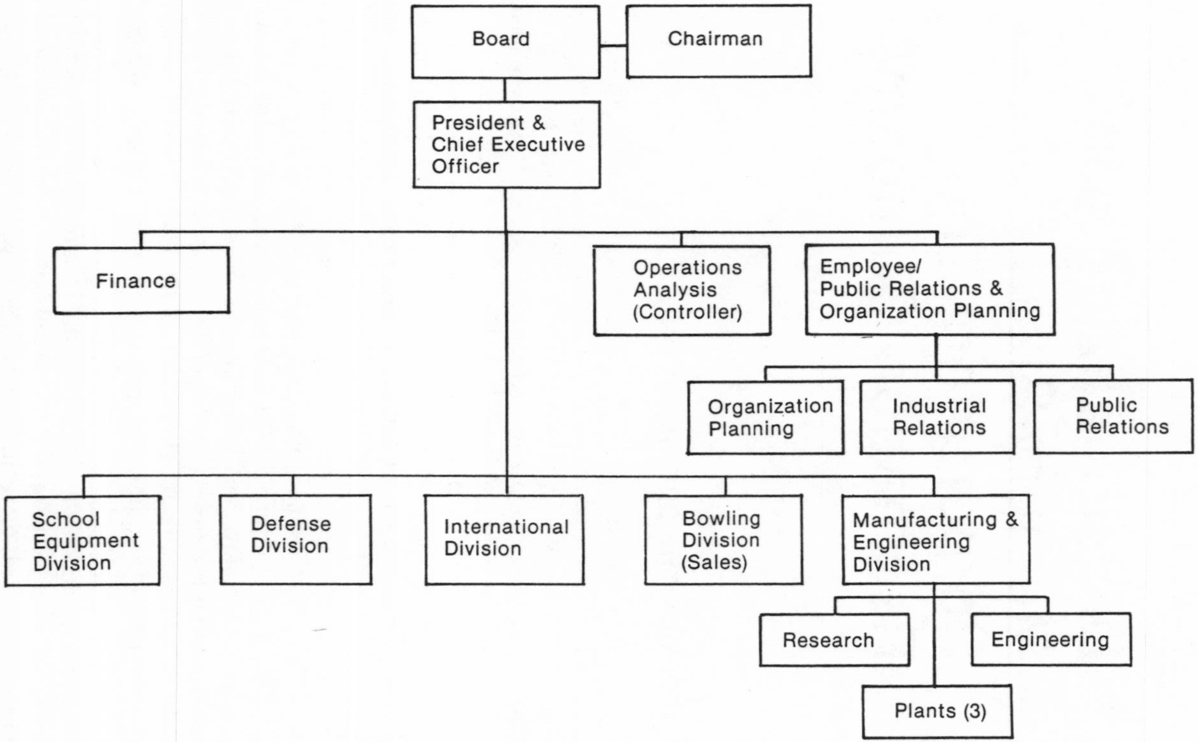

action, if taken, would have a very depressing effect on the price and market for new equipment. Since the equipment was built to last for twenty years or more with good maintenance, there was not much hope for a substantial replacement market.

Fortunately, while the stock was at its peak value, the management was wise enough to see that it was risky to have bowling equipment account for over 80 percent of the annual gross revenues of about $50 million. For exchange of stock, the management then began to purchase several companies in the fields of recreation, health, education, and defense. It acquired a hospital supply company, which manufactured and distributed a proprietary line of medical supplies and surgical equipment; a manufacturer of sports clothing and equipment; a manufacturer of fishing rods and reels; a company that manufactured large boats with inboard engines; a small manufacturer of plastic boats; and a manufacturer of outboard motors and related accessories.

An organization chart showed nine product divisions which contained thirty-nine plants. The annual sales volume had increased to about $360 million and the number of employees to over 18,000. Because of this explosive growth the profits began to decline rapidly. The organization structure had been just about the right size to manage three plants on a functional basis. It was not strong enough, however, nor did the company have the policy framework and specialized skills required for the profitable management of a highly diversified, conglomerate corporation of that size. The vice president-employee/public relations and organization planning could see that the most urgent problem that faced the company was to develop a policy program and a policy manual that would permit the top executives to manage the strong divisions by policy. The only policy manual they had originally was a discredited three-volume operations manual, which contained outmoded evaluation job descriptions and about five corporate policies and procedures. It took the staff about one year to develop a policy presentation, which was given to the chief executive officer and to the board of directors. It was approved and implemented as far as was possible with the limited number of corporate functional staffs that existed at that time. There were no staffs at all in four critical control areas, i.e., marketing, manufacturing, research and development, and public relations. There was no chief operating officer and there were no full-time group executives. This structure threw a tremendous overload on the position of chief executive officer, who had little time to spend on strategic planning and on the external problems of the corporation. In spite of this overload, much of the chief executive's time was spent at his home in Bermuda. Absentee leadership aggravated the already difficult top-management control problem. Fortunately, the chief executive was knowledgeable about professional management, having read heavily in the field and taken many management courses and seminars.

TOP-MANAGEMENT REORGANIZATION

To permit the implementation of the policy program, the staff first made an organization study of the company, relying heavily on previous studies of conglomerate structure and divisionalization made by the staff of the Automobile Company (see Chapter 6).

In summary, the following structural changes were recommended:

1. Establishment of a new position of president and chief operating officer.
2. Establishment of four group executive positions.
3. Creation of four new corporate staffs under the chief operating officer as follows:
   A. Corporate marketing staff.
   B. Corporate research and development staff.
   C. Corporate manufacturing staff.
   D. Corporate public relations staff.
4. Changing the corporate controller to report to the vice president-finance instead of directly to the chief executive officer.
5. Elimination of the unnecessary staff group executive position over the industrial relations and organization planning staffs. Changing the organization planning staff head to report directly to the chief executive officer. Changing the industrial relations director to report to the chief operating officer.

These changes were approved in broad concept by the chief executive officer and the board. The CEO then filled three group executive positions by promoting division heads. He also reestablished the corporate public relations staff. Finally, he went to the outside and filled the position of president and chief operating officer with an executive who had been for many years the general manager of the electrical products division of a glass company and more recently president of a jointly owned subsidiary. As a provision of his employment contract, he asked for and received, under his direction as president and chief operating officer, the director of industrial relations, the director of organization planning, and the corporate controller; then he made the organization planning staff a section of the industrial relations department and elected the director of industrial relations a corporate vice president. He then decided that the company was not large enough to have group executives and eliminated these positions. The incumbents were returned to their former jobs as division heads. The president and chief operating officer then appointed a former general manager of the television division of a major electrical products company to fill the new position of corporate marketing vice president. Later, a corporate research and development staff was created under a technical vice president. Finally, a corporate manufacturing staff was created. The marketing director was then promoted to vice president over the public relations, marketing, and industrial relations staffs. The chief operating officer also created a bowling centers division to operate repossessed bowling centers (see Chapter 8). Repossessed equipment was taken back into the books of the corporation at the price of used equipment (see Exhibit 7.2).

ANALYSIS AGAINST THE BONDS OF ORGANIZATION

Identification Activities

During a period of cost reduction, the public relations staff had been abolished. It was reactivated only as a result of the staff's recommendations. Although heavily sales-oriented, this staff did a reasonably good job of promoting the institutional identity of the Recreation Company over the strong objections of the division heads.

PERPETUATION ACTIVITIES

Personnel

A good job of bringing in staff professional talent was accomplished at the middle management level. Where the chief executive or the chief operating officer did the recruiting job personally to fill top line positions without properly using professional recruiting assistance, men with inapplicable experience were employed and a high executive failure was the result.

Finance

The vice president-finance was responsible for replenishing the capital resources. This was a very difficult job, since over $400 million in marginal pinsetter receivables were outstanding. That is why protection of these receivables and freeing up the tremendous contingency reserves were critical problems and such a threat to the survival of the company.

Thoughtways

The chief executive officer gave lip service to the new divisionalization concepts and policies of the company, but was unwilling really to believe in and conform to them himself in a crisis situation. We believe this failure was due to lack of skill in managing a divisionalized corporation. As a result, he did not display the "will to manage" and to enforce the discipline of the system.

Exhibit 7.2 Organization Plan (Phase II): Recreation Company

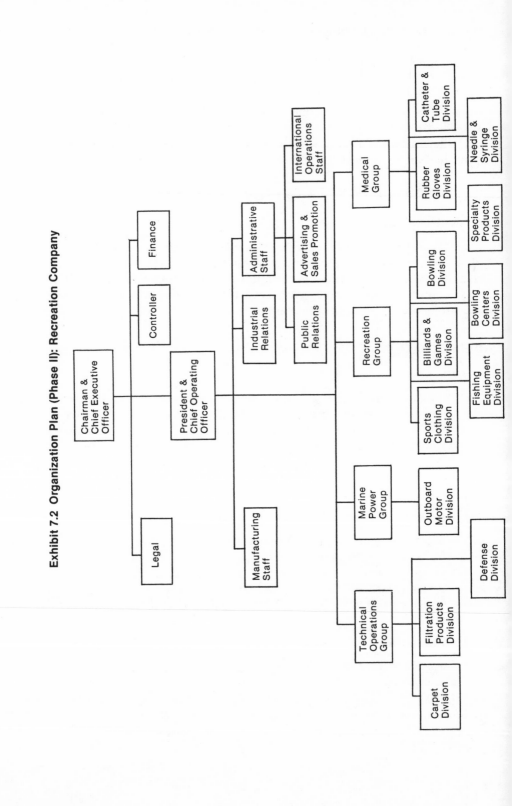

WORKFLOW ACTIVITIES

Production

These activities were carried out in the plants of the operating divisions. A major weakness in structure was the fact that, at first, there was no corporate manufacturing staff with the responsibility for the coordination of the production activities throughout the corporation.

Distribution

These activities were carried out in each of the divisions of the corporation. Another major weakness in structure was the fact that before the reorganization, there was no corporate marketing staff to coordinate distribution and warehousing activities throughout the entire corporation.

CONTROL ACTIVITIES

Directive

There were many signs in the company that the directive activities were weak. They were performed on an absentee personal and verbal basis rather than on a systematic, consistent, and written-policy basis. Even though there was a clearly defined policy manual, these policies were violated almost at will by the executives that authorized them, including the chief executive officer. There was little will to manage by system.

Motivation

Since the chief executive officer made no effort to appraise managerial performance on a result-oriented basis, he had no real means for motivating and reinforcing outstanding division performance with financial and non-financial incentives.

Communication

Management information and policies were communicated effectively through the vehicle of the policy and procedures manual. There was, however, little effort on the part of the top executives to see that there was understanding and compliance by their subordinates, since they did not themselves comply with administrative constraints unless it was useful for their personal purposes to do so. Management training meetings were held, but they were given not by the internal staff experts in the subject, as at Ford, but by untrained line managers, from academic texts developed by the training manager in the personnel department. Two-way, frank, face-to-face communication was extremely limited.

HOMEOSTATIC ACTIVITIES

Fusion

The fusion process was very effective in the case of the long-service employees who had a very warm feeling for the company. This sense of loyalty and commitment also existed in the case of the newer staff employees of the company in the Chicago office, who were management professionals in various fields of specialization.

Problem-Solving

The vice president-employee/public relations and organization planning was aware of the survival crisis facing the company. He was one of the few top executives with enough professional management experience really to understand the scope of the problem and what had to be done about it.

At the end of World War II, a management consulting firm had conducted an organization survey for the chief executive officer. The consultants pointed out the need to reset the executive compensation structure and redo the management incentive plan in order to attract outside talent. The first phase of the work of the organization planning staff, therefore, was largely devoted to this project. As a result, the salaries and incentives became competitive and it was possible to bring in from the outside the high-priced talent that was necessary to plan the divisionalization program. At first there was no effort to change the top-management organization structure in any major way. A little reorganization work was done at the division level as part of the installation of the salary program whenever the division head seemed to be receptive. The organization planning director hoped that by demonstrating the value of sound organization planning at the division level, the staff's reputation would be such that he would be asked by the chief executive officer to do the same kind of organization planning work at the top-management level. However, the staff was never asked. It acted finally on its own initiative. The surveys of the company by management consultants were available in the library and they proved to be very helpful. The problem had been explored in sufficient detail for those on the staff who had had experience in the divisionalization of other companies to identify the weaknesses in the top policy and organization structure of the Recreation Company. The organization planning head saw the need for activating a formal long-range planning process in the corporation and was very hesitant to recommend any top-management organization changes of significance until this had been done. On the other hand, others on the staff felt that the chief executive officer was so overloaded, because of the weak top organization structure, that there was little hope that he could devote much time to long-range planning until the top-management organization had been clarified and strengthened first. However, the staff could not issue mandatory organization policy documents until the policy on administration of policy had been issued and the concept of mandatory documents and policy compliance was clearly understood by the CEO and the other top executives. In spite of the many presentations the staff made on the need for policy enforcement, there was no real awareness of this basic problem. Otherwise, the chief executive officer and the chief operating officer would have complied with the mandatory goal setting and performance appraisal policy. The problem was carefully and thoroughly explored and understood by the trained management analysts of the organization planning department.

The Character of the Situation

The situation presented the company with a very serious survival threat. By acquiring so many strong companies and diversifying so rapidly without first strengthening the top policy and organization structure, the company was rapidly becoming "atomized," i.e., it was literally being torn apart by the strong divisions. The top structure that had provided the framework for the successful management of three plants was wholly inadequate to manage nine divisions with thirty-nine plants and over 18,000 employees. Finally, in one year the company lost $75 million. Critical to its survival was a clear understanding of the root-cause of the problem. The solution did not require necessarily a larger top-management organization structure, but an entirely different one in design, functions, and skill requirements, and one specifically tailored to facilitate management of a large, diversified, divisionalized corporation. This, in a word, was the character of the situation and failure to strengthen the top-management structure presented a serious threat to economic survival. The situation became rapidly worse as more and more of the bowling equipment customers ran into financial difficulty and defaulted on their installment payments. With the possible exception of the outboard motor division and the hospital supply division, none of the acquired companies proved to be substantial money makers. The small boat division and the yacht division had so much trouble financially that they were finally sold.

The banks and insurance companies that had loaned the company over $400 million were carefully watching to see that the proper equity level was maintained as prescribed by the loan covenants. How long the company could have continued to dismantle and warehouse repossessed equipment is, of course, problematical. In the staff's opinion, however, the situation was deteriorating rapidly. The creation of a bowling centers division came just in time (see Chapter 8).

Creditor banks and insurance companies were importantly affected by this crisis. If they had decided to press for a change in the management of the corporation, then the top executives would have been removed and others brought in from the outside. The finance vice president fortunately had the confidence of the insurance companies, as did the credit manager. They performed well in retaining this confidence in spite of the company's difficulties.

The decision to write off millions in reserves to protect the pinsetter receivables shows how much capital is required to protect solvency and how quickly it can be dissipated. The poor financial condition of the organization was not likely to impact on the creditors, unless the situation was permitted to deteriorate to a point where the equity of the company was so low that the creditors in case of bankruptcy could not recover on the debts outstanding. Normally, creditors move to force a change in management before that time, and this action appeared likely to occur.

Recommended Solution

In recommending a plan of management organization to the chief executive, all feasible alternative solutions and plans of organization were thoroughly explored. The staff recommended that several of these alternative plans be presented to the chief executive, together with the suggested criteria to help him make a wise decision. The organization planning head's experience in the management consulting field had led him to believe it was not wise to present any more than one alternative to a client for fear he might select the wrong one. For this reason, only one plan was presented. Others on the staff with experience as internal consultants had found through their experience that more learning, understanding, participation, and commitment takes place when the line executive is required by the staff man to select from more than one of the feasible alternatives. Of course, he must at the same time be given the criteria and techniques of analysis that will help him make a wise selection from among the alternatives recommended. In view of some of the past executive selections of the chief executive, the staff was very concerned that he might not put into the new president and chief operating officer's position a man experienced in successfully changing an organization from a functionalized structure to a fully divisionalized structure. For this reason, the staff carefully wrote up the man specification for this job so this ability was a minimum requirement.

Decision

The proper structural decision was made by the chief executive officer. It was clear-cut and it was thoroughly communicated to the executives that were to carry it out. There were at least ten separate presentations on the proposal made by the staff head to small groups of top executives, as well as to the board of directors.

The objectives to be achieved by both the policy program presentation and the top organization presentation were clearly defined and justified, and there was little or no objection voiced by any of the top executives or members of the board of directors. Job specifications and standards for the proposed reorganization were drawn up. Assignments were clearly made and the authority and accountability of each executive was specified in a detailed short-term action program.

Action

The pathology in the problem-solving process lay in the way the plan was implemented by the chief executive officer and in the inapplicable background of the men with whom he staffed the new positions in the structure, particularly, the crucial position of the president and chief operating officer.

Leadership

In view of the chief executive's selection of unqualified executives to man the revised organization structure, there is no doubt that there resulted a serious dysfunction both in the leadership and perpetuation activities. The chief executive officer should have relied more heavily on the advice of the organization planning staff that developed the plan and wrote the position specifications to guide him in the filling of these positions. In almost all cases of organization changes at the Automobile Company, the organization staff had been asked what kind of men to put into the new or changed positions and whether or not those currently being considered were qualified to meet the minimum specifications.

Conclusion

With the exception of the four group executives and the reporting of the controller to the finance vice president, all the structural organization changes the staff recommended were carried out as proposed. The problem proved to be staffing the structure with unqualified men, and the lack of enforcement of discipline and conformance to mandatory policy.

At the Automobile Company there was a reluctance to go to the outside and find the professional management talent to staff the new organization. In the Recreation Company there was no reluctance to go to the outside, but the chief executive officer sought talent with inappropriate skills and experience. He should have gone to the large diversified companies that had successfully and profitably weathered the transition from a functional to a divisionalized structure. There he could have found a qualified executive who had piloted the change-over. The experience of such a man in the new position of president and chief operating officer no doubt would have brought profit improvement to the company much sooner.

ORGANIZATION OF ORGANIZATION PLANNING

In the mid-fifties, when the Recreation Conmpany began its explosive growth, a junior professional was the supervisor of organization planning. He had developed a management operations manual. It consisted of three large volumes of out-of-date position descriptions that were being used to evaluate management positions in a depressed salary structrue. This manual also included three or four salary administration policies and procedures. This organization analyst reported to the vice president-employee/public relations and organization planning, who, in turn, reported to the chief executive officer. The vice president-employee/public relations and organization planning was in a sense a staff group executive. He had been a systems analyst and a public relations manager in a large divisionalized company and also had a broad experience in the personnel field. He could foresee the tremendous organizational problems that diversification and rapid growth through acquisition had brought to the company. For this reason he wisely recruited a seasoned organization planning staff. A management consulting firm had made an organization study of the corporation just after World War II and, among other things, had recommended the resetting of the salary structure on a more competitive basis, and the revision of the management incentive compensation plan. Granting of the year-end bonus had, under this plan, become so automatic and fixed in amount that each participant considered it as part of his base salary.

Most of the initial work of the staff was focused on the installation of the new exempt and non-exempt salary programs. This included revision of the management bonus and stock option plans. Next, one of the staff developed and gave a presentation to the chief executive and the board recommending documentation and issuance of all mandatory corporate policies, procedures, and organization documents in one manual. This manual proved to be a monumental undertaking and was finally issued in the sixties. It is still in effect today, without substantial change.

Another staff man was placed in charge of planning the move to a modern new building that was in the process of construction. He also directed the office services staff. Other members of the staff were largely concerned with exempt job description writing and evaluation. One man specialized in non-exempt job evaluation. The staff director also recruited a librarian and began to build up a management library.

Shortly after the staff's inception, the staff held a three day seminar away from the city. The vice president-employee/public relations and organization planning and the director of industrial relations also attended. The staff was concerned with the backlog of work that was rapidly building up. They found they were facing a two year project backlog. Because of the staff head's consulting background, he never fully understood the proper method of organizing a functional control, proactive organization planning staff. As a result, the division managers at the Recreation Company never learned much about performing their reserved responsibilities for organization planning. They relied far too heavily on the services of the free corporate organization planning staff to do their organization work for them. The fact that the staff would have to change its role was clearly evident in deliberations at the seminar.

The staff head wanted to apply staff expertise in conducting an organization survey of the corporation as a whole; however, he thought the way to receive such an assignment would be to establish an outstanding reputation by conducting free organization surveys for the division heads. As a result, the chief executive would hear about it and ask him to conduct a similar survey for the corporation. The chief executive, on the other hand, was apparently waiting for the staff to conduct the study on its own initiative. This became evident when the staff gave the policy presentation to the chief executive and he asked some very probing questions, which left little doubt that he had been exposed to advanced divisionalization and organization planning concepts through attending management seminars. For example, he asked asked if the company had any group executives in the accepted sense of the term; if not, should it have any and, if so, how many? Based on this encouragement, the staff made an organization survey of the top-management structure using the previous management consulting survey report as a start. This study resulted in many recommended changes dcesigned to strengthen the top organization structure.

At present, only two men are left from the original staff. One heads management development; the other maintains the compensation program. The chief executive made the mistake of thinking that once the major reorganization and strengthening of the top structure of the company had been completed, the structure would stay well designed and he would have no need for such a high-talent—and highly paid—organization and compensation planning staff. The role of the staff is now largely restricted to maintaining the corporate policy and procedures manual and performing routine compensation and benefits planning work assignments. Essentially, the staff has now completed its life cycle and is back in the relatively unimportant role it played originally. Of course, the professional staff had some impact. The salary structure is better; the top-management structure is stronger; there is a corporate policy and procedures manual that is reasonably up-to-date; and there is a management library. But top-management organization structure does not stay well designed without the constant attention of a highly qualified staff working closely with the chief executive officer. This is the concept of the *Principle of Continuity*.

In this experience in the organization of an organization planning staff, we see the same life cycle that was so obvious at the Automobile Company. First, the organization planning work is performed poorly. Next, a professional staff is organized independently of the personnel function to help the CEO with a major reorganization. These men are broad-gauged, experienced organization planners and internal consultants who are required to help the chief executive reorganize the top-management structure. Once the reorganization is completed, however, the staff then is placed under the personnel director and they limit their activity to compensation planning. The structure again becomes outmoded and another traumatic reorganization is required. The staff must again be established outside the personnel department and restaffed with experienced organization planners, who are capable of helping the chief executive with a reorganization of such scope.

If we can learn anything from these experiences, it is to keep the staff small, proactive, and manned with a few very experienced organization planners. The staff should not be used as a free internal organization consulting service, but as a small functional guidance and control staff that primarily serves only the chief executive officer. In addition, it teaches the division and corporate staff heads to do their own organization planning. It reviews their organization change proposals for the chief executive and issues and maintains the organization and policy manual. If the divisions have so many organizational planning studies that the division head cannot do this work alone without neglecting his other managerial duties, then he should have his own organization planning specialist on his staff reporting functionally to the corporate organization planning staff. Compensation planning should preferably also be a continuing part of the corporate organization planning responsibility. Ideally, the staff should not be a part of the corporate personnel function. The organization staff may be called upon to make recommendations of a critical nature regarding the personnel staff itself, and it must be in a position to do so with complete objectivity. This is not normally possible if the staff itself reports to the personnel director. Further, the staff director must report directly to the chief executive if he is to advise him when major organizational changes are confidentially under consideration.

TOOLS AND TECHNIQUES OF ORGANIZATION PLANNING

The staff director frequently said he had never seen an up-to-date organization manual, and an out-of-date one could cause much misunderstanding. For this reason, although he never actively prevented issuance of organization documents in the corporate policy and procedures manual, he showed very little interest in formal structural documentation. The lack of an organization planning policy, such as the policy on planning of the structure (see Exhibit 1.2), vigorously enforced, was one of the reasons the staff frequently first learned of major organizational changes through "Chalk-Talk," the company newspaper. Of course, if there was a salary increase involved, they learned quickly enough, since they processed all salary changes before they went to payroll. Normally, however, the staff learned of changes only after irreversible staffing commitments had already been made. There was no organization survey guide, since the staff head was more interested in making the organization surveys for the division heads than in teaching them or their staffs to conduct such surveys for themselves. For this reason, the functional guidance and control tools and techniques of organization planning were non-existent. The compensation and job evaluation tools and techniques were, on the other hand, very well done. This was the area of primary concentration for most of the members of the staff.

PRINCIPLES OF ORGANIZATION PLANNING

When the staff prepared the top-management organization presentation to be given to the chief executive, the principles of organization as listed in Chapter 1 were included. These principles were used in analyzing the weaknesses in top-management organization structure. Here the staff found that the most critical weakness was the overload on the chief executive as was also the case at the Automobile Company. This overload violated the *Principle of Balance*. The staff found cases of improper staffing where one incumbent was filling two or more key positions. The *Principle of Specialization* was not followed in the case of the position of vice president-employee/public relations and organization planning. He was responsible for several unrelated specialized staff functions. The *Principle of the Objective* was violated, since several key corporate functional control staffs—public relations, marketing, manufacturing, and research and development—were missing. The *Principle of Coordination* was violated by having the vice president-finance and the controller report independently to the chief executive. This situation still exists, even though many of the other structural weaknesses have been corrected. The *Principle of Responsibility and Authority* was, and still is, violated in the sense that there is very little policy control exercised over certain of the divisions. Because there were no organization documents, and titles were in many cases misleading, there was violation of the *Principle of Definition*. There were position descriptions but they were used for evaluation purposes only and were not generally communicated in manual form. There was never an up-to-date chart of the top-management organization structure distributed generally for the guidance of the top executives and employees. There is still none available for distribution. Most of all, perhaps, the *Principle of Centralization* was violated, since central policy direction and control were almost non-existent until the staff's policy recommendations were carried out. Even now policy control is not exercised over certain divisions. The chief executive did not believe in living by and enforcing his own policies when a strong corporate executive or division head objected. Enforcement of corporate policy is a way of life in successful divisionalized companies, and this is one reason the company has been so long in achieving anticipated profit results from its divisionalization program.

STRATEGY AND STRUCTURE OF THE RECREATION COMPANY UP TO THE PRESENT

The group executives were reestablished to reduce the operating span of control. Marginally profitable divisions (the School Equipment Division, the Small Boats Division, and the Yacht Division) were sold. To avoid a hostile takeover, the highly profitable medical divisions were also sold. Two highly profitable boat divisions were acquired. The positions of president and chief operating officer and four group executives were eliminated. Currently there are seven staffs and eight operating divisions reporting to the CEO. This broad span of control throws a heavy overload on the CEO (see Exhibit 7.3).

Sales are currently up to $1.54 billion and net earnings are $110 million. Return on shareholders' equity is 21.1 percent. Employees are over 26,800.

The Corporate Policies and Procedures Manual is being currently updated in line with organization changes. Coverage has not been expanded to include new policies, procedures, and organization documents. No top-management organization chart has been distributed for several years. The management compensation program has been maintained substantially without change, except for the addition of an incentive compensation plan for bowling center managers. There is no organization policy like the one in Exhibit 1.2. There is no organization planning staff. Management position descriptions are maintained for evaluation purposes only.

Exhibit 7.3   Organization Plan (Phase III), 1988: Recreation Company

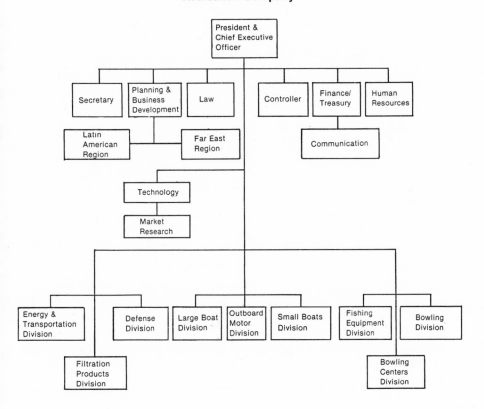

8

Establishing a Division in the Recreation Company

In all the other cases in Part II the problems concern the improvement of an existing organization structure. This book would be incomplete without an example of the design and staffing of an entirely new organization component. As an example of such a problem, we will discuss in this chapter the establishment of a new profit center in the Bowling Division of the Recreation Company—the bowling centers section. Establishment of this unit required the preparation of a long-range manpower plan of considerable complexity. For this reason, the example clearly demonstrates the close relationship that exists between strategic planning, organization planning, and manpower planning. It is then a short step to placement, recruitment, performance appraisal—on an MBO basis—then training. These are all key management functions.

WHAT IS MANPOWER PLANNING?

Manpower planning—like any other planning process—focuses on the future. The process starts with the strategic plan. The strategic plan begins with the corporate philosophy of the company. It concerns the markets and industries in which the company participates and their place in the economy. It considers the position of the company in the industry. It anticipates changes in the nature and scope of the business or the component. It anticipates developments and major changes in the business. It considers the long-range purposes of the organization. If there is already a formal company strategic plan, this is reviewed; then it tries to determine what future work will be required to achieve these goals.

BASIC PRINCIPLES OF MANPOWER PLANNING

Anticipation and analysis of future work and organization structure is the essential first step prior to the selection, training, or recruitment of the manpower to do the work. This process aims at providing balanced human resources to meet both the present and future requirements for staffing the organization structure. It must integrate the needs and interests both of the individuals and the component with respect to management personnel resources and their development or outside recruitment. At the same time the planning process must preserve equality of opportunity for promotion from within according to individual ability, interests, effort, performance, and results. This process is not limited to finding the additional personnel required. It must also provide for continuity through adequate depth of management, functioning in a sound organization structure. Manpower planning is a reserved responsibility of every manager, which he cannot and should not delegate.

THE THREE PHASES OF MANPOWER PLANNING

There are three phases in manpower planning:

1. Long-range manpower planning—at least as far into the future as the strategic plan (normally five years)
2. Short-range manpower planning—the foreseeable future (normally eighteen months)
3. Providing continuity and depth of management

LONG-RANGE MANPOWER PLANNING

This first phase concerns the analysis of the strategic plan to determine specifically what organization structure and skills probably will be required in five years to carry out the plan. This includes comparing the future structure to the present structure and making policy decisions on internal manpower development needs and outside recruitment sources. The planner should develop a manpower trial balance sheet, showing when he will need to use the manpower and the source. The action needed now should also be shown.

SHORT-RANGE MANPOWER PLANNING

This phase includes the development of a short-term organization phase plan toward the long-range organization plan developed in the previous phase. After assessing the difficulty he will have internally developing or externally recruiting the skilled manpower he will need to staff the long-range organization plan, the planner should estimate how far he can go toward staffing the long-range structure with currently available manpower within the foreseeable future—eighteen months. He can now begin to think in terms of specific individuals, who may be elsewhere in the organization or on the outside, who have the potential to staff the short-term organization structure. The planner should particularly concentrate on developing and getting approval of a qualified candidate list from which the head of the unit can be selected. This task is given priority by the planner, because it is urgent for the head of the unit to begin as soon as possible to participate in the organization and staffing process and to initiate the activation of the unit. The preliminary evaluation of the key positions is an important step in this process.

CONTINUITY AND DEPTH OF MANAGEMENT

The third and last phrase concerns the problem of building depth into the short-term management structure. When the head of the component is on the job he must begin developing at least one successor—and preferably more than one—for each key executive position within his organization. These men must not only have the potential to achieve outstanding performance in their present jobs, they must also have the ability immediately—or after a reasonable training period—to be prompted to a higher rated position. Then the manager must in turn think of selecting understudies for these men. This is a complex problem that can best be analyzed through the technique of a Replacement Chart (see Exhibit 8.1). This analysis then feeds back information for the decisions made in phases I and II. This process helps to integrate the organization needs with the manpower resources.

Now let us turn to the specific problem—the establishment of the bowling centers section in the Bowling Division of the Recreation Company.

PHASE I—THE LONG-RANGE MANPOWER PLAN

First the organization planning staff concentrated on the key business problems facing the Recreation Company. The company had over $400 million of questionable receivables outstanding because of selling pinsetters and lanes to unqualified customers on long-term contracts. These customers frequently had poor credit, no recreation center management ability, and very little wholly owned capital. It is little surprise that after a year or two the customer began to default on his payments. When threatened with legal action, he responded by suggesting that the company repossess the equipment. The company began at first to warehouse the equipment, because selling it on the open market would be likely to depress the market for new equipment. If properly maintained, a pin-

Exhibit 8.1 Replacement Chart (Phase I):
Bowling Centers Section

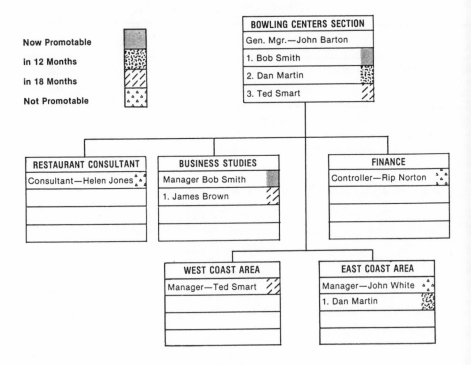

setter would have a useful life of twenty years or more. The strategic plan contained a statement of purpose to counteract this serious threat to the survival of the company.

Since the company had never operated any bowling centers in deference to their customers, none of their employees had the skills required to operate a profitable chain of bowling establishments. No equipment manufacturer had ever managed a bowling chain before and there was no experience from which to borrow. Since bowling establishments are small businesses located from coast to coast and overseas, the section would have to be organized on a geographic basis, with the headquarters located in the central United States. The staff thought the structure should be patterned on the dealer development organization of an automobile company.

In brief, an automobile dealer development program works something like this. Anyone who has had successful experience running an automobile dealership for someone else on a salaried basis and has a good reputation can apply to the automobile manufacturer for a dealer franchise. If he can raise 25 percent of the wholly owned capital required to start the enterprise, then the automobile company will furnish the other 75 percent. The dealer will at once begin to buy-out the company equity from his income until he owns 51 percent of the stock in the dealership. The automobile company, however, runs the dealership in the interim period. This is accomplished through the dealer development organization. Under such an arrangement, the automobile company representative never has any more than six such dealerships under his direction at any one time. Dealer development representatives work out of regional offices. The support staffs are in Detroit.

First, the staff conceptually determined what major functions would have to be performed by the new organization. Initially it would have to evaluate each delinquent bowling establishment in order to decide whether or not, with good management, it could survive and be made profitable. Next, someone with public relations experience would have to handle the adverse local publicity that might result from the takeover of a bankrupt bowling center. Then the center would need a trained recreation center manager. Finally, a uniform and sound accounting system would be required so that accurate and frequent financial reports would be available to the section on the profitability of the operation.

In order to convert these goals into work elements, the staff prepared an Activity Strength Analysis Chart (see Exhibit 3.3).

In determining how these essential activities should be grouped for managerial coordination, the staff next prepared a Grouping Analysis Chart (see Exhibit 3.4). On this chart, in the left column the three key line management positions were listed, for example, the section general manager, the area manager, and the bowling center manager. Their basic functions were also listed. In the right hand column of the chart the staff listed the essential activities that support the basic functions of each manager.

With these analytical tools the staff was able to sketch out several alternative long-term plans of organization. Only one is shown (see Exhibit 8.2). Finally the staff analyzed the authority flow in the structure through the use of a Decisions Analysis Chart (see Exhibit 3.5). This analysis both helped the staff determine the lowest level at which each type of strategic decision could effectively be made in order to maximize delegation, and provided another check on the proper placement of each staff, since a staff exists almost exclusively for the purpose of fact-finding and improvement of the quality of line management decisions. Improper staff placement can seriously impair its proper and effective functioning.

By exhibiting the descriptions for the positions specified, the chart provides a guide to the major decision-making authorities that should be included. The reader should remember that these analytical charts are considerably simplified so that the methodology will be easy for the reader to follow and successfully apply.

The final step in Phase I is to prepare the manager manpower trial balance. List in the first column the positions on the long-range organization chart, as well as the year they should be filled and the number of incumbents who will be required to staff them. Next, list the losses that can be expected among these incumbents during this period owing to attrition for various reasons. By adding these two figures the total number of employees required to fill each job during this period can be determined.

PHASE II—SHORT-RANGE MANPOWER PLANNING

In this phase the objective is to determine how much of the long-range organization structure can be achieved during the foreseeable future. For example, it was the plan to have the section purchase certain supporting service, such as personnel, from the incubating Bowling Division. During this stage, the candidate list for the appointment of the section general manager was prepared and approved. From this list the candidate was selected by the general manager of the Bowling Division and recommended to the chief executive officer of the Recreation Company, who approved the selection. Working with him, the organization planning staff and the personnel staff filled the key positions and activated the organization.

**Exhibit 8.2 Proposed Organization Plan (Phase I):
Bowling Centers Section**

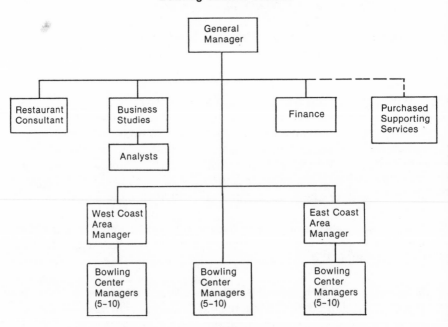

- - - indicates services purchased from Bowling Division.

PHASE III—CONTINUITY AND DEPTH OF MANAGEMENT

In the third and final phase, the organization planning staff turned its attention to the problem of organizational depth and continuity through the use of a Replacement Chart (see Exhibit 8.1).

The reader will note that, if John Barton should resign, Bob Smith is now qualified to replace him. However, if Bob Smith also resigns, Dan Martin would not be ready to replace him for twelve months. So Martin's training must be intensified. Vacations provide excellent opportunities to find out which of the understudies actually performs best in the higher job.

THE BENEFITS OF ORGANIZATION AND MANPOWER PLANNING

Most companies facing a crisis of this kind would do little advanced planning of the organization structure. The chief executive would simply pick his best man and tell him to get together a few "good" people to run the bowling establishments by "x" date, and to get started at once. The section head under such heavy pressures from his superior would no doubt pirate as many men internally or externally whom he could find who were "available" for recruitment. Without carefully thinking through the organization plan and the work structure, however, the section head may find that the men he had recruited were good at doing the things they had been doing, but not necessarily the things that he needed to have done.

For example, policy decisions have a heavy impact on management position specifications. When the section was first established, top executives disagreed as to whether the company should try to make money through operating the biggest bowling chain in the world in direct competition with its customers, or whether it should establish the centers on a "buy-out" basis, similar to the practice in the previously discussed dealer development programs of the automobile companies. The former course was decided upon, and this had a considerable influence on the qualifications sought in the candidates for bowling center managers.

In staffing the new section, the Recreation Company soon found out that there was no one among their employees who had ever run a bowling center profitably and successfully over a long period of time. They found that the best candidate to manage a bowling center was a person who had successfully managed a small "mom-and-pop" business, like a convenience market. If the company had decided on a buy-out program, then this type of experience plus sufficient wholly owned capital, and an interest in running his own business would be critical qualifications for the candidate, in order to be hired. If there was no buy-out opportunity, then the desire on the part of the candidate to own and run his own bowling center could actually be a negative factor.

Good long-range manpower planning minimizes the danger of serious recruiting errors of this kind. It does so by forcing a thorough thinking-through of the organization and staffing plan, and in this way provides time for the proper sourcing of qualified talent. Manpower planning minimizes expedient decisions, affecting the careers of individuals, that are tragic in their effect not only on the performance of the organization, but also on the lives of those concerned. Good planning also provides enough manpower to take care of the expected turnover and attrition of key managerial personnel and avoid disastrous surprises. It provides time to transfer personnel who fail to perform through no fault of their own to more suitable jobs. Finally, depth is built into the organization so that a highly qualified and trained individual is ready at all times to fill an unexpected key vacancy. Good manpower planning frequently is the difference between the success and failure of a new enterprise.

STRATEGY AND STRUCTURE UP TO THE PRESENT

In 1988, the Bowling Centers Division is a separate division of the Recreation Company (see Exhibit 8.3). It operates 250 bowling centers and is the largest bowling chain in the world. It contributes substantially to the profit of the corporation (see Chapter 7).

Exhibit 8.3 Organization Plan (Phase II), 1988: Bowling Centers Division

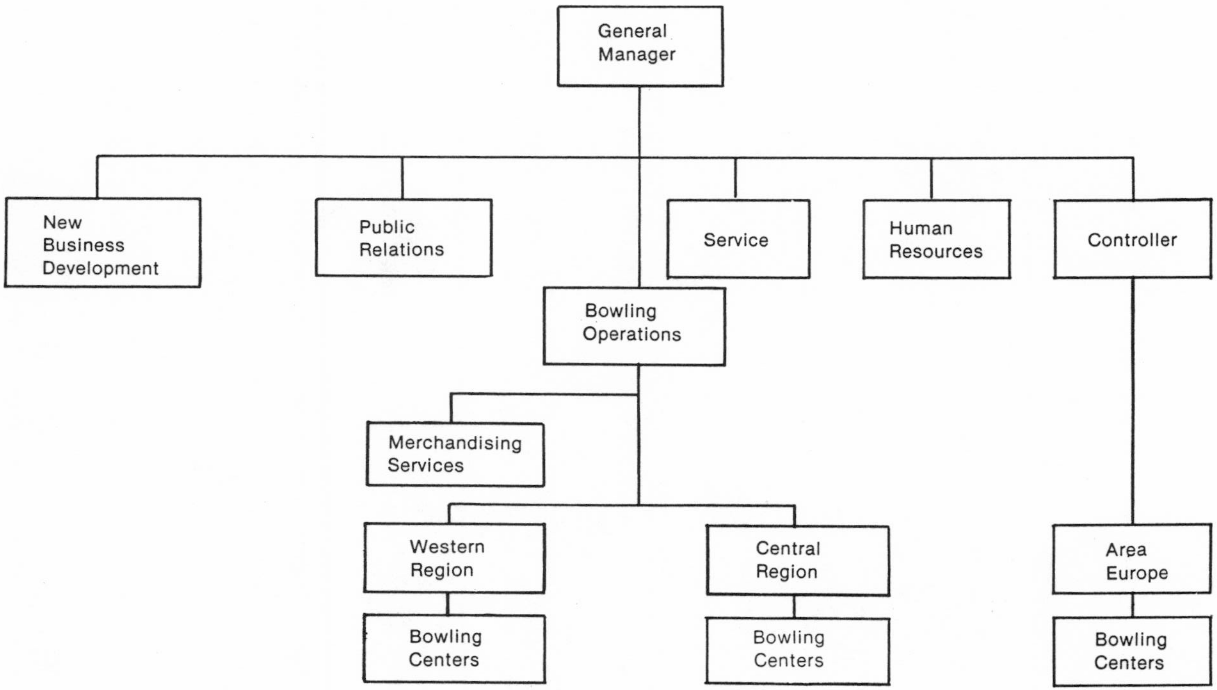

9

A New Organization for an Old Church: The Church Diocese

HISTORY OF THE CHURCH DIOCESE

The diocese grew rapidly in the first twenty-five years of its existence. Souls doubled in number from 47,000 to 95,000. Property values tripled from $26 million to $64 million as the number of churches grew from 114 to 172. The number of baptisms increased annually from 1,700 to 4,200, and confirmations from 1,500 to 3,600. In scope, the diocese covered the eastern half of the state. The number of church members per square mile decreased rapidly from the southern, densely populated area around the city of Metropolis to the sparsely populated wooded areas of the northern part of the state. The administration of such a rapidly growing organization began to weigh heavily on the shoulders of the bishop. The problem resulting from growth reached a point where he felt he was not able to do justice to the spiritual responsibilities of his position. There were many professional managers in his flock of laymen; one was chief executive of the Automobile Company, who persuaded the bishop that the application of sound principles of organization and modern management such as they had applied in his company might be the answer. The bishop called a meeting of the executive council of the diocese, which adopted the following resolution:

That there be appointed an administrative assistant to the bishop for the purpose of making a study of the organization of the diocese and investigating the possibility of its reorganization.

At another meeting of the same body an advertising executive was appointed to act as administrative assistant to the bishop in conducting this study. He was also appointed chairman of a committee to help him conduct the study. For over a year he conducted the survey and at the end of that time he prepared a report with his recommendations known as the Johnson Report. At that time a continuing internal committee, called the committee for the reorganization of the diocese, was created under the chairmanship of a pastor, whose regular job in the church was executive director of the industrial mission. To aid in implementing the reorganization, the Automobile Company provided the services of a member of the organization staff. The man was appointed a member of the reorganization committee.

THE JOHNSON REPORT

The following were the major recommendations of the Johnson Report:

1. Subdivide the diocese into three districts
2. Provide a suffragan bishop to head each district
3. Reserve to the bishop general overall supervision with power to rotate within the diocese the assignment of suffragan bishops to districts
4. Preserve overall financial control
5. Otherwise let each district become substantially autonomous
6. To further recommendation five, strengthen the convocations by increasing their power and responsibility
7. Simplify diocesan organization by (1) consolidation of the functions at the top level and (2) delegation of the burden of performance to the district organization
8. Integrate the organization of the women's auxiliary into the reorganized diocese

It will be noted from the organization charts (Exhibits 9.1 and 9.2), designed by the committee, that it recommended the following additional changes not in the Johnson Report:

1. Establish a new position of controller
2. Establish a new position of planning director
3. Establish an administrative committee as a policy-making and decision-recommending body of the diocese to integrate the activities of the three districts through developing and enforcing a mandatory policy framework

IMPLEMENTATION OF THE RECOMMENDATIONS

The position of planning director was established and a layman (a trained public relations consultant) was appointed on a full-time basis to fill it. The reorganization committee was renamed the planning commit-

Exhibit 9.1 Organization Plan (Phase I): Church Diocese

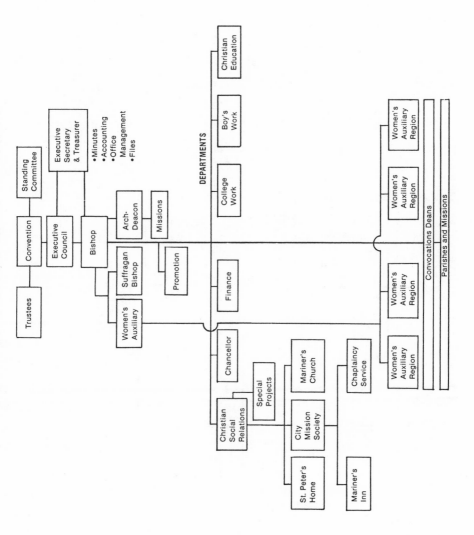

Exhibit 9.2 Proposed Organization Plan (Phase I): Church Diocese

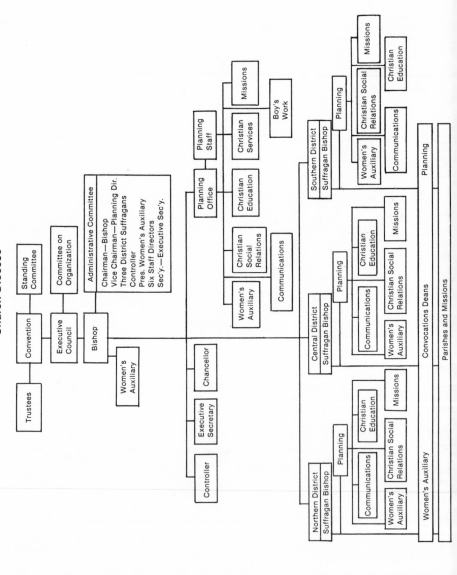

tee with the same membership under the chairmanship of the planning director. The three districts were created. The planning director disagreed with the reorganization committee recommendation that he have line supervision over the specialized staffs as shown in Exhibit 9.2. He was afraid he would get bogged down in day-to-day matters of staff supervision instead of planning. The bishop never required that he assume this managerial role, even though the committee warned the bishop that there were too many staffs reporting directly to him if he desired any relief from this cause of his overload. Next, the administrative committee was activated. It began to review and act on the recommendations of the planning director and the planning committee.

As changes began to be carried out, there developed a hard core of resistance to the reorganization program in the form of the diocesan executive secretary, a clergyman, and the finance chairman, a layman. This opposition took the form of criticism of the cost of the recommendations. These two men actively opposed the appointment of a professional controller for this reason, although no doubt they could foresee loss of their own financial power if such a man was appointed. Although the committee recommended the activation of a formal long-range planning process, this action was never taken.

The convocations did not become strong enough to carry out their key role in this process. The planning director was kept busy enough with the implementation of other phases of the Johnson Report without trying to institute a formal planning process. Ultimately the planning director was dismissed by the bishop in a cost-cutting move.

BENEFITS AND COSTS OF THE REORGANIZATION

We are sure, by districting the diocese and by having archdeacons to head the districts, the bishop was relieved of the load of personally managing the dioceses. Also, much more attention was paid to the local problems of the growing diocese by the three archdeacons than the bishop could have accomplished by himself. The costs were the salaries of the three archdeacons.

The real benefits that could have accrued from doing a professional job of strategic planning and budgeting were not realized, however, because of the opposition of the executive secretary to the appointment of a professional controller and the refusal of the bishop to carry out the plans as originally conceived by the planning committee.

ANALYSIS AGAINST THE BONDS OF ORGANIZATION

Organization Charter

The canon laws of the church are the charter of the diocese. The bishop, once elected, is, to all intents and purposes, in office for life. He is independent and the national church exercises very little policy direction over him. His is a political office and he feels more accountable to the members of his diocese who have elected him than he does to the national church organization. Every year there is a political convention and the bishop must report to this convention on his stewardship of the diocese .

PERPETUATING THE BASIC RESOURCES

Personnel

There were a few members of the clergy who were very capable and progressive managers, like the head of the industrial mission and the pastor of Christ Church. The majority, however, seemed to be out of touch with the problems of the secular world, even though many were extremely dedicated men. The real resources of the church, i.e., the laity, did not seem to be used very effectively.

Finance

Funds for the support of the diocese were always in short supply, but lack of money did not threaten its existence. Money came largely from the contributions of local churches. Part of these funds went also to support the national church. Reliance on this source of capital, of course, weakened the control of the diocese over the local churches as well as the control of the national church over the diocese. Supply of capital was always inadequate to do all the things the bishop wanted to do. If there had been better planning, however, and communication of this planning to the constituency, we believe funds would have been made available.

Thoughtways

Problem-solving and innovative ideas are not always welcome in the staid environment of the church. Mr. Johnson discovered that one or two of the dioceses had, in the past, engaged management consultants to conduct surveys of a limited nature to deal with specific problems. Not one, however, had ever undertaken an overall management survey of such scope as the one undertaken by this particular diocese. This fact, in itself, is very significant. The office of planning director was created in order to help the bishop develop some new ideas and directions in the organization and management of the diocese. In the past, the whole organization had been oriented toward performing the same routine service—Sunday after Sunday after Sunday. Strategic planning and goal setting, as it is done in progressive businesses, was all but unknown in the church. Personnel policies, such as job evaluation, hospital insurance and benefits, were very much behind the times. Serving God should be enough reward for any man—this was the attitude of the bishop. As a result, salaries were depressed. Thoughtways activities were inadequate. That was the reason for creating the positions of planning director and controller and for initiating a formal planning process.

CONTROL ACTIVITIES

Directive

The directive activities were very weak at both the diocesan and national church levels. The financial rewards system was also weak in view of permanent tenure of the bishop, the political method of his selection, the depressed salary level, and the absence of job evaluation.

Motivation

For purposes of motivation, the only rewards the bishop had at his disposal to offer the laity were non-financial in nature, such as letters of commendation and the like.

Since the reinforcements were weak, the motivation to perform was weak. The diocesan activities were primarily service activities for the parishes. Functional guidance and control was unknown.

Of all the service activities, communications were the strongest. It was not only extremely important that the services of the diocese be well performed, but that this fact be well publicized to the bishop's constituency in order to merit generous financial and political support. The bishop, in addition to his personal skills in this field, was assisted by a trained communications director, who had formerly been a newspaper man. This accounted for the excellent story in a business publication on the reorganization of the diocese. Ordinarily, however, the communications director had few innovative programs of general interest to communicate in the diocesan news bulletin.

HOMEOSTATIC ACTIVITIES

Fusion

The fusion process was very effective. The full-time employees were spiritually committed to their jobs and the goals of the diocese in spite of the poor compensation they received. Some were forced to accept second jobs in order to support their families. Generally they did so without either complaint or thought of leaving the organization.

Problem-Solving

Because there was more of an opportunity than a threat in the problem of bringing good management to the diocese, the agents became aware of the problem in plenty of time to take appropriate action. There was, however, no financial crisis that seriously threatened the existence of the diocese. The challenge was to improve performance of the bishop.

The Johnson Report thoroughly explored the cause of the problem. It was simply a result of explosive growth as shown in all statistics and the overwhelming burden it placed on one man, the bishop. This problem posed an opportunity to the organization, i.e., to deal more effectively—in advance of a survival crisis—with the funds available to meet the human and spiritual needs of the members of the diocese.

The problems resulting from growth had been rapidly becoming more complex. All the members of the diocese were affected. Although the parishioners grumbled about the many and varied donations to the church, they were not really likely to withhold their financial support so long as the routine church services and functions continued to be performed every Sunday.

Failure of the church to plan ahead and provide services that dealt with serious human problems—the decay of the inner-city church, increase of mental illness, and the like—was not likely to cause any threat to the survival of the church organization. At most, the parishioners would complain about the unnecessary uses to which their donations were put whenever more was requested. There was no real threat to the organizational charter or to the integrity of the organization, either short-or long-term. This major attempt at reorganization in itself reflects much credit on the efforts of the bishop. Many businesses reach a survival crisis before the chief executive is willing to undertake a reorganization of similar scope.

The interests of all the church members and even of community, in general, stand to benefit if the problem was solved and the services of the diocese were more effectively rendered in terms of urgent real-life human needs. There were only a few members in the organization itself with sufficient exposure to business to see the tremendous potential of applying management techniques to the problems of the diocese and at the same time had enough experience to make a practical contribution to their solution.

At least five feasible alternative reorganization plans were thoroughly discussed with the bishop before the final one was selected. The committee even used a plan evaluation chart (see Exhibit 3.7) as a guide to final organization plan selection.

Implementation was the area in which the dysfunction existed. The bishop was not willing to exercise discipline in the execution of the plan so far as the executive secretary of the diocese was concerned. The latter complained about the cost of the reorganization plan whenever he could, in spite of the fact that it had been approved by the executive council. He did so without any rebuke from the bishop. Finally, the job of the planning director was abolished on the grounds of cost. Even today the bishop blames the cost for his failure to implement the plan. In a real survival crisis, this reason would be given little credence.

Leadership

Here, in this case, we find pathology in the leadership activities of the chief executive. Replacing the bishop was not feasible until his retirement.

ORGANIZATION OF ORGANIZATION PLANNING

The need for the reorganization was first recognized by the pastor of Christ Church and a layman in his parish. As a result of the Johnson Report, a position of planning director was established and filled by a layman who reported directly to the bishop. Although very dedicated and capable, he was essentially a public relations man, just as Mr. Johnson had been an advertising executive. Neither one had any specialized experience in long-range planning or organization planning. The bishop kept accusing the planning director—with some justification—of fiddling with the automobile engine and not giving enough attention to the direction of the journey. On the other hand, when the chips were down, the bishop gave the planning director and the implementation of the report very little understanding and support. The bishop made no effort to read and learn about professional management in order to give knowledgeable backing to the reorganization effort. At the first sign of opposition from his "palace guard," in the person of the executive secretary, the bishop abolished the position of planning director, giving cost as the reason. The districting did take place, as did the creation of the administrative committee and integration of church women into the structure, but little else was done to implement the plan.

This is an excellent example of a poorly organized planning function and one that received very little support and understanding from the chief executive. Although the bishop attended meetings of the planning committee, he apparently never really believed in what the committee was doing. Results and benefits in relation to the great potential for implementing the Johnson Report were minimal until after his retirement.

TOOLS AND TECHNIQUES OF ORGANIZATION PLANNING

A broad management study was made. Although an organization and policy manual was recommended, none was ever prepared. There were no administrative constraints. This was one reason none of the key men ever really understood his changed role in the new organization structure or changed his performance accordingly. There was no organization planning or titling policy. The formal long-range planning process never got off the ground even for one cycle, so that no self-correcting mechanisms were activated. Alternative plans of organization were, however, considered using a plan evaluation chart. Techniques of activity analysis, grouping analysis, and decisions analysis were not required. Organization charts and brief statements of functions were used in selling the new plan of organization to the executive council of the diocese. The planning was sound, but the implementation was weak, due to inadequate support of the planning function by the bishop and his lack of will to manage.

PRINCIPLES OF ORGANIZATION PLANNING

On reviewing the organization structure, we find a one-man chief executive with the resulting heavy overload on this position. This was a violation of the *Principle of Balance* and the *Principle of Centralization.* The *Principle of Responsibility and Authority* was also not being followed, since there was little feeling of accountability to the bishop on the part of the parish priests and deans. Since there was no organization and policy manual, the key positons were not defined and communicated to all concerned. The organization planning function was so poorly organized and supported that the *Principle of Continuity* was violated. Proper organization implementation and control never took place as planned, until after the prior bishop retired.

STRATEGY AND STRUCTURE OF THE DIOCESE UP TO THE PRESENT

In 1978, the bishop retired and was replaced by a new bishop, who is much more interested in the planning, strategy, and structure of the diocese. A pamphlet entitled *People and Program* setting forth the mission, the goals, the priorities and the organization structure of the diocese was issued by the bishop, based on a report from a new goals and priorities committee. This committee had replaced the planning committee. This pamphlet instructed that there were three districts each under an archdeacon. Within these districts were fourteen convocations, each headed by a dean. The number of souls were down from 95,000 to 80,000 served by 340 clergy. The annual budget was about $1 million. One of the goals was stated as follows:

VI. Structure and Process—provide structure and process that will anticipate needs and will enable maximum feasible participation in decision making. (From the Report—The Goals and Priorities Committee)

There was an executive assistant to the bishop on special ministries and assistants to the bishop on human resources development, administrative and finance, town and country, urban affairs, financial stewardship, school of theology, chancellor of the diocese, treasurer of the diocese, financial adviser to the bishop, and chief accountant (see Exhibit 9.3).

Exhibit 9.3 Organization Plan (Phase II), 1988: Church Diocese

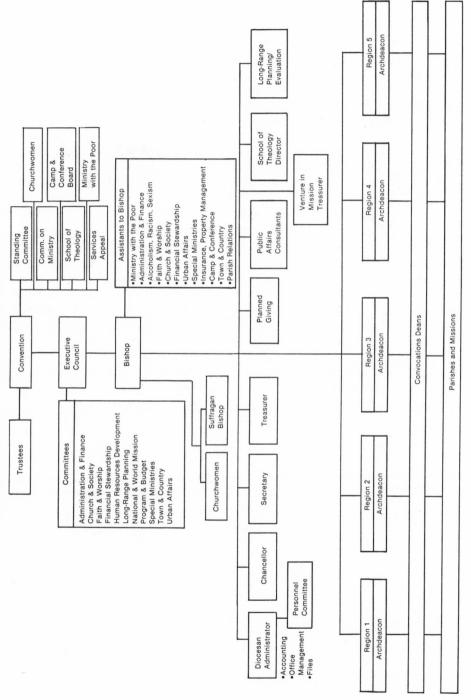

In 1987, the *People and Program* 1986-1987 pamphlet showed the following additions to the structure. The position of suffragan bishop has been added to assist the bishop with confirmations. The regional archdeacons cannot officiate at confirmations. There are new assistants to the bishop.

There is a new position of diocesan administrator over the accounting, clerical, and personnel staff as well as new public affairs consultant positions. Treasurer of the diocese and chancellor of the diocese remain unchanged. Strategic planning and structure in the diocese are at last now being given much needed emphasis with the advent of the new bishop. Salaries and benefits are competitive as well. The three districts have been changed to five regions, each under an archdeacon; although there is no administrative committee, the bishop meets once a month with the five regional archdeacons to coordinate their efforts.

In this case, we see clear illustration of the importance a change in CEO's can have in the implementation of a reorganization plan. The new bishop immediately appointed a Goals and Priorities Committee to recommend written goals and priorities for the diocese. These were stated in the *People and Program* pamphlet, together with a mission statement and a detailed description of the organization, including the committees and their functions.

Even though the number of souls is down to 60,000, income is up to $15 million. Salaries and benefits are more competitive. The bishop now has a full-time lay volunteer as assistant to the bishop-long-range planning and evaluation. There is a *Salary and Benefit Manual* and a Vision Statement for the year 2000, adopted formally by the convention in 1987.

10

Rejuvenating an Unpaid Organization: The Management Association Chapter

HISTORY OF THE MANAGEMENT ASSOCIATION CHAPTER

The management society was formed shortly after the turn of the century; its founder is generally known as the father of the scientific management movement. Out of this movement came today's concepts of modern management as a profession.

The nominating committee of the chapter in the sixties had the charge to come up with a slate of officers for the next season. At the first meeting of the nominating committee, the executive vice president eloquently defined the problem of the chapter.

The fortunes of the chapter had sunk to a very low ebb. There was little activity in the chapter except the monthly meetings at which only about thirty out of the four hundred and twenty chapter members attended. The inactivity of the membership was alleged to be a result of the activities of a former group of officials of the chapter who had used the society for their personal ends, rather than for trying to advance the goals of the society and the chapter. It was the job of the nominating committee to replace these officers and plan for the reorganization of the chapter.

The committee came up with an outstanding slate of officers. They had enlisted the services of some well-known professional management authorities in the local area. These candidates had agreed not only to lend their prestige to the letterhead, but to attend board of directors luncheon meetings. This was perhaps the most important move leading to the rebirth of the chapter. The minds of these men working together on the board gave the essential guidance and support the chapter needed to increase the active participation of the members.

The chapter had no paid staff. Initially, the board spent much time trying to guess why the members did not attend the monthly meetings, in spite of the fact that some of the most outstanding management professionals in the country addressed the group.

The board finally decided to send out an attitude questionnaire to all the members. This questionnaire was designed by the president of a professional marketing research firm. The board found that the members were generally of such stature that they knew as much or more about the subject given at the monthly meetings than the speaker did. They consequently felt that they could learn little from attending. Being members of many professional associations themselves and very active in at least one, many of them did not feel that they should spend their limited discretionary time attending more meetings, unless they could feel some sense of active participation in the advancement of the goals of the society, or could receive some help in solving their current management problems. The chairman of the membership committee asked each inactive member to appear before his committee to explain the reason for his inactivity. The committee, armed with the attitude questionnaire, went into the background of each member and found out his abilities and interests in participating in the activities of the chapter.

First, the membership committee filled the vacancies on the chapter organization chart (see Exhibit 10.1). Then the committee began to form special interest groups in many areas based on the expressed desires of the inactive or new members. They also appointed functional vice presidents in administration, research and development, manufacturing, and marketing management. It was the job of each functional vice president under the general direction of the executive vice president to chair each monthly meeting in his area of expertise. A professional public relations consultant was appointed the public relations director. The chief executive instituted a very professional newsletter, which was combined with the monthly meeting announcement. A few days before the meeting, he sent out a reminder, in the form of a self-addressed and stamped postcard, which he also used as a basis for estimating attendees. In addition, each member of the membership committee was assigned twenty members to call personally, get to know them, and invite them to attend the monthly meeting. Unfortunately the efforts of the membership committee to stimulate attendance at monthly meetings by telephone calls did not prove successful. Finally, however, as a result of these efforts, over one hundred members were attending the monthly meetings of the special interest groups.

The chapter officials decided to define formally the structure, policies, and procedures of the chapter in a chart and operations manual. They

**Exhibit 10.1 Organization Plan (Phase I):
Management Association Chapter**

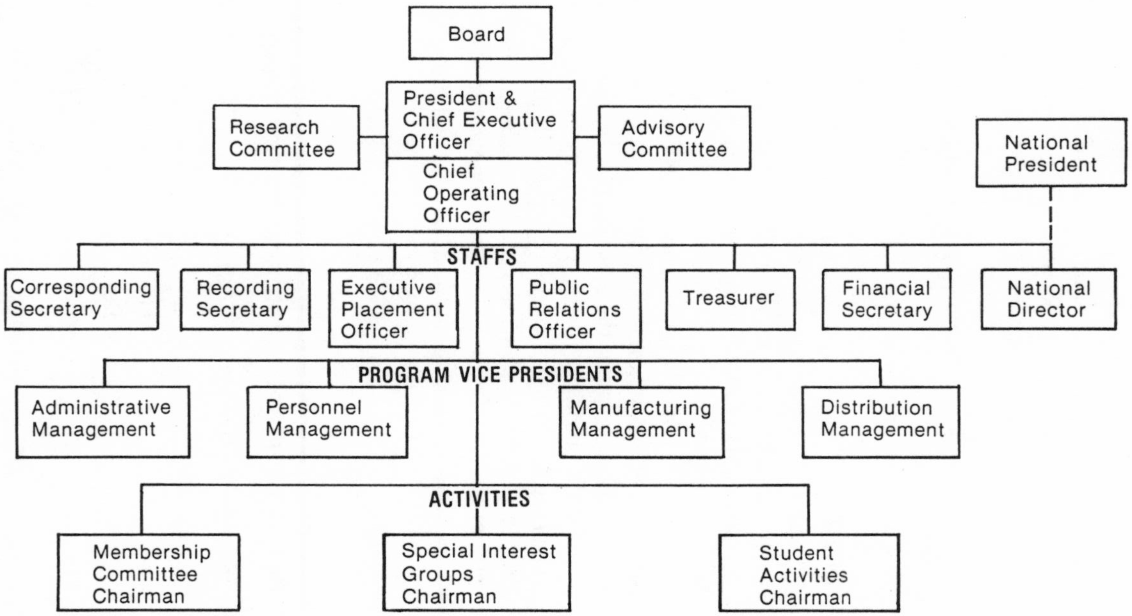

also established a long-range plan to carry out the objectives of the chapter with dates and accountabilities established for each official on the chart.

The activities of the special interest groups proved to be most successful in increasing the interest and participation of the inactive members of the chapter. These activities were designed to help the members fill their specific developmental and problem-solving needs and gave them a feeling of participation in the work of the chapter. One special interest group, the organization planning workgroup, was later spun-off from the chapter and became a professional society on its own, the Organization Development Council.

The successful reorganization of the chapter, in spite of its small size, proved to be the most difficult organization problem in this book. No doubt this difficulty was caused by the fact that there was no paid staff. The only rewards system that could be used was non-financial in nature, and it was not an effective motivator. The chapter members were working only for personal professional benefits. Achieving fusion proved to be very difficult in respect to the members, with the exception of the small hard core of committed officials of the chapter who met every month at board meetings and got to know one another very well; fusion was excellent in their cases. Except in the special interest groups, too few of the members met each other frequently enough to develop a strong interpersonal relationship or to feel any sense of accomplishment in furthering the aims of either the national society or of the local chapter. We have concluded that this is an example of the organizational involvement and commitment that can be generated by giving each member some specific productive work to do, rather than by expecting him passively to listen to an expert lecture.

ANALYSIS AGAINST THE BONDS OF ORGANIZATON

Identification Activities

These activities were very important in the chapter. At first they were performed poorly or not at all within the chapter itself. With the accession of the new president, he began a well-done monthly newsletter combined with the announcement of the monthly meeting. This newsletter contained articles by each chairman of the thirteen special interest groups. This was issued to the membership and others who might be interested in attending meetings and in becoming members. The national society seal was prominently used for the purpose of symbolizing the organization. The letterhead with the list of the officers and directors was also most important as an identifying symbol. The chapter issued a yearly calendar of programs and their dates to all the membership. The national society pamphlet and monthly publication of management articles were effective vehicles to stimulate member identification.

PERPETUATION ACTIVITIES

Personnel

The membership chairman was in charge of the job of getting new members and keeping the present members from resigning. The problem was not the quality or supply of human resources, but their motivation to become active in the work of the chapter.

Finance

One of the very real problems of the chapter was the allocation of its limited capital resources. Of the $60 annual dues submitted to the national organization, $5 of this was rebated annually for the support of the local chapter. With four hundred members this amount was not small. Most of it went, however, to defray the expenses for publicity for the monthly dinner meeting, which could not be completely financed through what the members paid to attend.

Because of the limited money in the treasury, the new president inaugurated the idea of a chapter development fund, through which the chapter would receive tax-free donations from the members and their companies, which were used to improve the newsletter and meeting announcements.

Thoughtways

The chapter officials and board of directors met every month in a luncheon meeting to perpetuate the ideas of the chapter. These meetings during the first days, were particularly concerned with the means of getting the finances in order and finding out why there was such poor attendance at the monthly meetings. Out of these deliberations came the idea of conducting the member attitude survey. The members were the customers. The chapter officials did not really know why they were not buying the products enough to become active. Since the society advocated applying the principles of scientific management to problems such as these, the chapter resolved to "practice what it preached." In developing an operations manual for the chapter, defining the duties and authorities of the officers and committees, and in developing a strategic plan for the chapter, the board was also applying principles of good management and organization to the work of the chapter. Each of the board meetings brought together some of the best management minds in the country in many areas of technical specialization. In this resource, the chapter was most fortunate. Ideas were never in short supply. Since the chapter had no paid staff, there were not enough members with time during working hours to carry out these ideas.

CONTROL ACTIVITIES

Directive

The chief executive was accountable for performing the control activities, with the assistance of the treasurer, who developed the operations manual and the long- and short-term strategic plan for the chapter; he also assisted the chief executive in the staffing of the organization and in evaluating the work of the officials in his role as chairman of the nominating committee. The executive vice president of the chapter also assisted the chief executive by coordinating the work of the divisional vice presidents in making the arrangements for the monthly meetings. The more this work was distributed among the officers of the chapter, the more the heavy overload on the shoulders of the chief executive was reduced. An important factor to recognize in evaluating the control activity is that there was no paid staff to control. For each member his job in the chapter was self-developmental in nature and took discretionary time from his family and extracurricular activities, i.e., church and community. For this reason, control of member activity by the chief executive was a difficult duty to perform successfully.

Motivation

There was no paid staff and the reward system was weak. A fellow award was given to the member who accomplished most for the profession of management and the national society through the work of the chapter. The most active chapter was annually given the Brody Trophy Award. Other awards were given by the national society to individuals for outstanding achievements in the field of professional management.

Evaluation

Evaluation activities, with the exception of those performed by the chapter nominating committee, were performed by appropriate awards committees in the national society.

Communication

Communications activities improved considerably with the issuance of the newsletter and the member attitude questionnaire, and with the efforts to get in personal touch with the members through the work of the membership committee. As members began to get to know one another by participation in special interest groups, the personal relationships and interaction between the members began to improve. The organization finally began to achieve cohesion and strength. Communication of society goals to the general public was not effective. With the possible exception of the chapter meeting on cybernetics, which received an excellent write-up in a national news weekly magazine, the monthly meetings received no publicity in the public press at all. This was partially because the chapter did not have services of a paid trained public relations specialist. The national society, however, received national publicity for its annual conventions.

HOMEOSTATIC ACTIVITIES

Fusion

The organization had a real problem with fusion. The members did not see why their active participation was needed in the chapter activities so long as they paid their dues. The president made his thoughts on this known to the members through the monthly newsletter. The membership committee helped him in personal interviews with each of the inactive members. Fusion gradually became more effective as the members began to take an active part in the work of the chapter.

Problem-Solving

The chapter executive vice president was fully aware of the problems of the chapter when he addressed the nominating committee. Originally, while member apathy was a troublesome problem, as long as the members remained, this problem did not pose a threat of survival as much as it presented an opportunity for improvement.

Failure of the organization to realize the promise in the situation meant that little was being done to advance the profession of management or the ideas of the founder locally. A few men—chapter officers and board members—were developing their own management skills through their close working association with each other at monthly board meetings. But the great potential impact of the organization, on management as a profession and the community in general, was being realized only in small part.

After the attitude questionnaire was sent out and the results had been tabulated and interpreted, then accurate judgments began to be made by the board as to the cause and the other pertinent aspects of defining the problem.

At first, when the board of directors met without any facts on the inactive members and their opinions and tried to guess why there was such poor attendance at the monthly meetings, there was a tendency to oversimplify or personalize the problem. Many of the pertinent factors were left out, such as the inadequate effort to promote interaction between members.

After the member questionnaire results were received, alternative strategies for correcting the situation were thoroughly explored by the board.

The necessary response activities were carried out according to plan, particularly by the membership committee. The possible exception was in making telephone calls to each member before each meeting to urge him to attend. There was some unfavorable response by the members to these calls; they construed this effort as exerting too much pressure to get them to the monthly dinner meeting in view of their limited interest in attending. This plan was modified in the light of this reaction. The committee made an occasional series of telephone calls to all members just to keep in touch with their attitudes toward services of the chapter, or toward some particular proposal on which the officials wanted membership reaction quickly. The board periodically reviewed the results of the strategy in increasing the member activity, even though the chapter never did very well in the competition for the Brody Trophy Award. The considerable activity in the special interest groups did not receive due recognition from the national organization in the point system, which determined the winner of this award.

Leadership

The chief executive, with the assistance of the membership chairman, did make changes in the chapter organization structure, in order to carry out the strategy and goals of the chapter. Through his dynamic leadership the chapter gradually came to life. After seven years, the chapter activity, as reflected in the newsletter, could be considered a complete success.

CONCLUSION

With the exception of the appointment of a professional public relations manager, all of the organizational recommendations made by the membership chairman to the chief executive were carried out. Elsewhere among the membership, there was no shortage of professional management talent. The problem was to get a member to serve in an active capacity, particularly when he had spent many previous years in serving the society. The young newcomers to the society and to the chapter were the likeliest candidates to become active. They had the most to gain from the learning opportunity resulting from working with the experienced professional management authorities who were officials and directors of the chapter.

In retrospect, it is apparent that more effort should have been made to publicize the work of the chapter and the benefits of professional management to its recipients, the general public. Awards should also have been given by the chapter for the professional achievements of its members. In spite of the tremendous importance of the role of the professional manager in the life of Ameirca today, relatively little had been done to publicize this key work.

ORGANIZATION OF ORGANIZATION PLANNING

It is not surprising that, in this case, we find effective organization for organization planning. The chief executive of the chapter was not only a man skilled in the function of organization planning himself, as all professional managers should be, but he believed in the practical value of the function as well. He assigned to his membership chairman, who was an experienced organization analyst, the job of preparing the long-range policies and objectives of the chapter, as well as designing the organization structure and writing the operations manual. He also participated in conducting a study of the problem of member inactivity through the attitude questionnaire. Once he knew more about member desires, interests, and professional needs, he was able to design a worthwhile program as well as an organization structure to carry it out. The primary problem was one common to all organizations without a paid staff—a weak rewards system. The members had little time during working hours to devote to the work of the chapter. What work was done, however, was very well organized and proceduralized.

TOOLS AND TECHNIQUES OF ORGANIZATION PLANNING

The long-range and annual program and organization manual, as well as the attitude questionnaire sent periodically to the members, were the primary organization planning tools. Goals, structure, programs, policies, and procedures were well defined in writing in the operations manual and sent out to all the members. Since activities were voluntary and there was such a high rate of turnover in the key positions, this communication of management information was important to the effective functioning of the organization. Because there were no paid staff members, there was no real reason for the use of sophisticated analytical tools in designing the organization structure. The national group gave the chapter guidance and encouragement in the preparation of the chapter operations manual.

PRINCIPLES OF ORGANIZATION PLANNING

The Principle of Definition was the most important principle applied to the organization of the chapter. The Principle of Balance was also important. The chief executive had a heavy workload, since there were only a few hard core members of the chapter who were willing to help him. The membership chairman developed the organization plan so as to use as many members as possible. In this way, he encouraged active participation and commitment. Putting on a monthly meeting was the most time-consuming job in the chapter. For this reason, the structure shows the chief executive and four functional vice presidents who chaired the programs in their areas of expertise. He applied the *Principle of the Objective* in determining what positions the chapter needed in its structure to carry out the annual and long-range program.

STRATEGY AND STRUCTURE UP TO THE PRESENT

In 1976 the chapter president reported that he still had a problem with member inactivity (see Exhibit 10.2). He did not continue the use of the special interest groups as such to maintain member activity. However, similar work was carried out through the regular organization structure. For example, the chapter public relations officer recently ran a special project that provided the management talent needed by a local drug rehabilitation clinic in order to apply for a federal grant-in-aid. Their efforts were successful and the chapter received much favorable publicity.

The president stressed the fact that he ran the chapter on an MBO basis by first agreeing with an officer on the result goals expected of him to be achieved by a specific date. If the officer did not work to help achieve these goals in a reasonable period of time, the president replaced the officer with another member who would. By thus vigorously applying the principles of result-oriented professional management to the work of the chapter itself, the president doubtless alienated some members who did not wish actively to advance the profession. Indeed, he had not pleased some members of the national organization who were more interested in the size of the chapter than in the member activity achieved. Even inactive members pay their dues. The membership of the chapter was now down from 400 to about 200 members; of this 200, however, at least 100 were active. This was better in the president's opinion—not necessarily in the opinion of the national organization—than having 400 members of which only 30 or so were active.

In 1982 the chapter discontinued its operations and returned its funds to the national organization. Apparently the competition from other management associations in a large city had made it too difficult to achieve active participation of a sufficient number of its members. Perhaps it was a mistake to discontinue the special interest groups that had been so successful in increasing member participation.

**Exhibit 10.2 Organization Plan (Phase II), 1975:
Management Association Chapter**

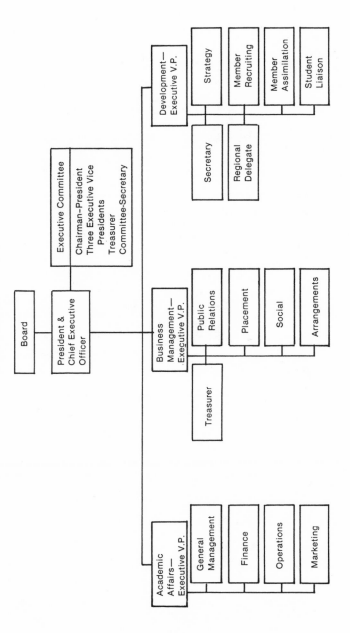

11

Rescuing a Small Non-Profit Organization: The Art Association

ORGANIZATION SURVEY OF THE ART ASSOCIATION

When the organization department of the Automobile Company was formed in the early fifties, long-service members of the staff knew little about the principles of organization planning or the techniques of making organization surveys. They visited several companies that were known to have organization planning staffs that had done outstanding work in this highly specialized field. One of the first and most outstanding of these was the department on organization of an oil company on the west coast. As an example of organization planning work and the techniques involved, the head gave members of the staff a copy of a survey report his department had made of the Art Association. He also gave them a copy of a manual of organization survey techniques developed by his department for the use of anyone in the company working on task forces with his staff members in making organization surveys. The techniques in this manual were used in making this organization survey, and the combination of this report and the techniques manual gave the inexperienced members of the organization staff of the Automobile Company a clear picture of the function of an organization planning staff, and the tremendous job that lay ahead of the staff in making surveys of the entire structure of the Automobile Company.

All the other cases in Part II were taken from the author's experience. An exception was made in this instance because the report on the organization survey is such an excellent illustration of the application of sound organization planning survey techniques in a very small organization. Because of the small size of the Art Association, the report is thorough and comprehensive. In the case of the larger organizations discussed previously in Part II, such a survey report not only would be impossible, it would be unwise to write such a comprehensive report on all the details of an organization. The only facts that are available on this case are those included in this survey report and those obtained in subsequent telephone calls to the current president of the Art Association. We hope the reader will understand this limitation and make the proper allowance in evaluating the treatment of the Art Association case.

THE HISTORY OF THE ART ASSOCIATION

As is pointed out in the survey report, during the years of the Vietnam War, the Art Association made money only in one year. In the last year, 1973, the association lost about $40,000. The survey (see Exhibits 11.1, 11.2, 11.3, and 11.5 at end of Chapter 11) was made as a public service by the professional staff of the department on organization of an oil company, in the hope that they might simplify work and eliminate jobs in such a way that the Art Association might become once again financially self-sustaining. Although it was a non-profit organization, the association's objective was, if possible, to recover expenses through current revenues. While it could solicit its members for charitable contributions, it did not wish, as a matter of policy, to do so. During these years it had covered its deficits by using some available reserves and they were at the point of being exhausted when the survey was made. The conduct of the survey, according to the plan, required twenty-five-man days. There were three men on the project; therefore, it must have taken them about two weeks full-time to complete the assignment. At $3,000 a month per man, the survey cost the oil company about $5,000. An outside consultant would have charged about $200 to $500 a day for each man. On this basis, this organization survey would have cost the Art Association more than $10,000. This donation, therefore, resulted in a substantial savings to the Art Association.

FINDINGS OF THE ORGANIZATION SURVEY

The objectives of the survey were two:

1. To develop a sound and workable plan of organization for the administrative staff of the Art Association
2. To develop, as necessary, improvements in policies, methods and procedures, records and reports, and related activities so as to ensure economical administration and to facilitate the progress of the association

The report pointed out certain findings that were outside the scope of the survey as originally outlined in the survey plan. The financial deficit that threatened the survival of the school of fine arts was a critical factor completely unknown to the task force members when the survey began. If the recommendations of the report were carried out, a saving of only perhaps $18,000 to $20,000 annually against the $33,000 deficit would be realized. For this reason, the report recommended that an overall economic study or business survey be conducted, with resulting valuations and estimates to be used as a basis for determining a future course of action for the association to correct the serious financial deficit. The study team foresaw the need to increase the enrollment of the art school possibly through attracting more of the older hobby artists and students from suburban areas. To achieve this result required strengthening the public relations and sales promotion activities.

It was also found that the director was overloaded with detail rather than managerial and fund-raising tasks. A new position of administrative assistant was created to permit the director to delegate more of the administrative routine to a qualified management analyst. It was also no doubt the purpose of this change to provide within the full-time staff a person who would be able to carry out the intent of the report and hold costs to a minimum. The work experience and skills of the director, although not given in the report, were probably limited largely to art teaching and related activities. In this case unneeded positions were eliminated. Total full-time positions were reduced from seven to five. After a more detailed study, it was thought that some reduction would be possible in the part-time help also.

ANALYSIS AGAINST THE BONDS OF ORGANIZATION

Identification Activities

The constitution of the Art Association was, of course, its formal charter. It stated that "the object of this organization shall be to maintain a museum of fine arts and school of fine arts, to provide for and conduct exhibitions and to unite in fellowship the membership of the association and to promote the cultivation of the fine arts."

Since the museum of fine arts was operated independently, the maintenance of the art school appeared to be the major activity of the Art Association. Further, the administrative staff activities of the association and the school were so closely interrelated that, for the purpose of the report, it was necessary to consider them as a single organization.

The organization survey team recommended as follows:

34. Consider the appropriateness of preparing a concise brochure which will set forth the history of the Art Association, its organization, its financial structure,

sources of income, membership, relationship to the school of fine arts, trust funds, endowment funds, or any other information pertinent to its past history and future programs. Such a production could serve several purposes in the field of public relations.

35. Prepare in some suitable form a statement of present personnel policies setting forth working conditions and hours, overtime, vacations, holidays, time off with and without pay and other related subjects, as appropriate, bearing upon employee relations.

Here is a recognition of the importance of strengthening the charter and giving it some publicity beyond the membership of the Art Association itself.

One of the key points in this report was that the Identification Activities needed considerable strengthening. This was accomplished by the creation of a new position, representative-public and art association relations. The salary was made competitive; the size of the office was increased; and the position was freed from any other major responsibilities. These changes permitted hiring a qualified publicity professional and fund raiser for the position.

PERPETUATION ACTIVITIES

Thoughtways

With the recommendation that the director be "ex officio" a member of the board of directors and the executive committee, and with the executive committee meeting more often for the purpose of giving the director their thinking, reaction, and ideas on possible improvements, it was hoped to generate some new ideas on alternative directions for the Art Association that would get it out of the deficit financing position.

WORKFLOW ACTIVITIES

There were only a few workflow activities connected with the work of the Art Association and the school of fine arts: billing the association members for their annual dues; registering the students at the beginning of each school year; managing the cafeteria and getting and paying the models. Each of these activities was carefully scrutinized by the task force to see if it was subject to any substantial economies. These were the procedures, methods, forms, and reports mentioned but not included in the report. These activities supported the two major workflow activities (educational and food services).

The cafeteria was a loss operation and the report suggested that the food service be farmed out to a professional catering service. All unprofitable courses should be eliminated insofar as possible. The legitimacy of all charges to the association by the state university should be carefully scrutinized.

CONTROL ACTIVITIES

Directive

These activities had apparently not been performed very effectively by the director because of his limited understanding of professional management. He was to be supported in these activities, owing to his lack of management skill and interest, by the new administrative assistant.

Motivation

A salary survey was made by the survey team to assure that the full-time employees were being paid fairly in comparison with their counterparts in other organizations in the area. Nothing was said in the report about goal setting and performance appraisals. These activities could have proven worthwhile once the board of director had set some overall directions for the organization. This apparently had not been done, at least with the presence and participation of the director.

Evaluation

Having no real goals, the goal setting and performance evaluation activities in the Art Association by the board must have been very limited, except in their repeated criticism of the operating deficits. By grouping all of the business management activities under the administrative assistant, it was the purpose of the recommendations in the report to provide a qualified person to help the director manage and control the organization.

Communication

The communication activities were weak, not only between the Art Association and its members, but also between the association and the general public. If the school was to survive, these activities had to be strengthened considerably. An attitude survey of art students and members would, no doubt, have helped in the survey considerably, as in the Management Association Chapter, in evaluating the performance of the Art Association staff. The fact that the director was not a member of the executive committee must have caused very difficult communication problems.

HOMEOSTATIC ACTIVITIES

Fusion

There was considerable confusion about the specific direction the school and the association should take in order for the school to survive. The objectives of the association were lofty goals with which few could argue. With the growth of the leisure, well-educated, middle class in the local area, there should have been a real place for the school in the adult education field. On the part of the full-time employees, there should not have been a fusion problem if the communications problem had been handled properly. That is the reason a personnel policy manual was recommended. Some employee training would then have been in order also.

Problem-Solving

Even though the task force members were not aware of the extent of the financial difficulties of the association when they took on the survey, the association director must have been aware of the situation. This awareness came in time, we believe, to take appropriate action.

Critical aspects of the problem were explored by the task force, but the scope was not broad enough to define all aspects of the problem and alternative solutions.

There was a definite economic threat to the existence of the school if not to the association itself. Since 1970 there had been financial deficits in varying amounts.

The students of the school and their families could be affected, although nothing was said about the existence and availability of other fine arts schools in the area. Only if there were few feasible alternatives was this factor likely to be of much importance; this possibility, however, should have been mentioned in the report. Alumni have certainly helped in other cases where privately supported schools have had financial difficulties. Public financing was another alternative.

Failure of the board to meet the financial needs could certainly cause the school to be discontinued.

Leadership

A leadership problem may have resulted from not having a professional association manager as the director of the Art Association.

CONCLUSION

In evaluating the survey report, on the whole it was an outstanding piece of work both in the techniques employed, in the thoroughness of execution, and in the breadth of its scope. If any problem developed in realizing satisfactory results from the survey, it probably happened during the implementation of the recommendations. Expanding the enrollment of the school proved to be extremely difficult. Cutting the excess administrative costs was easy by comparison. Perhaps a government grant to such a school, as is the case in foreign countries, could have been a short-term answer. Government subsidies for a fine arts education are not very common in this country.

ORGANIZATION OF ORGANIZATION PLANNING

The small size of the organization meant that providing a full-time organization planning specialist to help the director was impractical. The best that could be expected would be that the administrative assistant in the proposed organization structure would have some skills in the field of organization planning and analysis, and would be able to counsel the director in carrying out the organization and systems improvements recommended by the task force. More critical, of course, was finding a new director with professional management skills, of which organization planning would be the key skill.

Using experienced organization planners from the outside was important in conducting this organization survey as it was also in the conduct of the organization survey of the Church Diocese.

TOOLS AND TECHNIQUES OF ORGANIZATION PLANNING

In spite of the very sophisticated organization planning techniques used by the task force from the organization staff of the oil company (as outlined in their organization survey guide), an objective analysis of the survey suggests areas where there might have been improvement in both carrying out the survey and preparing the report. A key omission is that the task force did not prepare man specifications for the jobs as well as job descriptions.

If they had done this, they might have found that Mr. Johnson, the director, was an excellent art teacher, but had not the required management skills to qualify as director of the Art Association. In all fairness to the task force members, they might actually have done this by giving these recommendations to the executive committee and leaving them out of the formal report in the interest of sparing the feelings of Mr. Johnson. This apparent omission was almost as critical in importance as the fact that there had been no broad business survey of the affairs of the association prior to the organization survey. This action would have highlighted the serious financial condition of the organization and pointed out ways to acquire funds to cover the deficit. This problem could not be solved by the simple expedient of eliminating two unneeded positions through the techniques of organization survey as used by the task force. The report also contained too little information on the history of the development of the Art Association organization itself. This information was, of course, essential to the solution of the problem (i.e., the replacement of Mr. Johnson and expansion of school revenues). Too much time and attention in the report was given to improving the detailed paperwork procedures of the school in order to eliminate positions, and not enough to the establishment of the position of administrative assistant designed to support Mr. Johnson with some of the management skills that he lacked, or to the establishment of a professional representative-public and art association relations who could publicize the work of the school and conduct fund-raising activities. In this way the school could increase its enrollment and conduct some much needed fund-raising campaigns among the alumni group or association members. This action could bring in money and tide the association over its financial difficulties until the end of the Vietnamese conflict, when serious full-time students would become available again with student loans to fund the tuition. Perhaps the task force should have postponed their study until the broad business study of the association's affairs had been made. The staff might even have limited its recommendations to a proposal for the conduct of such a business study. The report should have also included an action plan in which the immediate next implementation steps were described in specific terms.

PRINCIPLES OF ORGANIZATION PLANNING

The application of the *Principle of Definition* was most important in the solution of this particular organization problem. The task force carefully charted the present structure before they proposed another plan. We believe they would have found the technique of linear responsibility charting helpful in this process of functional definition in such a small organization (see Chapter 3). They would have been sure that the position descriptions and man specifications that they developed fitted together properly. Linear responsibility charting is also an excellent technique for illustrating the proposed changes in duties. Application of the *Principle of the Objective* was important in illustrating the need for initiating new activities and two new positions in the organization structure required to ensure the survival of the school. Apparently the executive committee and its staff frequently interfered with Mr. Johnson's management of the art school. This was a violation of the *Principle of Responsibility and Authority*. Such actions might indicate a bypass of the director's authority. We have observed such violations of this principle frequently in the case of non-profit associations where there are full-time staffs headed by a staff director.

STRATEGY AND STRUCTURE UP TO THE PRESENT

In 1979 the president of the Art Association reported that the structure of the association existed very much as it had when it was restructured in the reorganization previously described. He had been on the board of the Art Association at the time of the reorganization, and it soon became evident to the board that the previous director did not have the management skills needed to carry out the recommendations in the organization survey report. The board then asked him to accept the position as president and he has been the president ever since. He said the reorganization had achieved the financial results anticipated. They were necessarily limited, however, as long as the Vietnam war lasted. When the war was over and the veterans returned with their desire for professional art careers and with government student loans to finance their tuition, the school enrollment quickly increased to over 400 students; the school had not been in financial difficulty since that time. This case illustrates the fact that circumstances beyond the control of an organization can have a drastic impact on its financial survival.

In 1988, the Art Association had grown to the size shown on the chart in Exhibit 11.4. The number of students has increased to over 700. Tuition has increased to $7,600 per year for a total $5.32 million tuition income. This contributed to a net income of over $200,000 last year. Employees have increased from five to forty-five. A sound organization structure has provided a firm basis for growth and financial success. Another survey might uncover some possibilities for staff reductions.

Exhibit 11.1
Organization Survey of the Art Association

Department on Organization — Oil Company

PROJECT WORK ORDER

Art Association — Administrative Staff

Title: Organization Study   Project No. 1

Requested by: L.L. Smith, T.I. Jones   Date Assigned: 4/21/74

Date due: 7/1/74   Assigned to: F.E. Brown and others

Estimated Time Required: 25 man days

OBJECTIVE:
1. Develop a sound and workable plan of organization for the administrative staff of the Art Association.

2. Develop as necessary improvements in policies, methods and procedures, records and reports, and related activities to ensure economical administration and to facilitate the progress of the association.

PLAN: (Principal aspects of work to be done, and schedule, as appropriate)

Section I

1. Through personal contact with each member of the staff, discuss and observe the working assignments, methods used, workload, currency of work, and related activities.

2. Evaluate the end purpose and the need for each activity; in this connection, study the various subjects listed in Section II, including such additional items as may be advisable for study or analysis as the review progresses.

3. Observe the working relationship with the School of Fine Arts and evaluate the services performed for the school.

4. Prepare position descriptions that will clearly state duties and relationships of each employee.

5. Prepare an organizational manual that will establish at the management level the basic functions, responsibilities, relationships, and authority for key members of the administrative organization.
   NOTE: This will include the relationships of the staff with the policy-making group, which will be specifically defined in the organization manual.

6. Evaluate each job for the development of a salary schedule.

7. At the conclusion of the review, prepare a report covering observations and recommendations for changes considered necessary to achieve the foregoing objective.

Section II

Study the various subjects listed below, including such additional items as may be advisable for study or analysis, as the review progresses:

1. Plan of organization.

2. Policies.

3. Methods, procedures, records, and reports, including those pertaining to accounting controls over expenditure authorizations and vouchering systems involved in each accounting.

4. Required number of employees to accomplish the essential work.

5. Budgetary preparation and use as a control over costs.

6. Need for a position of managing director.

7. Operation of the art supply store and the profit and loss realized therefrom.

8. Operation of the cafeteria by association employees and the possibility of arranging for such services to be rendered by a caterer.

9. Personnel policies.

10. Preparation of a concise brochure, which will set forth the history of the Art Association, its organization, its financial structure, sources of revenue, membership, relationships to the Institute of Fine Arts, trust funds, endowment funds, or any other information pertinent to its past history and future progress.

11. Adequacy of auditing procedures.

12. Purchasing system.

13. Validity of charges from other groups, such as state university charges for accrediting services.

14. Need for publicity and appropriate staff personnel to perform such service.

15. Need for secretarial assistance to all members of the staff and to the policy-making group.

16. Effectiveness of part-time help from students and the control over the use of such help.

17. Contemplated programs and commitments.

18. Methods, time, and cost of registering students.

19. Building arrangements and facilities, including operating costs.

20. Financial or tuition support given to students.

OIL COMPANY
October 1, 1974

ART ASSOCIATION
SURVEY OF
ADMINISTRATIVE STAFF

BOARD OF DIRECTORS,
THE ART ASSOCIATION

This report summarizes the findings and recommendations resulting from the survey of the administrative staff of the Art Association and its School of Fine Arts made at your request.

PURPOSE

The principal purpose was to develop:

1. A sound and workable plan of organization for the administrative staff.

2. Improvements as necessary in policies, methods and procedures, records and reports, and related activities to ensure economical administration, and to facilitate the progress of the association.

SCOPE OF THE REVIEW

The review included an overall survey of the functions and activities of the respective members of the association's and school's salaried staff, other than personnel engaged in academic endeavors.

The internal review was conducted mainly on the basis of discussions with key personnel; review and analysis of work performance information; analyses of operating records and statistical reports; review of correspondence and published material; and general observation and review of the application of policies and procedures.

SUMMARY OF PRINCIPAL FINDINGS

The principal findings, developed from the review, are summarized as follows: *Administrative Staff-Combined Salaried Personnel of the Art Association and School, except Academic Personnel*

1. The Constitution of the Art Association states that "The object of this organization shall be to maintain a Museum of Fine Arts and School of Fine Arts, to provide for and conduct exhibitions . . . and to unite in fellowship the membership of the Association and to promote the cultivation of the Fine Arts."

   Since the Museum of Fine Arts now operates independently, the maintenance of the School of Fine Arts appears to be the major activity of the Art Association. Further, the administrative staff activities of both the association and the school are so closely interrelated that, for the purposes of this review, it has been necessary to consider them as a single organization.

2. The present plan of organization is not the most effective type to provide fully coordinated and economic control over the various activities of the staff, in that operations are conducted on a separate and largely self-contained small unit basis, each requiring the immediate supervision of the director. In a small organization, this highly functionalized plan is not an efficient type of operation. In addition, this arrangement has resulted in rigidity in the assignment of workload and is conducive to the exercise of individual prerogatives to the extent beyond that considered economical in a small organization.

3. The administrative detail burden placed upon the director arising in connection with other than academic activities, i.e., operations and publicity, is wasteful of his time and effort. This is due in part to the organizational arrangement whereunder he is obliged to coordinate and supervise details that normally would be concentrated in certain supporting positions. The present arrangement of offices, to some extent, fosters self-containment and inefficiency.

4. The present arrangement of a separate salaried secretary for the Art Association does not appear warranted. Art Association relations, school outside relations, and overall publicity and public relations are sufficiently similar in conduct and common in end purpose that such closely related functions should be combined

for more effective administration and maximum utilization of the salaried personnel, under the immediate supervision of the director. Service to the Art Association would continue to be provided as required under such an arrangement.

Art Association School of Fine Arts
Beyond the scope of the requested review of the administrative staff, the following findings have come to attention. They bear upon the continued or long-range existence of the school.

1. A deficit situation, as reflected in the annual audits, has persisted since 1969, and the trend appears to challenge the continued existence of the school. The following are total figures and include, in the 1973 revenue, the "single-shot" advantage of the Special Contributions Campaign proceeds of approximately $24,000.

Fiscal Year Ending June 30	Revenues	Expenses	Effect
1969	$306,800	$289,600	$17,200 Gain
1970	350,000	360,000	(10,000) Loss
1971	276,000	308,000	(32,000) Loss
1972	261,600	271,000	(9,800) Loss
1973	195,400	235,000	(39,600) Loss

It is our understanding that the foregoing deficits have been alleviated by calling upon available surpluses and use of some unrestricted funds (that have now or will become practically exhausted). This appears to represent a true condition of the finances, rather than a calculated deficit policy to be capitalized upon for financial support publicity.

2. The forecast of income and expense prepared for the fiscal year ending June 30,1974, indicated that a net loss of about $33,000 will be sustained. The major breakdowns in income and expenses are as follows:

Income

Membership dues	$15,000	
Tuition	101,000	
Store sales gross profit	11,400	
Miscellaneous	14,600	
Total		$142,000
Expected Donations		6,000
Total		$148,000

Expense

Salaries—Faculty	$70,000	
Administrative	72,000	
Total		$142,000
Utilities	$7,400	
School Advertising	4,000	
Bulletin Printing	3,000	
Telephone and Telegraph	2,200	
Stationery and Supplies	2,200	
Insurance	2,000	
Catalogs	3,400	

Miscellaneous (prizes, exhibits, etc.)	14,800	
Total		39,000
Total Expense		181,000
Net Loss		($ 33,000)

NOTE: An examination of the income and expense to the end of the fall term indicates a loss of about $24,000 to January 31, 1974. A rough projection through the spring term indicates a substantial loss to the $24,000 by the end of the spring term. This generally substantiates the deficit condition as forecasted at the beginning of the fiscal year.

3. It will be seen from the above condensed figures that the greater part of expense consists of items not susceptible of large economies. Some saving in time and manpower will result from adoption of recommendations contained in this report, probably amounting to the salaries of about two positions, less some offsetting part-time assistance and some minor operating economies, both resulting in a total savings of possibly $8,000 to $10,000 annually.

4. The survey points up the need for consideration of basic problems that will be faced by the school within the immediate foreseeable future:

   A. Need for additional funds with which to meet essential expenditures. It is estimated that operations can be carried to June 30, 1974, without exhausting the principal of a trust fund (Helen K. Jones Fund) that can be used for the purpose (about $46,000). Unless the number of students can be increased (this requires intensive advertising and publicity), the prospect of using the entire fund principal is almost a certainty during the next year.

   B. Need for necessary repairs and replacements to buildings and improvements.

   C. Need for long-range planning giving consideration to retention of the present buildings and grounds. Total area of the land is about 90,000 square feet, upon which the building occupies about 20,000 square feet, leaving 70,000 square feet of valuable property unused. The building itself has about 40,000 square feet including all levels, corridors, locker rooms, and so forth. About 30,000 square feet is actually being used. Upkeep of the building involves considerable expense.

   One problem that must be faced by the board of directors is whether the land and buildings should be sold and more suitable, compact, and comfortable quarters found elsewhere. If the decision is made to retain the present location, then necessary repairs and replacements must be considered. Further, consideration should be given to either (1) selling or leasing the unused portion of real estate or, (2) erecting suitable facilities for income producing purposes.

5. Additional possibilities for improvement in financial condition are:
   A. Elimination of all possible non-profitable academic courses.
   B. Expansion of present publicity program designed to attract potential part-time and full-time students from outlying areas.
   C. Institution of additional academic courses designed to attract the "Sunday" or "hobby" type artist.

All of these matters are major policy decisions that must be made by the board of directors. It would perhaps be desirable to conduct an economic study with valuations and estimates to be used as a basis for determining a future course of action.

Major Recommendations—Administrative Staff

1. Assign to the director full responsibility for all activities of the administrative staff of the School of Fine Arts and Art Association, with direct accountability to the executive committee of the board of directors for proper fulfillment of such duties under suitable working arrangements with the respective other committees of the board. Approve the proposed Management Guide for the position of director, provided as a part of this report, setting forth such responsibilities and authority.

   Appoint the director as an ex officio member of the executive committee and board of directors to be present at all meetings, except when specifically excused, to provide full information regarding the academic and operating progress of the school, and such related subjects as arise therewith.

2. Make greater use of the executive committee, as a means of executive control as provided in the bylaws, to reduce the need for full board of directors meetings as practiced now and to reduce frequency of board meetings.

3. Redesign the administrative staff organization structure to relieve the director of the substantial detail currently performed, and to permit greater freedom for attention to major school projects considered essential to future progress.

4. Concentrate in a single organization unit under a new position of administrative assistant all functions and activities relating to finance, office operations, student registrations, and related services, bookstore conduct, purchasing, building maintenance, and other subjects normally considered as subject to recognized business controls and appraisals. Eliminate the present position of registrar.

5. Concentrate in another single organization unit under a new position of public and art association relations representative all functions and activities relating to school publicity, public relations, Art Association services and programs, bulletin, motion picture presentations, and speaker scheduling, advertising, shows and exhibits, and other subjects recognized as being within the broad field of public or outside aggressive endeavors. Eliminate the present position of executive secretary-Art Association, and also eliminate the present position of public relations, publicity, and secretary to director.

6. Rearrange the office space occupancy to provide for maximum supervisory efficiency and to achieve full flexibility in the assignment of the current workload to office personnel.

7. Reassign the essential functions and activities to the positions as proposed in the attached manpower summary and organization chart (see Exhibits 11.2 and 11.3).

8. Institute the proposed improvements in methods of operation, service, accounting procedures, and general activities, as set forth in detailed recommendations elsewhere in this report, to achieve greater overall economy and efficiency.

9. Beyond the scope of the requested administrative staff review—board of directors to inaugurate an economic study with valuations and estimates to be used as a basis for determining a future course of action.

Conclusion

Mr. James Johnson, the director, and other members of the administrative staff rendered splendid support and cooperation throughout the entire course of the review. Certain of the proposals contained in the report are the result of suggestions offered by members of the organization.

In conclusion, we wish to express our appreciation for the complete and excellent assistance received during the entire review from the director and all members of the organization.

T. I. Jones, Organization
Counsel-in-Charge
F. E. Brown
J. W. White

Endorsed by
L. L. Smith, Manager, Organization
Planning, The Oil Company

DETAILED RECOMMENDATIONS

Administrative Staff

1. Assign to the Director full responsibility for all activities of the administrative staff of the School of Fine Arts and Art Association, with direct accountability of such duties under suitable working arrangements with the respective other committees of the board. Approve the proposed Management Guide for the position of director, provided as a part of this report, setting forth such responsibilities and authority.

2. Appoint the director as an ex officio member of the executive committee and board of directors to be present at all meetings, except when specifically excused, to provide full information regarding the academic and operating progress of the school, and such related subjects as arise therewith.

3. Make greater use of the executive committee, as a means of executive control, as provided in the bylaws, to reduce the need for full board of directors meetings as practiced now, and to reduce frequency of board meetings.

4. Redesign the administrative staff organization structure to relieve the director of the substantial detail currently performed, and to permit greater freedom for attention to major school projects considered essential to future progress.

5. Concentrate in a single organization unit under a new position of administrative assistant all functions and activities relating to finance, office operations, student registrations and related services, bookstore conduct, purchasing, building maintenance, and other subjects normally considered as subject to recognized business controls and appraisals. Eliminate the present position of registrar.

6. Concentrate in another single organization unit under a new position of public and art association relations representative all functions and activities relating to school publicity, public relations, Art Association services and programs,

bulletin, motion picture presentations and speaker scheduling, advertising, shows and exhibits, and other subjects recognized as being within the broad field of public or outside aggressive endeavors. Eliminate the present position of executive secretary-Art Association and also eliminate the present position of public relations, publicity, and secretary to director.

7. Assign to the director's position full responsibility for the direction of the respective organization units, and arrange for all important reports and related matters to be subject to release by the director.

8. Rearrange the office space occupancy to provide for maximum supervisory efficiency, and to achieve full flexibility in the assignment of the current workload to office personnel. Such an office revamp will be in accord with the proposed organization arrangement. This will involve the removal of one wall, installation of a suitable counter at standing height, moving the director to the present location of the registrar and moving the present Art Association office to the main floor (see Exhibit 11.5).

9. Reassign the essential functions and activities to the positions as proposed in the attached manpower summary and organization chart (see Exhibit 11.3) and as indicated in the attached list of position duties.

10. Authorize the following salary schedule for the administrative staff positions to be administered under a merit policy as determined by the board of directors:

Suggested Salary Ranges
Administrative Staff Positions
Art Association
School of Fine Arts
Monthly Salaries Based Upon 35-Hour Week

	Minimum	Community Average	Maximum
Director-School of Fine Arts (As Established by Executive Committee)			
Class I—Administrative Assistant	$1,005	$1,125	$1,275
Class II—Representative-Public and Art Association Relations	900	1,005	1,125
Class II—Accountant-Clerk Typist	900	1,005	1,125
Class III—(Open) Full Secretarial Work—Part-Time Hourly Equivalent of:	720	810	900
Class IV—(Open) Limited Secretarial Work—Part-Time Hourly Equivalent of:	645	720	810
OPERATING EMPLOYEE—Building Maintenance Man—Janitor (40-Hour Week)	765	840	930
PART-TIME EMPLOYEES—Various	(As Established by Director)		

Cafeteria

11. Discontinue the operation of the cafeteria by the present position of registrar. The cafeteria should be operated either by a professional catering service, the

student council, or individual members of the student body. The School of Fine Arts should retain responsibility for ensuring compliance to proper standards of service, quality, and sanitation.

Registration

12. Discontinue preparing daily penciled record of registrations, and discontinue typing two copies of this record. Rely on position of accountant to maintain record of numbers of student's registration forms as received, as a control to preclude unauthorized withdrawals from stores.

13. Discontinue preparation of student record form and rely on copy of student registration form for required information.

14. Establish a program for record keeping that will provide the following:
    A. Review of all material prior to filing, destruction of material not required to be filed, and notation of a destruction date on material not requiring permanent retention.
    B. Review of all material in files at the close of each year and destruction of all material not requiring permanent retention.
    C. Segregation of student records between active and inactive to facilitate reference.
    D. Removal to storage of all material over two years old.

15. Discontinue preparation and maintenance of student files listing name, address, telephone number, class schedule, and locker number. Rely on file of student's registration form for required information.

16. Discontinue preparation of duplicate copy of notification to models to report to work. Rely on schedule that is prepared three weeks in advance, and make notation on such schedule when models indicate acceptance of assignment.

17. Discontinue using receipt form to obtain receipt from models upon payment of fees. Prepare two copies of authorization for payment of model form and obtain signature of models on one copy of such form as support to petty cash fund.

18. Utilize the services of the position of librarian to assist in performing activities of the administrative staff that can be accomplished in the library, such as stuffing envelopes, mailing bills and bulletins, and miscellaneous typing, etc.

19. Eliminate petty cash fund now maintained by position of receptionist, and cause all petty cash payments during the daytime to be made by position of accountant.

20. Revise the present method of billing members of the Art Association so that annual dues for all members fall due at the beginning of the fiscal year. To accomplish this, compute dues on a monthly basis, and bill members for the number of months between the anniversary date of each membership and the close of that final year. All future billings can then be made once each year for all members at one time. Arrange to have bills prepared and mailed by a commercial Addressograph label concern. Transfer all files relating to membership dues to the custody of the accountant.

21. Eliminate the position of receptionist and transfer the duties now performed

by that function to other positions as indicated:

A. To the proposed position of administrative assistant: (1) Interviewing; (2) Receipt of all incoming telephone calls from 9 A.M. to 11 A.M.; (3) Receipt and distribution of mail.

B. To the position of accountant: (1) Preparation of checks; (2) Scheduling and payment of models; (3) Assignment of lockers and maintenance of cash deposits and records; (4) Billing of Art Association membership. See additional recommendations on this subject.

C. To the position of librarian: (1) Receipt of all incoming telephone calls from 11 A.M. to 5 P.M.; (2) Miscellaneous typing; (3) Mailing of catalogs and other similar items; (4) Maintenance of catalog mailing list; (5) Maintenance and posting of bulletin board.

Accounting and Related Subjects

22. Institute the pegboard system for writing basic accounting documents in one operation and avoid copying the same figues from one record to another; this procedure is particularly adaptable to accounts receivable, accounts payable, and payroll. This will require the purchase of a speed writing board and a posting unit to hold accounts receivable ledger cards (total cost approximately $50, plus some small cost of forms). It would be advisable to place the accounts receivable feature into effect at once, but defer accounts payable and payroll until present expensive forms are depleted and the accountant has acquired familiarity with the system.

A. Discontinue present type of receipt form. One receipt form should be designed to serve all purposes.

B. Discontinue present type of ledger sheet for accounts receivable.

C. Discontinue separate posting to accounts receivable.

D. Discontinue posting detail to "Record of Cash Received." Post totals only as prescribed by recommended procedure.

When possible, as mentioned, adopt a similar system for accounts payable and the payroll. At that time, remittance advice can be discontinued and copies of invoices can be returned to vendors as evidence of payment. All data, under this system, will be prepared in longhand and not typed for both the payroll and accounts payable. The company systems men will render free assistance in establishing this system and the design of necessary forms. The Country School for Boys uses the system as described. The system can be seen in operation, if desired.

23. Cause the position of accountant to take over certain record-keeping duties of other positions, as described elsewhere herein.

24. Cause the position of administrative assistant to reconcile the bank accounts in the interest of improved internal control.

25. Grant check-signing authority to the position of administrative assistant for checks drawn on the general fund, and release officers of the Art Association from this routine detail. Retain officers' authority for trust fund and other account fund withdrawals.

26. Discontinue detailed posting of names, dates, expense information, and account numbers to the office fund voucher. Post summary to voucher only for

posting to ledger. Receipts show all essential information and are the original source documents for audit purposes. Tally on a working paper the use of models in classes for analytical purposes at the close of each term, as follows:

	CLASS #						
Voucher Date	*104*	*103*	*102*	*101*	*100*	*99*	*98*
2/17/74	11	1	11	1	1	11	1
3/31/74	111	11	111	1	1	1	11

27. Restrict the use of Storeroom Requisition—C-503 to items not in stock that must be ordered from vendors to meet instructors' needs. Cause the position of administrative assistant to approve requisitions.

28. Institute the use of standing orders on vendors for supplies ordered frequently; phone call can be made direct to vendor for material; packing slip that arrives with material can be initialed and sent to the accountant as authority to pay invoices against the standing orders. Cause accountant to check invoices against all deliveries, tags, and receipt of material copies.

29. Discontinue maintaining stores ledger on withdrawals by veterans. Work from yellow copies of standard register forms.

30. Discontinue preparation of purchase and sales report on stores. Prepare profit and loss for the month on average retail mark-up basis.

31. Arrange to dispose of obsolete stock in stores through making a deal with Flax* or others to take over such items at a discount, and credit the school for future purchases. This includes unpopular paint kits, reducing glass, dry flow ink, paints, construction paper, unpopular and expensive books, etc.

32. Subdivide shelves so as to prevent double-stocking that causes great inconvenience in handling fast-moving items.

33. Provide some minimum shelving for storing surplus stocks in the loft above the store.

General

34. Consider the appropriateness of preparing a concise brochure that will set forth the history of the Art Association, its organization, its financial structure, sources of income, membership, relationship to the School of Fine Arts, trust funds, endowment funds, or any other information pertinent to its past history and future progress. Such a production could serve several purposes in the field of public relations.

35. Prepare in some suitable written form a statement of present personnel policies, setting forth working conditions and hours, overtime, vacations, holidays, time off with and without pay, and other related subjects, as appropriate, bearing upon employee relations.

36. Utilize professional office service organizations during beginning of school semesters to assist in peak workload situations to avoid excessive overtime, and to permit maintaining permanent paid staff at a minimum consistent with normal workload.

*Name of art supply store where they buy their art supplies.

ART ASSOCIATION – SCHOOL OF FINE ARTS
BALANCE SHEET AS OF DECEMBER 31, 1973

ASSETS

Cash in Northern Trust Company Account	$ 5,874.92	
Cash in Holding Account	1,000.00	
Cash in Bank	200.00	
A. Branden Savings Account	7,835.48	
Albert N. Bend Revolving Fund	20.00	
Petty Cash Accounts	1,270.00	
AA Building Maintenance Account	19,612.40	
Total Cash on Hand and in Banks		$ 35,812.80
Accounts Receivable—Non-Veterans and		
and Vietnam Veterans	$ 6,418.76	
Accounts Receivable—346 Veterans	4,646.42	
Accounts Receivable—16 Veterans	650.02	
Accounts Receivable—Veterans		
(State University)	569.00	
Accounts Receivable-Others	202.06	
		12,486.26
Accounts Receivable—Trust Funds		2,913.74
Store Inventory as of 7/1/73		19,343.46
Janitor Supply Inventory as of 7/1/73		747.54
Unexpired Insurance		3,117.78
Land and Improvements	$819,051.96	
Less: Reserve for Depreciation	361,438.26	
		457,613.70
TOTAL ASSETS		$532,035.28

LIABILITIES

Accounts Payable		$ 9,644.12
Accrued Payroll Taxes		1,361.34
Sales Tax Payable		160.48
Agency Funds: Women's Auxiliary	$1,188.30	
Alumni Association	31.26	
Student Association	(115.66)	
Artists' Council	693.42	
		1,797.32
Special Funds: Memorial Fund	$ 734.26	
Robert Fur		
Memorial Fund	381.50	
M. Cunning Memorial		
Fund	750.00	
A. Brand Memorial		
Fund	7,985.48	
Bend Revolving		
Memorial Fund	9,000.00	

Other Funds	2,900.28	
Prize Fund	550.00	
		22,301.52
Suspense Account		38.00
Helen Jones Fund Loan Payable		9,000.00
TOTAL LIABILITIES		$ 44,302.78

Capital		$533,709.38
Less: Surplus as of		
June 30	$37,104.38	
Loss 7/1/74 to		
12/31/74	8,872.50	
Total Decrease in Capital		45,976.88
		487,732.50
TOTAL LIABILITIES AND CAPITAL		$532,035.28

ART ASSOCIATION

MAJOR EXPENSE
REPAIRS AND REPLACEMENTS
REQUIRED IN NEXT YEAR OR TWO

Water System	$20,000
Roof	2,000
Painting and Miscellaneous Repair	4,000
Furnishings	4,000
Lighting	4,000
Necessary Expansion of Library Facilities	5,000
Repairs Required by Fire Department	1,000
TOTAL	$40,000

ART ASSOCIATION

GROUND AND BUILDING AREAS

	SQUARE FEET AREA	TOTAL SQUARE FEET	
Students			
Drafting Rooms	5	3,000	
Studios	8	8,300	
Shops and Laboratories	5	6,000	
Class and Lecture Rooms	2	2,500	
			19,800
Faculty Offices			1,000
Administrative Offices			1,000
Library			1,200
Gallery			1,000

Cafeteria		1,200
Supply Store		1,000
Rest Rooms and Locker Rooms	Approx.	4,000
Total Space Actually Used		30,200
		75%

APPROXIMATE TOTAL SPACE	
(Includes Corridors, Stairs, Locker Rooms)	40,000
Lot Area—Approximate	90,000
Portion Occupied by Building	20,000
Excess Lot Area	70,000

REPORT EXHIBITS

NOTE: A complete set of exhibits was made up from (1) the various stationery forms now used by the school proposed for discontinuance or simplification and (2) the suggested new forms and procedures, and *are included as a part of the master copy* of this report to be furnished to the director for installation, upon approval of the recommendations by the board of directors.

MANAGEMENT GUIDE
DIRECTOR
SCHOOL OF FINE ARTS

I. *FUNCTION*

Executes the policies of the board of directors. Responsible for overall direction, control, and coordination of the School of Fine Arts within the scope of such board policies, including the formulation and execution of approved programs involving planning and direction of the administrative staff and faculty, enlisting and maintaining broad community, and other participation in the school's program, publicizing its art education activities and programs, either personally or by direction, and other related activities.

II. *RESPONSIBILITIES AND AUTHORITY*

The responsibilities and authority stated below are subject to the provisions of the bylaws and other policies of the board of directors.

A. *Activities*

1. Plans, directs, and coordinates the activities of the School of Fine Arts in meeting the overall objectives of the Art Association.

2. Formulates, recommends, and executes approved programs pertaining to the immediate academic endeavors of the school in its respective fields of art education, including necessary faculty arrangements and assignments.

3. Develops and recommends long-range plans of school development and improvement; proposes such short-time expedients as are practicable to meet current situations.

4. Plans and directs the efforts of the administrative staff in the conduct of all phases of the school's student and business affairs to achieve full utilization of personnel assigned and maximum efficiency of operation.

5. Promotes the public acceptance and continued success of the school in meeting the objectives of the Art Association through dignified public relations and publicity through all available channels. Directs the effort of the staff in planning, developing, and accomplishing the fullest public acceptance of the school.

6. Conceives and assists with new programs, methods, and measures to increase the influence and effectiveness of the Art Association in its particular efforts to gain the maximum financial support of the School of Fine Arts, including the development of any detailed steps required.

7. Integrates the activities of the administrative staff to the fullest extent in providing assistance and support to the efforts of the various committees of the Art Association in the conduct of programs relating to their particular objectives as they affect the school.

B. *Organization*

1. Develops and establishes the plan of organization for the administrative staff and faculty designed to meet the current requirements; reviews and alters this plan as desirable.

2. Adds, alters, or eliminates positions within the organization plan as appropriate, maintaining manpower consistent with needs and within approved limits of expenditure budget. Recommends in cases involving reallocations of budgeted amounts.

3. Arranges for the preparation of position or job description, and recommends changes in position appraisals.

C. *Personnel*

1. Selects, assigns, and separates administrative staff employees and faculty members.

2. Administers personnel programs, consistent with approved policies. Recommends on changes in personnel policies, as conditions change and as the need arises.

3. Develops and administers equitable schedules for the remuneration of staff employees, reviewing and recommending modifications as circumstances require.

D. *Finances*

1. Prepares and submits an annual budget showing current financial status, anticipated revenue, and estimated operating, capital, and special project expenditures; recommends revisions as appropriate.

2. Develops improved methods of extending present available finances to greater areas of education consistent with the objectives of the Art Association.

3. Directs the purchasing activities relating to all phases of the school and related activities to assure that proper standards of quality and perfor-

mance are maintained, and that such purchases are consistent with the overall Art Association interest. Maintains adequate controls over inventories to obtain maximum utilization.

4. Establishes and administers effective internal controls to safeguard the assets against loss through dishonesty or negligence.

III. *LIMITS OF AUTHORITY*

A. *Capital Expenditures:* Authorizes capital expenditures previously approved in the budget, with major individual items subject to specific approval by the executive committee. Recommends on items not in the budget.

B. *Operating and Maintenance Expenditures:* Authorizes operating and maintenance expenditures approved in the budget, and recommends as to items not included in the budget.

C. *Execution of Contracts:* Executes contracts on behalf of the School of Fine Arts for the purchase of materials, equipment, and services to be rendered to the school for items within the director's authority. Refers contracts beyond his authority to the executive committee.

D. *Sale of School Assets:* Recommends to the executive committee sale of any school assets.

E. *Scholarships:* Authorizes expenditures for scholarships approved under established arrangements; and approves credit or offset to tuition charges for working scholarships under existing educational finance policies.

F. *Expense of Employees:* Approves expense reports of school's employees, including minor expenses of the director consistent with established practice of the executive committee. Refers extraordinary expenses to the executive committee.

G. *Bank Accounts:* Recommends to the executive committee school policies relating to banking practices and procedures.

H. *Public Relations and Other Expenditures Relating to the School and Art Association Publicity:* Authorizes expenditures approved in the budget and recommends items not in the budget.

I. *Salary Administration:* Approves initial salaries of the administrative staff and faculty and salary increases within the limits of the salary schedules and policies established by the executive committee.

J. *Personnel Policies:* Authorizes application of personnel policies as established by the executive committee.

K. *Other Expenditures and School Policies:* Recommends them to executive committee and authorizes within specifically approved limits.

IV. *RELATIONSHIPS*

A. *Executive Committee*

Reports to and is accountable to the executive committee. Advises, consults with, and informs the executive committee on matters affecting administrative staff, faculty, school, Art Association, and related activities, making regular or special reports as required, or as the director deems necessary. To the extent appropriate, serves in a liaison capacity among the individual members of the executive committee in rendering assistance and relieving them on detail matters.

B. *Other Committees of the Art Association*

Works closely with, and provides assistance to, the various other committees of the Art Association in carrying forward their respective programs toward achieving the objectives of the Art Association.

C. *Other Schools and Art Associations and Museums*

Maintains appropriate relationships with other schools, art associations and museums of a character consistent with the school's prestige and effectiveness in its fields of education endeavors.

D. *Public*

Meets with individuals and various groups on matters bearing upon the educational, financial, and other aspects of the school's and Art Association's activities; resolves the problems, or makes suitable recommendations to the best advantage of all parties concerned.

Meets with representatives of the press, radio, and television; prepares news releases and other informative materials for publication.

E. *Other Organizations*

Maintains appropriate relationships with professional, social, civic, and other associations and organizations, as desirable, in the interest of the School of Fine Arts and the Art Association.

APPROVED:_____

DATE: _____

POSITION DUTIES

Administrative Assistant

Provides relief to the director on administrative detail and supervises the functions and activities relating to finance, office operations, student registration, and related services, student employment services, bookstore conduct, purchasing, building maintenance, and other matters primarily of business character. It includes acting as registrar of students and performing general office activities as necessary in addition to providing assistance on administrative details, such as correspondence, reports, visitors, student matters, and other subjects as assigned.

Representative—Public and Art Association Relations

Provides assistance to the director on all matters relating to public and Art Association relations. This involves such publicity matters as news releases, advertising, brochures, posters, catalogs, The Bulletin, and other forms of publicity. It includes public relations requiring outside contacts, such as radio, press, television, and various public groups and all activities of the Art Association and its various committees, Women's Auxiliary, and Artists' Council. It extends to all forms of relationships that arise in promotion of the school's new motion picture film and related programming of exhibitions and speakers. This position, broadly speaking, generally is to develop, recommend, and carry out all types of relationships that are designed to increase the prestige and recognition of the school and Art Association with fields of art education and art appreciation.

Accountant/Clerk

As supervised by the administrative assistant performs the accounting activities arising in connection with the maintenance of the necessary financial records and reports of the Art Association and School of Fine Arts. Prepares regular and special statements as necessary. Performs general office clerical activities in connection with the student and business affairs, as assigned. Performs such necessary typing as may be required.

Building Maintenance Man—Janitor

As supervised by the administrative assistant, performs essential janitorial service throughout the School of Fine Arts main building and related buildings, including such grounds upkeep as is necessary. Performs minor and emergency building maintenance activities as required, and such other services of a general character as may be assigned from time to time.

Part-Time Employees and Working Scholarships

As supervised by the administrative assistant, or representative-public and Art Association relations, performs such services assigned as part-time work. Makes such reports and schedules of work assignments as requested to facilitate proper administrative control over such activities.

Exhibit 11.2 Organization Plan (Phase I): Art Association

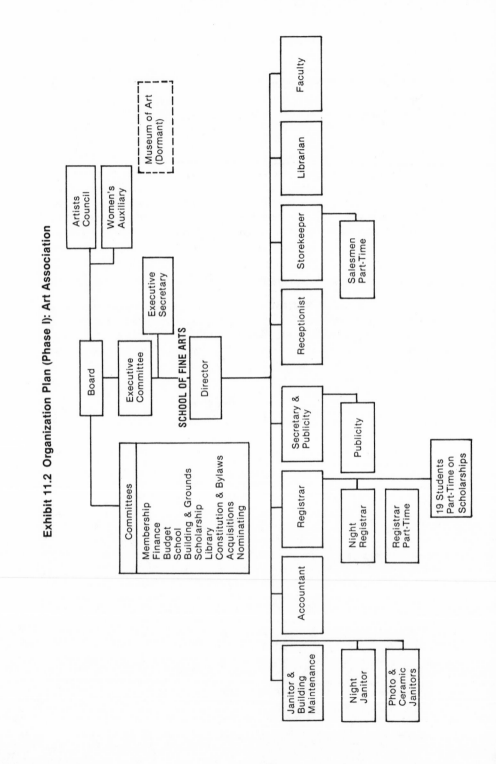

Exhibit 11.3 Proposed Organization Plan (Phase I): Art Association

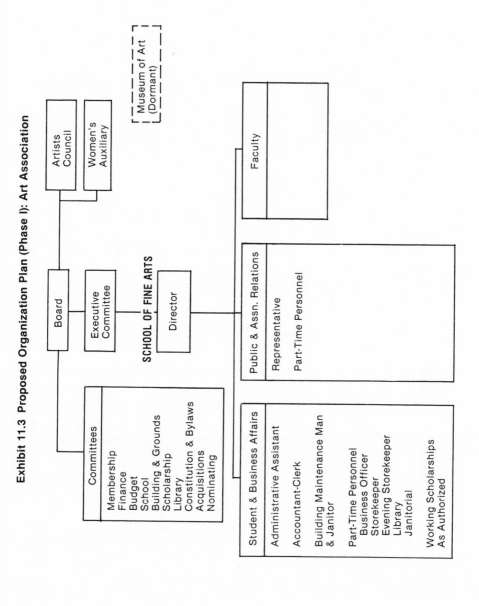

Exhibit 11.4 Organization Plan (Phase II), 1988: Art Association

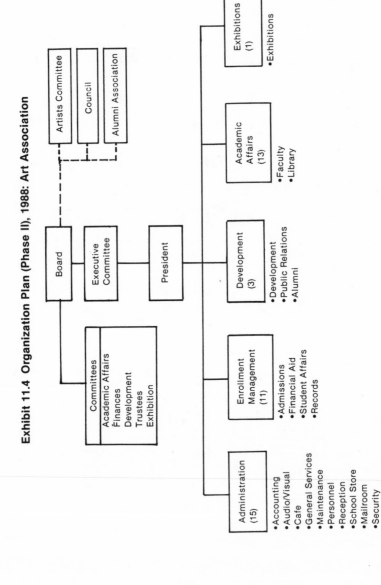

Note: Numbers in parentheses are numbers of full-time employees.

220

Exhibit 11.5 Office Arrangement (Phase I): Art Association

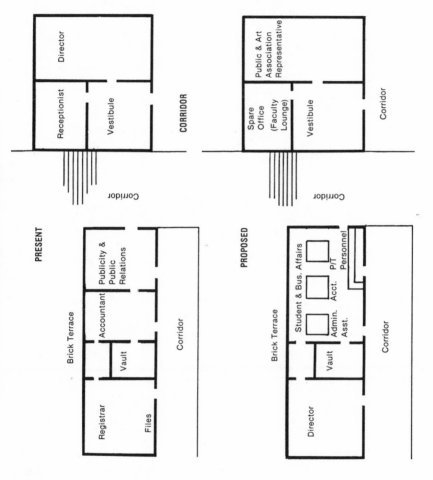

Part III

The Future

12

The Future of Organization Planning

At the beginning of this chapter we wish to recall the aims and limitations of this book. We have sought to provide a workbook for managers on how to apply the principles to design and control the organization structure. For purposes of illustration, actual cases have been taken from the author's experience. Two case examples concern large business organizations in planned transition from functional to divisionalized structures; we have tried, however, to help the average businessman analyze his own organization structure by including in our examples other types of smaller organizations undergoing planned structural change. We have used, for comparative analysis, three sizes of business enterprises (an automobile company, a recreation company, and a hard rubber company), a church diocese, a local chapter of a management association, and an art school. These reorganization experiences were not given briefly just to give substance to our analysis. They were given in detail and in extended time span so as to give the businessman concrete examples through which he could learn to assemble the necessary facts, analyze them and solve complex problems of organization structure and design. Proven techniques of compilation, analysis, and plan evaluation are thoroughly explained using actual cases as illustrative examples. Any manager or staff man should have no difficulty in evaluating the structure of his company or component using these techniques of organization analysis and design. We have also attempted to reappraise and add knowledge to the findings of Ginzberg and Reilley on successfully how to achieve planned structural change in the light of the experience in these cases. This book has been exploratory in nature with the following objectives:

1. To clarify the important organization planning function
2. To assess the strategic factors involved in the successful performance of this function by the chief executive working together with his organization planning staff
3. To consider how the joint efforts of the chief executive, his organization planning staff, and the line and staff managers at all levels can achieve and maintain a more effective top-management organization structure
4. To suggest the outline of future investigations likely to yield new knowledge and improvement in top-management organization planning and control practices

CLARIFICATION OF THE ORGANIZATION PLANNING FUNCTION

We have done all the above objectives through presenting concrete examples of the work of the chief executive and his organization planning staff in real-life cases of organizations undergoing major planned change. Further, the organization of the organization planning staff, the tools and techniques of organization planning, and the application of the principles of organization have been described in each example. We have understandably not included cases on hospitals and other types of special purpose service organizations with which we have had no organizing experience. We have concerned ourselves primarily with the structure and not with the dynamics of organization.

STRATEGIC FACTORS IN THE SUCCESSFUL PERFORMANCE OF ORGANIZATION PLANNING

In discussing each example we have analyzed the successes and, more important, the failures in the performance of the organization planning and control function so that the reader could clearly understand the strategic factors involved in the successful performance of this vital activity. We have given some suggestions for the professional manager on how to achieve and maintain a sound, well-designed organization structure, both overall and within the staff and division components.

HOW TO IMPROVE THE WORKING RELATIONSHIPS BETWEEN THE CHIEF EXECUTIVE AND HIS ORGANIZATION PLANNING STAFF

We have listed several ways for the chief executive of a large corporation to support his organization planning staff and several ways for the staff to merit his support. We have highlighted this as the critical strategic factor in the successful performance of the organization planning function.

FUTURE INVESTIGATIONS

In Chapter 4, we evaluated the experience from our case examples against the experiences and findings of Ginzberg and Reilley and pointed out some fruitful methods for more successfully effecting planned change in organizations of various sizes and types.

We have also borrowed from the social sciences and psychology a framework of comparative analysis—the Bonds of Organization—that should contribute to a better understanding of the dynamic nature of an organization as a multi-institutional system of response. The Bonds of Organization were outlined by E. Wight Bakke in his *Concept of the Social Organization*. We hope that this book will be but a first stage of a continuing investigation into successful, practical ways of making planned change in organization structures that will improve group performance and results.

The following presents a summary of the principal findings, and suggests the directions that hold promise for better understanding of the organization planning and control function and practices.

THE IMPORTANCE OF TIME

Our experience has thoroughly confirmed the importance of time as a finding of Ginzberg and Reilley. At the Automobile Company, top-management executives were expecting profit results only two years after the divisionalization program had been started. This was a completely unrealistic time frame in the light of the time it took Ford and other companies to get profit results from a similar divisionalization of their organization structures. It took Ford and the Automobile Company over six years; it took the Recreation Company over twelve years.

A BALANCE SHEET APPROACH

We fully agree with the finding of Ginzberg and Reilley that it is important to weigh the potential benefits against the costs before deciding to undertake a major top-management reorganization. In the cases of the Automobile Company and the Recreation Company, as has been true in the case of many other companies making a change to divisionalization, the change was in response to a survival crisis. To use the balance sheet approach in such an instance would be almost as ludicrous as a man with cancer counting up his pennies to see if he could afford an operation. However, we fully agree that the chief executive should never embark on a major reorganization without fully understanding the time, costs, and distasteful decisions that would be required in order to weather this traumatic experience successfully.

THE CRUCIAL ROLE OF THE CHIEF EXECUTIVE

In these and other major reorganization experiences, we have found effective participation of the CEO to be the critical success factor in the performance of the organization planning function. At the Automobile Company, results were never achieved until a trained professional manager replaced the lawyer as chief executive. At the Recreation Company, the limited "will to manage" of the founder's grandson seriously restricted the results of the reorganization effort. The bishop prevented the complete and full implementation of the reorganization plan in the church diocese because he lacked the motivation, the will, and the management skill to fully implement the reorganization plan. His replacement implemented the plans.

EFFECTIVE COMMUNICATION OF
ORGANIZATION STRUCTURE

The problem resulting from failure to communicate the new roles in the organization structure to key managers goes back to the crucial role of the chief executive officer, for he is, and must be, the chief communicator of any new overall plan of organization. When he does not understand the new plan, he cannot communicate it through his subordinates to the lower levels. At the Recreation Company, the organization planning staff gave many visual presentations on the new plan to the top executives, but the lack of in-depth understanding of the plan on the part of the chief executive prevented effective personal communication of the plan to his key executives and his subsequent assignment of tasks in accordance with the plan.

LEARNING NEW SKILLS AND NEW WORK PATTERNS
BY KEY EXECUTIVES

At both the Recreation Company and the Automobile Company the key executives did not learn their new roles, because both chief executives knew too little about the new plans to teach the key executives their new roles under the plan.

ALIGNMENT AND REINFORCEMENT

At neither company were the chief executives sufficiently knowledgeable about the new roles to use reinforcements effectively, such as performance appraisal, compensation, and management incentives, to encourage the necessary change in the performance of key subordinates.

BALANCED PROGRESS

At neither company were there effective written monthly progress reports from the organization planning staff to the chief executive officer. At the Recreation Company, the chief executive thought he had completely implemented the organization change when he had filled the four new positions of group executives and the position of president and chief operating officer. When that staffing job was accomplished, he felt he had no further need for a strong organization planning staff. He did not understand that the change required not only putting men into the new positions, but that these men had to be qualified, and they had to be further trained by him in their new roles. The chief executive did not ask for, and did not get, any progress reports from the staff; he felt fully capable of assessing staff progress on a personal basis. We fully agree, however, that the program should be thoroughly planned in every step and that there should be periodic progress reports going to the chief executive as these steps are accomplished (see Exhibit 6.1).

UNIQUENESS OF THE ORGANIZATION

Here our findings thoroughly support the findings of Ginzberg and Reilley. In our case examples, we have made every effort to give the reader enough of the unique history of the organization so that he could evaluate the basic problem, the staff's approaches to the problem, the organization changes that took place, and the results in improved performance. Every organization survey should go thoroughly into the unique history of the development of the organization structure over the past five or ten years in order for the analyst to understand the reason for abnormalities in the present structure. In developing these cases, we were careful to describe the history of the organization prior to analysis of structure, and to present our conclusions. We were also careful to recommend a complete manpower inventory, including the work histories, abilities, and aptitudes of the key executives, because such an inventory as well as the structure, are unique.

In addition to the above findings, which in general reinforce the findings of Ginzberg and Reilley, we have some new findings to present.

NEED FOR A BROAD BUSINESS SURVEY
AND STATEMENT OF OBJECTIVES

While it is true that an organization planner can develop some specific objectives for the organization in order to design the structure through interviews and discussions with the key executives, and through reading their speeches, this is usually not enough to provide a sound basis for major changes in structure. Preferably a broad business study should first be conducted by trained market and financial analysts. This should cover the position and objectives of the company in each of the major product businesses in which it participates, including the product line, financial resources, and many other factors. At the Automobile Company, the marketing staff made such a study of the air conditioning business before the organization planning staff was finally able to design the structure of the air conditioning division properly. Once the decision was made to stay in the air conditioning business and make the large capital investment required to redo the product line completely, it was then feasible for the organization staff to recommend a suitable top-management organization structure in order for the division to carry out this strategy.

NEED FOR MAN SPECIFICATIONS

We have found that it is not enough to recommend new position descriptions in the organization survey report; they should also be accompanied by man specifications for each key position in the new structure. In this way the capability of the present personnel to fill the new positions can be more effectively determined. More important, their training needs can be ascertained for the guidance of the chief executive officer.

NEED FOR A SHORT-TERM ACTION PLAN

In spite of the thorough nature of the organization survey report on the Art Association, it contained no proposed list of immediate next steps that should be taken to implement the recommendations. Such an action plan tends to clarify and pinpoint the specific steps required to implement the survey proposals and provide a basis for reporting progress in specific terms.

FREQUENT INTERACTION BETWEEN THE CHIEF EXECUTIVE AND THE ORGANIZATION PLANNING STAFF

At Ford Motor Company during the divisionalization program, it was reported that Breech, the chief operating officer, was a frequent visitor to the offices of his organization planning staff. It is logical to assume that Breech wanted to make his goals and viewpoint known to his organization planning staff and to get their personal reaction to some of the organization and management changes that he was considering. The contacts between the administrative vice president of the Automobile Company and his director of organization took place weekly and were of one to two hours duration. As a consequence, the work of the organization planning staff was very effective during this period. We would not hestitate to conclude that this particular chief executive's understanding of his role and his personal contact with his staff was a strategic factor in the success achieved by the staff during this period. At most other times, in our experience, for reasons we are at a loss to explain, there was almost no personal contact between the chief executive and his organization planning staff in their offices.

INTERNAL TRAINING OF THE MEMBERS OF THE ORGANIZATION PLANNING STAFF

In none of the cases has there been any opportunity or time provided for the more experienced members of the organization planning staff to train the less experienced members, or for the senior staff men to teach each other. At the Recreation Company, the plans were made for such training, but the director of organization planning did not see that this was done.

ORGANIZATION PLANNING AS A FUNCTIONAL GUIDANCE AND CONTROL STAFF

Organization planning is largely functional guidance and control work at the corporate level, and the planners should not be expected to perform free organization surveys as an internal consulting service for all the various corporate staff and product division heads. The staff should perform services for the chief executive only. It should teach and functionally guide the corporate staff and division heads in conducting their own organization surveys, and review their organization proposals for the chief executive. If the division is large enough to warrant an organization planner to help the division head conduct these studies, then the corporate organization planning staff should help select and exercise functional guidance over the work of this staff specialist. To be in a position to exercise functional control effectively, however, the organization planning staff must use the most proven and perfected tools and techniques of organization planning possible, which include: issuing and maintaining an organization and policy manual, an organization survey guide, an organization planning and control policy, a titling policy, an announcements policy, and authorized organization principles, as well as salary administration policies, if salaried job evaluation is included in the functions of the staff.

COUNSEL OF THE ORGANIZATION PLANNING STAFF ON KEY MANAGEMENT APPOINTMENTS

If it is important that the organization planning staff develop man specifications for the key management positions, then it is also important that this staff be consulted whenever the position is to be filled to determine whether the proposed candidate meets the minimum requirements of the position specification. A negative opinion from the staff should be given heavy weight by the chief executive to a point where it is an actual right to veto an appointment. The organization planner should not be held accountable for performance within a structure he has recommended when the structure is staffed with executives that do not meet the man specifications he has developed. A well-designed structure, staffed with qualified men, should be able to perform successfully, if properly trained and motivated by the chief executive officer. The danger of staffing a new or changed plan of organization with unqualified men without first consulting the organization planning staff is such an important finding that it cannot be overemphasized as a strategic success factor. An unqualified key executive not only performs badly in the management phases of his job, there is a strong tendency to organize away from him, as in the case of the sales vice president at the Hard Rubber Company. This tendency further compounds the problem of achieving a soundly designed structure.

USEFULNESS OF ORGANIZATION PLANNING PRINCIPLES

For a more complete discusison of the usefulness of the generally accepted principles of organization planning, we refer the reader to Chapter 4, where this subject is discussed in some detail. In summary, we found the *Principle of Definition*, the *Principle of the Objective*, the *Principle of Specialization*, the *Principle of Coordination*, the *Principle of Span of Management Control*, the *Principle of Balance*, the *Principle of Minimum Levels*, and the *Principle of Responsibility and Authority* were the most useful in identifying weaknesses in organization structures. The *Principle of Continuity* was the most important in clarifying the need for organization planning as a continuing staff function. In reference to application of the other principles, violations were not found in these specific cases to result in any critical dysfunction in these organizations. This fact alone, however, does not invalidate the use of the other principles. They were not important in these cases.

USEFULNESS OF THE TOOLS AND TECHNIQUES
OF ORGANIZATION PLANNING

Again, for a more complete discussion of the usefulness of the tools and techniques of organization planning, we refer the reader to Chapter 4. The most important of these tools is the organization and policy manual. This should contain the organization planning and control policy, the titling policy, the announcements policy, position descriptions, and the generally accepted principles of organization planning that should be applied in the design of the structure and in proposing organization changes in it. The organization survey guide is also helpful as a training tool. The most helpful techniques used in assembling and analyzing organizational information are the organization chart, the position description, the man specification, the work distribution or linear responsibility chart, the activity analysis chart, the grouping analysis chart, the decisions analysis chart, and the organization plan evaluation chart. Illustrations of the use of these powerful techniques of data assembly and analysis are found in Chapter 3.

IMPORTANCE OF THE ORGANIZATION PLANNING FUNCTION OF THE FUTURE

Is the importance of sound organization design increasing, or is it declining like the skills of the buggy-whip maker? Big knowledge organizations, in spite of the efforts of the Department of Justice to break them up, are with us now, and we believe they will continue to be with us for some time. Researchers report that large corporations account for most of the output, most industrial employment, most of the profit, and most of the innovation today. Forecasters see even larger organizations in the future. The advanced position of American industry is grounded in the systematic application of science and technology to the making of goods and provision of services. The strengthening of organization structure of American businesses and the continuing improvement of managerial skills likewise depends on organization research. While rapid change has for some time been an accepted fact of modern life, the planned and deliberate control of organization change in private enterprise and in voluntary and governmental organizations has only just begun. While there may never be a large number of staff organization planners, just as there may never be a large number of long-range planners, every large organization should have a few qualified men in these fields. More important, all professional managers, all chief executives, group executives, division heads, and controllers, as well as subordinate executives and administrative personnel, including systems men, compensation executives, and job analysts in all organizations, large and small, would do well to be highly skilled in the analysis and design of organization structure.

CONTRIBUTIONS OF THE SOCIAL SCIENCES TO ORGANIZATION PLANNING

We believe the confusion that currently exists about the work of the social scientists and the organization planners arises because the public generally does not know what these specialists do. The organization planner is basically a management analyst. He is concerned with the design of organization structure and jobs and not with the behavior of specific individuals who may be occupying the jobs at any one particular point in time. Of course, an organization structure—no matter how well designed—is not much good without the qualified people to staff the structure. It is like a racing car without a driver and without any gas in the tank. If the driver is qualified and the gas meets specifications, then the better designed car should win the race. The social scientist is, on the other hand, more concerned with the *dynamics*, i.e., the behavior of the specific human beings in their interaction with other human beings in small face-to-face groups. He has found if they are open and honest in their dealings with one another and if their superiors treat them in the same way, they will do better work no matter what it is. No matter how skilled the members of a football team are, if their interpersonal relationships are bad off the field, it could conceivably adversely affect the play and teamwork on the field. The social scientist can help with problems of this kind. The organization planner would be concerned with the plays. What does the end do regardless of who the end is at any particular time; how can the position be best played so that the team gets the most touchdowns and wins the game? The question is often asked: What will the social scientists contribute to organization planning? Not often is the question asked: What will organization planners have to contribute to the social scientists? We will respond to the first question by continuing with our analogy to the racing car and driver. The study of specific human beings has contributed substantially to the science of automobile engineering; for example, where to place the dials so that they can be read; how large should the figures be. Substantial as this contribution is, it is only a small part of the knowledge that must be acquired by an automotive engineer. A good organization planner must have a good working knowledge of the social sciences. He must also see the organization as a biosystem. But this is only a small part of his knowledge requirements. More important, he must know how to apply the principles of professional management. He must know work simplification techniques, forms design, systems analysis, management position design, job evaluation, records management, organization design, long-range planning, performance appraisal, recruiting, interviewing, and many other skill areas that are of only peripheral interest to the social scientist.

Social scientists have done considerable work in studying organizations as responsive biological social systems. E. Wight Bakke, in particular, has given the organization planners a much broader perspective from which to view organization structure as a biosystem. The terms he uses also can be helpful in discussing the common features of very diverse kinds of hierarchical organization structures. For this reason, we have used his framework and terminology to analyze the organizations in this book. Although perhaps unfamiliar to the businessman when first exposed to them, these terms, we believe, will ultimately become more generally used in business, particularly by organization planners, position evaluation analysts, systems analysts, and others who must, as part of their work, deal with organization problems of increasing complexity. An example of such a study may be found in the Conference Board Study No. 154 (1972) by Wilbur McFeely entitled, *Organization Change: Perceptions and Realities.* This is a study of fifteen member companies that have gone through reorganizations to achieve divisionalized structures. The organization planners use social science terminology and concepts to give them greater insight, and perhaps a slightly different viewpoint, in evaluating their reorganization experiences. We have tried to do much the same thing in this book, particularly in the divisionalization reorganizations of the Automobile Company and the Recreation Company. In the future, we see such studies increasing in their importance and sophistication.

13

Making Knowledge Organizations Fully Effective

ORGANIZATIONS THAT ARE LARGER AND MULTI-NATIONAL IN SCOPE

Only recently we have seen the general advent of large multi-national corporations, most of which are based in the United States. They have not been welcomed in all countries by the societies and governments they serve. They have, for example, been accused, by the labor unions particularly, of draining the United States of jobs. If they are to become fully effective, they must apply the modern management tools that have made it possible for an organization the size and scope of GM to be managed profitably and effectively internationally for so many years in the competitive automobile industry. These tools include:

1. Management by system, not personality
2. Fact-oriented approach to problem-solving
3. Respect for human resources and talent
4. Central policy control and decentralized operations
5. The divisionalization concept of organization and management
6. Centralized cash management
7. MBO performance appraisal
8. Management incentive plans
9. Formalization and communication of policies and organization concepts in writing

GE also has made its contributions to the successful management of large international organizations.

We believe the effective planning and control of the organization structure of these large organizations will become a vital factor governing their continued effectiveness, if not survival. The careful planning and control of the problem-solving and decision-making structure will be vital, since the automation of the management information systems—as in the case of automated manufacturing processes—makes their change a time-consuming and costly proposition. Off-the-cuff organization changes will be a thing of the past. Note the stability of the GM organization structure. Management decison-making processes and information gathering will be a subject of considerable study, simplification, and formalization. Fact-finding will be automated wherever feasible. This, of course, will encompass the design of the organization structure and the positioning of the technical staffs and top-management committees that assist in the planning and decision-making processes. If communications are to remain viable, then the management levels must be held to a minimum through broadening the spans of management to a far greater extent than they are at present, and holding down the percent of managers to workers by some of the organizational techniques perfected by General Electric Corporation (see *Professional Management in General Electric* [New York: General Electric Company, 1954]). Rational organization design and careful and effective control of the organization structure, the evaluation of management jobs as well as MBO performance appraisal and its use as a basis for management incentive awards determination will increase in importance. More and more systematic management will replace intuitive management.

FUTURE DIRECTIONS FOR RESEARCH

Comparative Analyses

It is hoped that the comparative analyses of these carefully selected cases out of the author's experience will provide the basis for sorting out the unique from the generic factors in organization planning, and thus they will help to highlight sources of strength and weakness in carrying programs of planned organizational change.

These cases are taken from domestic hierarchical profit and non-profit organizations. One organization had no paid employees on the local level. It would appear that mission, rather than size, plays the most important role in influencing the process of change in organization. Size, of course, plays the most important role in requiring the change from a functional to a divisionalized structure of organization. We have, unfortunately, because of limited experience, not been able to include among the cases examples from all types of business, governmental, and service organizations, i.e., hospitals, insurance companies, and the like.

Limitations of the Experimental Approach

The case studies have, therefore, used the empirical rather than the experimental approach. Controlling all aspects affecting changes in large organizations in a laboratory setting would be extremely difficult, if not impossible.

Studies of the Decision-Making Process

Advanced studies of the decision-making process in organization structures may hold the key to more effectively positioning the necessary staff functions and committees within the structure. Such support mechanisms exist largely to facilitate and improve the fact-finding and decision-making of the line executives.

Since knowledge organizations in the pluralist society of the future probably will increase in numbers and size, investigations should be made into the alternative and more efficient ways of planning and controlling the structures of these organizations. These structures must be extremely well designed and controlled if they are to be effective, yet at the same time be manned at minimum cost. We have observed that monthly management meetings are most useful in facilitating the learning processes wherever rigid behavior patterns of long-standing must be changed in as short a period as possible. Such meetings were not used at all at the Automobile Company and were only of a generalized type at the Recreation Company. The content of the training presentations was prepared by the corporate training director rather than by the company specialists in the particular functional area.

It is believed that this book represents one of the few investigations into organizational change involving real-life situations in a variety of special purpose groups in a power hierarchy, and is one that has focused on the top-management structures of these organizations; it is hoped that it will not be the last.

While change has always characterized organization structures, finding the means to plan systematically and control this change is new. Industry's intense current interest in organization planning stems, we believe, from a general recognition of the fact that the well being and productivity of our society can be substantially improved if we can learn to organize and manage large and complex organization structures so that their very size will not jeopardize their effectiveness.

We hope this book will make some small contribution toward this end. Further, we hope it will contribute to a reduction in the many organizational mixups we see happening every day; such ineffectiveness and inefficiency adds up to a staggering waste of the nation's human resources.

The practical application of the organization planning knowledge that already exists is limited to a very few well-managed companies like General Electric. Organization planning, we have observed, is a much neglected and underrated managing process; in fact, businessmen often have disdain rather than respect for organizational planning. By showing in the case studies better performance and results that have been contributed to substantially by improving the clarity, stability, and design of organization structure, we hope we have replaced with respect any disdain the reader may have had in the past for this process, for organization planning is a powerful management tool that should, in the future, be better understood and more extensively applied in business.

OBTAINING ORGANIZATION CHARTS OF OTHER COMPANIES

If you would like to know how other similar organizations are organized, the Conference Board has an organization chart exchange service. The board maintains charts on over 400 U.S. corporations. These charts are updated annually. A fee is charged to cover the cost of the service. If you wish to order charts, call (212) 759-0900 or write: The Conference Board Chart Collection, The Conference Board, Inc., 845 Third Avenue, New York, NY 10022.

Bibliography

Allen, Louis A. *Professional Management*. New York: McGraw-Hill, 1973.

Alpander, Guvenc G. *Human Resources Management Planning*. New York: AMACOM, 1982.

Andersen, Richard C. *Management Strategies*. New York: McGraw-Hill, 1965.

Appley, Lawrence A. and Keith Irons. *Management Manpower Planning*. New York: AMACOM, 1981.

Bakke, E. Wight. *Bonds of Organization*. Hamden, Conn.: Archon Books, 1966.

_____. *Concept of the Social Organization*. New Haven, Conn.: Yale Labor and Management Center, 1959.

Barnard, Chester I. *Organization and Management*. Cambridge, Mass.: Harvard University Press, 1948.

_____. *The Functions of the Executive*. Cambridge, Mass.: Harvard University Press, 1938.

Bower, Marvin. *The Will to Manage*. New York: McGraw-Hill, 1966.

Brown, Alvin. *Organization: A Formulation of Principle*. New York: Hibbert Printing Co., 1945.

Chandler, Alfred D., Jr. *Strategy and Structure*. Cambridge, Mass.: The MIT Press, 1962.

Cordiner, Ralph J. *New Frontiers for Professional Managers*. New York: McGraw-Hill, 1956.

Dale, Ernest. *Organization*. New York: AMACOM, 1967.

_____. *Planning and Developing the Company Organization Structure*. New York: American Management Association, 1952.

Desatnick, Robert L. *Business of Human Resource Management*. New York: John Wiley & Sons, 1983.

_____. *Innovative Human Resource Management*. New York: AMACOM, 1972.

Dively, George S. *The Power of Professional Management*. New York: AMACOM, 1972.

Dooher, M. Joseph and Vivienne Marquis. *The Development of Executive Talent*. New York: American Management Assocation, 1952.

Dougherty, David C. "The Function of Top Management Organization Planning and Control in a Manufacturing Corporation." *Personnel*, January 1954, pp. 275-85.

Drucker, Peter F. *Innovation and Entrepreneurship*. New York: Harper & Row, 1986.

_____. *Management: Tasks, Responsibilities, Practices*. New York: Harper & Row, 1974.

_____. *Age of Discontinuity*. New York: Harper & Row, 1968.

_____. *Managing for Results*. New York: Harper & Row, 1964.

_____. *Practice of Management*. New York: Harper & Row, 1954.

_____. *Concept of the Corporation*. New York: The John Day Co., Inc., 1946.

Famularo, Joseph J. *Organization Planning Manual*. New York: AMACOM, 1979.

Fayol, Henri. *General and Industrial Management*. London: Sir Isaac Pitman & Sons, Ltd., 1949.

Fisch, Gerald G. *Organization for Profit*. New York: McGraw-Hill, 1964.

Fombrun, Charles J., Noel M. Tichy, and Mary Anne Devanna. *Strategic Human Resource Management*. New York: John Wiley & Sons, 1984.

Ginzberg, Eli and Ewing W. Reilley. *Effecting Change in Large Organizations*. New York: Columbia University Press, 1957.

Glueck, William F. *Organization Planning and Development*. New York: AMA Research Study No. 106, 1971.

Grove, Andrew S. *High Output Management*. New York: Random House, 1983.

Gulick, Luther H. and Lyndal F. Urwick. *Papers on the Science of Administration*. New York: Institute of Public Administration, 1937.

Henrici, Stanley B. *Company Reorganization for Performance and Profit Improvement*. Westport, Conn.: Quorum Books, 1986.

Higginson, M. Valliant. *Management Policies*. New York: AMA Research Report No. 76 and No. 78, 1967.

Holden, Paul E., Lounsbury S. Fish, and Hubert L. Smith. *Top Management Organization and Control*. Stanford, Calif.: Stanford University Press, 1941.

Holden, Paul E., Carlton A. Pederson, and Gayton E. Germane. *Top Management*. New York: McGraw-Hill, 1968.

Iacocca, Lee and William Novak. *Iacocca: An Autobiography*. New York: Bantam Books, 1984.

Kappel, Frederick R. *Vitality in a Business Enterprise*. New York: McGraw-Hill, 1960.

Learned, Edmund P., David N. Ulrich, and Donald R. Booz. *Executive Action*. Boston, Mass.: Harvard University Press, 1951.

McConkey, Dale D. *How to Manage by Results*. New York: American Management Association, 1965.

McCormack, Mark H. *What They Don't Teach You at Harvard Business School*. New York: Bantam Books, 1984.

McFeely, Wilbur M. *Organization Change: Perceptions and Realities*. New York: Conference Board Report No. 561, 1972.

Mooney, James D. and Alan C. Reiley. *The Principles of Organization*. New York: Harper & Brothers, 1939.

Neuschel, Richard F. *Management Systems for Profit and Growth*. New York: McGraw-Hill, 1976.

Nevins, Allan and Frank Ernest Hill. *Ford: Decline and Rebirth*. New York: Scribner's, 1963.

Odiorne, George S. *Management Decisions by Objectives*. Englewood Cliffs, N.J.: Prentice-Hall, 1969.

Professional Management in General Electric. New York: General Electric Company, 1954.

Rock, Milton L., ed. *Handbook of Wage and Salary Administration*. New York: McGraw-Hill, 1983.

Sampson, Robert C. *The Staff Role in Management: Its Creative Uses*. New York: Harper & Brothers, 1955.

Sherman, Harvey. *It All Depends: A Pragmatic Approach to Organization*. Montgomery: University of Alabama Press, 1966.

Sloan Alfred P. *My Years with General Motors*. New York: Doubleday, 1964.

Smith, George Albert, Jr. *Managing Geographically Decentralized Companies*. Boston, Mass.: Harvard University Press, 1958.

Steiner, George A. *Strategic Planning: What Every Manager Must Know*. New York: Free Press, 1979.

_____. *Managerial Long-Range Planning*. New York: McGraw-Hill, 1963.

Taylor, Frederick W. *Principles of Scientific Management*. New York: Harper & Brothers, 1947.

Walker, James W. *Human Resource Planning*. New York: McGraw-Hill, 1980.

White, K. K. *Understanding the Company Organization Chart*. New York: AMA Research Study No. 56, 1963.

Wortman, Max S. and JoAnn Sperling. *Defining the Manager's Job*. New York: AMACOM, 1975.

Wright, J. Patrick. *On a Clear Day You Can See General Motors*. Grosse Point, Mich.: Wright Enterprises, 1979.

Zimet, Melvin and Ronald G. Greenwood. *The Evolving Science of Management*. New York: AMACOM, 1979.

Index

ABOUT THE AUTHOR

DAVID C. DOUGHERTY is Managing Director of David C. Dougherty & Associates, which provides organization and personnel consulting services to manufacturing companies and banks. He was formerly an organization planner at Chrysler, Brunswick, Keebler, Amerace, The First National Bank of Chicago, and Allied Products Corporation. He is president of the Chicago Chapter of the Society for the Advancement of Management as well as fellow and honorary life member. He has lectured on organization at the AMA Management Course and at numerous seminars and courses. He has written an article in *Personnel* entitled, "The Function of Top Management Organization Planning and Control in a Manufacturing Corporation."